The LIBRARY
of the
PARRISH
Art Museum

Donor   MR & MRS HANS NAMUTH
1980

M

CZECH GOTHIC PAINTING

We always remember you with love - and shall never forget.
Our very best for X-mas to you, dear Mrs. Carmen, and to children!

Yours

Jos. Čermáška. -

+ Alžběta Čermásková.

Pilsen 24. XII. 1951.

CZECH GOTHIC PAINTING

1350–1450

by

Antonín Matějček & Jaroslav Pešina

Melantrich Praha 1950

FOREWORD

The late medieval art of Bohemia, from the establishment of Prague in 1348 as the capital of the Empire of Charles IV to the outbreak of the Hussite Wars in 1419, has long been recognised as a decisive meeting ground of styles where the so called „International Gothic" manner achieved one of its most remarkable manifestations. Here more than anywhere in Europe a culture was consciously built up with careful borrowings from other centres, Matthias of Arras, the architect from Avignon, Peter Parler, the architect and sculptor whose father had worked on Cologne cathedral, Tomaso of Modena, the painter, from Treviso. Already in the papal court at Avignon a fusion was taking place between Italian and Gothic forms. Prague became a second centre where Giottesque idioms were adapted to more Northern tastes. But it was no one way traffic from the schools of Italy. In Milan, Verona and Venice the new graciousness of line, the soft thickly falling folds, the friendly birds and beasts which people landscapes interpreted with a new sense of space, are as frequent and apparent as in Avignon, Paris or Prague. The forms may be a synthesis, but they are adopted because they answer to a need which the clear cut brilliance of earlier Gothic work or the massive gravity of Giotto did not satisfy. „The soft style" it is sometimes called from its swaying, slightly blurred treatment of drapery, and it had in fact a gentleness of spirit, a liking for the fanciful and pretty, which seems to have pervaded Europe. It was an art commissioned by wealthy patrons who liked pleasant things, but its vogue transcended any particular class.

The course of Bohemian art in the fourteenth and early fifteenth century can best be followed in illuminated manuscripts, of which many have survived, or in the architecture and carving of the cathedral at Prague. But there is a rich survival also of panel paintings, and it is these which Professor Matějček has catalogued and analysed, giving us for the first time a comprehensive list, carefully documented and with most useful information, only obtainable through recent cleaning and restoration work, as to the state of the pictures. Few of these works can be securely dated and almost all must be assigned to anonymous masters, with the exception of Theodoric, Charles IV's painter at Karlštejn, and he, though a distinct and accomplished artist, is a shadowy personality, whose place of origin is not known. Professor Matějček has arranged the material into an approximately chronological order on the basis of stylistic development. Such a procedure cannot have finality, for the personal element, the span of an artist's life, the conservatism of a workshop, elude exact placing. In England there is less familiarity with and confidence in style analysis than there is on the continent, an unfamiliarity that is reflected in the absence of recognised terms and at times the extreme difficulty of finding an English expression to render a phrase of continental speculation, so that any translation seems clumsy and inadequate. But such analyses are an essential part of the statement of art historical problems. Professor Matějček's book has advanced the subject to a new stage of intelligibility, and the admirable illustrations which it includes make possible comparative work which will lead to a fuller understanding of Czech medieval art in relation to the rest of Europe.

To the English reader, Bohemia under the Luxembourg Emperors has a particular interest. In 1382 Anne, daughter of Charles IV, married Richard II. She came to England with a train of Bohemian attendants and there has been much argument as to whether this new connection led to relations between English Lollards and the doctrines of Hus. It is tempting to think also that the arts, for which Richard's court became a centre, owed something to Bohemian influences. Certainly it is then that the international style flourishes in England, and there are, particularly in illumination, some clear affinities between the two countries. But it is a difficult period for disentangling art relationships. Never was art so genuinely European in its scope, at least North of the Italian Alps, and in England the same elements were being absorbed into the traditional patterns as somewhat earlier had given a new impetus in Bohemia. The naturalism of Bohemian painting, its liking for strongly characterised portrait heads, finds some reflection in English taste. Richard II is the first English king visually recognisable. But this was a practice widely spread in France, and it is probably the Paris of Charles V rather than the Prague of Charles IV that provided English models. The repertory of forms and subjects was common to all centres, and the influences of one upon another are too uncertain for definition. The indisputable fact is that in this international style, the achievement of Bohemia was outstandingly rich and varied.

Prof. T. S. R. BOASE,
President of Magdalen College, Oxford

*T*his English edition of ČESKÁ MALBA GOTICKÁ *(Czech Gothic Painting) is an adaptation of the book which originated in the work of the Charles University Institute for the History of Art, headed by Professor A. Matějček, of which the Czech edition appeared in 1938, the German edition in 1939. Externally, certain changes have been made in the course of adaptation. The introductory passages have been extended and the critical catalogue and the bibliography abridged, while some of the reproductions have been left out, and others added instead. Of greater significance are the changes made internally. The discovery of further relics of Czech Gothic painting has brought about a change of opinion on a number of related problems, just as the new research made on the memorials of the first half of the XV*th *century brought about great changes in the judgments and conclusions on the art of that period.*

The shortening of the catalogue and bibliographical data, which proved necessary from the point of view of the publishing house, has not detracted from the scientific value of the book. Even the specialist will find in this edition all he needs for his researches. Should he nevertheless require a wider choice, he will have to turn to the new Czech edition, which is being published simultaneously with the present volume. This English version of the manuscript is the work of J. C. Houra.

Prague, March 1947

A. Matějček and J. Pešina

INTRODUCTION

The golden age of Czech panel painting was at its height during the reign of the two kings of the Luxembourg dynasty who followed each other on the Bohemian throne and in the Roman Emperorship, Charles IV and Wenceslas IV. It was a period of glory for the Kingdom of Bohemia, which from the hands of an alien dynasty received all that the last Přemyslides had striven for in vain — the leading position in the German realm for the lands of the Bohemian Crown. What blessings accrued to Bohemia through the entry of Charles into its political and cultural life is familiar history. Born with both German and Czech blood in his veins, brought up at the French Court, Charles was a living symbol of that political and cultural synthesis which he set himself as his life's task as a sovereign ruler. He linked his personal and dynastic interests with grandiose plans of statesmanship; he strove to strengthen the royal authority in his kingdom and in the German realm; he intervened inspiringly in the political and ecclesiastical affairs of Europe, and made the economic, moral and cultural improvement of the kingdom he had inherited his first and foremost aim. In him the perspicacious political realist was balanced by the man of profound erudition and great cultural attainments; a personality imbued with a deep, mystically tinged Christianity was complemented in him by a being affected by the first throbbings of the incipient humanism and aestheticism of the Renaissance. In constant touch with European culture in the west and south and with prominent personalities of the Europe of his day, he sought ways of improving his kingdom and its capital, Prague, by all attainable means, both material and spiritual. Sensitive to the manifold spiritual currents of his day, he grasped at and made use of anything capable of raising the standard of Czech life. His endeavours to improve the level of education, which found their expression in the founding of Prague University, crossed paths with his efforts to give a religiously ethical trend to spiritual life. His desire to better the country and its metropolis competed with and even outstripped the steadily growing interest of his times in aesthetic values, and gave a mighty impulse to the fine arts.

In these efforts of his the King was greatly supported by a whole company of dignitaries of the Church, all men of learning and concerned with the new spiritual currents then flowing through contemporary Europe. At their head was the first Archbishop of Prague, Arnošt of Pardubice, who had spent his student years in Italy. In his footsteps followed the high clergy, the bishops and directors of the King's Chancellery. Jan of Středa, bishop and chancellor, an admirer of Petrarca, himself a poet and cultivator of hymns spiritual, loved literature as much as art and was the first bibliophile on a grand scale. Like their august master, Arnošt of Pardubice and Jan of Středa also both had spiritually split personalities. The medieval man in them, seeking his soul's salvation in firm faith and the zealous observation of the bonds of the Faith, was welded together with the awakening, modern man, projecting his inmost being into the mundane world and trying to enhance it with a religious individuality and aesthetic culture. This spiritual culture of Bohemia, although permeated with and nurtured by currents from many lands, had nevertheless a preponderantly national tinge. From the Caroline chancellery in which Jan of Středa grew into prominence (to become later its head) there sprang efforts towards a purification and ennoblement of the German language which also enriched the German literature of that time; Jan of Středa did pioneer's work in this literature, as a translator and poet at least on the formal side. This interest in linguistic and literary matters passed, simultaneously, too, into the Czech language and literature, which was cultivating spiritual drama and allegory, knightly and legendary epic poetry and hymnology - though only in the form of translations from and adaptation of Latin and German models. So, too, the Czech literary language developed and grew into an artistically effective medium of expression. The early years of the latter half of the XIVth century saw the compilation of Latin-Czech dictionaries, and these efforts culminated in the dictionary of Bartholomew of Chlumec, an author known as Claretus de Solencia, whose collaborators were the Emperor himself, Bishop Jan of Středa and other prominent personalities amongst the intellectuals at Court. The Czech language in the second half of the XIVth century was already so flexible and expressive that a work of such artistic quality as the Legend of St. Catherine could come into being — a work written by an unknown poet in whose art scholastic learning was blended with a mystically exalted imagination.

This striving for a formal culture of the Czech tongue is a manifestation of the aestheticism of the period, stirred up by the rising Italian humanism, which is also perceptible in the sphere of the visual arts. The latter, bound by medieval tradition until then, emancipated themselves from their backwardness and provincial dependence and sought new modes of expression, absorbing ideas of all kinds from both the west and the south. In architecture the development proceeds from the academicism of High Gothic to the reforming influence of Peter Parléř, which opens up the way for Modern Gothic; sculpture and painting strive to acquire a character of their own by vehement, often revolutionary forward plunges. Even though there is still a hard struggle here between medieval spiritualism and a steadily growing realism, the guiding idea was to try to find a beautiful and eloquent expression corresponding to the new conceptions of beauty.

These artistic efforts developed against an agitated background of a spiritual life which, slowly freeing itself from medieval fetters, began to strive for inner freedom. The latter half of the XIVth century was the epoch when the first cracks began to show in the thousand-years old spiritual structure of Christianity - cracks which revealed the shifting of the soil, the shaking of the foundations upon which the Church had built its power over men's souls. At the secular crossroads between the Middle Ages and the New Era, men began to long for a new basis and a new core of the life spiritual. There were sporadic attempts at reform of the Christian life, which grew more intense as the XIVth century progressed. But parallel with them, though much more timidly, new urges and longings clamoured in the breast of man, urges which already went beyond the scope of the medieval outlook on life and the world. True enough, the irresolute medieval relation to the world and life remained, like a scaffolding — however insecure — round the growing new view of the world. But gradually human thoughts and feelings underwent a change under the pressure of new perceptions, experiences and emotions. There was a gradual shifting from the level of rigid abstractness of conception, to one of a concrete and pictorial representation of abstract ideas. Symbols and allegories began to acquire significance as a means of expressing and making comprehensible the results of theological speculation - which by then had already passed its zenith. Symbol and allegory came to be used for the interpretation of biblical texts, and in the legends, in life stories of the saints and fables, people sought examples of the standards of the God-fearing life. This bringing together of the life transcendent and the life mundane was made more easily and firmly because of the irrationality of medieval ways of looking upon the real world as the scene of miracles and of believing in the activities of hidden, occult forces. The mind of man in the XIVth century divined a transcendental content and meaning behind natural phenomena and events, and it sought strenuously for a linking-up with the transcendent region by what were often rather crude means. This phenomenon might be explained — thought incorrectly — as the reflection of mysticism penetrating into wider human circles. But it was really a different spiritual force which was manifesting itself. Mysticism in the real sense of the word remained even in the XIVth century the spiritual affair of a class trained in speculative thought, and was a region inaccessible to the broad masses. But the longing for subjective participation in, and a more intensive experience of, the truths of the Christian teaching which in the XIVth century spread among the lay classes in the towns, made men seek some link with the transcendental sphere by means that thrilled the mind and at the same time gave free play to the elements of feeling. Hence the growth of sorcery, the yearning for miracles and an unprecedented cult of relics. Hence the fondness for dramatic depiction of the sufferings and death of Christ, the sorrows of Mary, and the martyrdom of the saints. Hence, too, an intensified cult of the Virgin Mary, and veneration of statues of the Virgin and of miracle-working images. It is true that influences of mysticism played their part in all this, both on the spiritual side and on the practical religious side, but, taken all in all, this longing for the personification of religious life represented a wider movement to which mysticism contributed little more than the outward trappings. In this case, as always, it was mainly the activities of the preachers which brought about the diffusion of this new religious sensibility and popularized the concept of the human soul mystically merging with God.

This bipolarity of religious feeling, manifested in a yearning for deep personal religious experience attained through emotion stirred up by sensual ideas, had an extraordinary influence upon the character of art in the XIVth century. To the antithetic working of these forces corresponds the twofold aspect of this art, which wavers between Gothic idealism and naturalism with far more rapid oscillations than did the art of the XIIIth century. The XIIIth century had achieved a temporary balance between these forces, but from the beginning of the XIVth century naturalism once more raises its head in an attempt to achieve dominance over the spiritualism and idealism of Gothic art, and its aggressiveness is strengthened, if not directly evoked, by a state of mind demanding emotional excitement through powerful sensual impressions. Only thus is it possible to explain the naturalism of the typical Crucifixion, the dramatic interpretation of the dead Christ and of the grief-stricken Mother in the Pietàs, or the progressive degree of the tragic in the pictures depicting the sufferings of the Redeemer. In all these naturalism is at work as a force seducing Gothic art from its idealistic path and abstract conventionalism to the field of realism, based on the experience of the senses, a realism which only with the Renaissance made secure its dominion as the triumphant principle in creative art.

In Bohemia, where as early as the latter half on the XIVth century ideas of religious regeneration and reform had begun to take root, not only the forces just mentioned but also new currents of thought had begun to operate, currents which formed part of the historical spiritual synthesis known as 'early humanism'. This movement, which flourished for but a brief space in Bohemia, had its ground prepared by the reformed Augustinism introduced to Bohemia from Italy by Bishop Jan of Dražice. This dogma attempted a synthesis of the new piety with the budding humanistic learning. Augustinian monasteries, founded and supported by the princes of the Church, the Emperor and the Bohemian nobility, became centres of culture in which learned studies were coupled with a religious zeal that fructified Bohemian cultural life in many directions. It was there that the Czech illuminated and illustrated book attained a world stature, from there issued the impulse to work in the sphere of art, especially painting, probably to a far greater extent than we surmise. Archbishop Arnošt of Pardubice and Jan of Středa, the Chancellor, were prominent intermediaries between this new intellectual sphere and Czech plastic art and painting, the spiritual foundation of which had steadily deepened from the middle of the XIVth century and the creative energy and capacity of which had steadily grown. From there came that intensified cult of the Virgin which was reflected in the numerous orders for canvases given by Arnošt of Pardubice, and which also found expression in the literary activities of Jan of Středa. At Prague the cult of the Virgin was propagated by the College of Mansionaries, established by Archbishop Arnošt of Pardubice and Charles IV. From this college there issued on the initiative of Arnošt the famous Lectionarium Mariale, and it was there that Jan of Středa wrote and compiled prayers and hymns to the Virgin. It was from there that the popularisation of Latin prayers in the national languages, Czech and German, was promoted, passing from Court circles to the convents and monasteries, to the popular religious Orders and to the ranks of the townspeople. From these Court circles, permeated with Augustinism, began a propagation of the doctrines of the teachers of the Church, mainly those of Augustine, which spread to lay circles. From this spiritually awakened environment, the basis of the later 'devotio moderna', there issued finally the attempts at reform which culminated in the revolutionary Hussite movement.

These spiritual currents are reflected in Czech art, particularly in sculpture and painting, although it is imposible for the moment to fix the extent and depth of their effect. The reason for this, on the one hand, in spite of its abundance, is the fragmentary character of the material that has come down to us; and, on the other hand, the lack of depth in our knowledge as yet of the art of the era of Charles IV. That the echo of these spiritual forces should have been stronger in the art of the Court circles is all the more comprehensible because works which were created in a burgher environment by the hands of inferior artists, were created in dependence upon an art prompted and supported in line with their own development by the noble class. The influence of the Court was so strong that as late as about the year 1400, when the efforts at reform had already begun to have the character of a popular movement, and thus set even against contemporary aesthetic culture the cult of beauty of form, which culminated in the field of sculpture in the group of Madonnas known as the 'beautiful' and even penetrated into the sphere of painting, and indeed dominated plastic art and painting. Art in the reign of Wenceslas was, in all its sectors, directly saturated with the refined culture of the Court, and the Court style and aesthetics penetrated into that section of art which was already serving the classes more profoundly affected by the reform movement. It is well known that these efforts at religious and moral reform were at the outset common to both the Czech and German population of Bohemia, but as they developed they carried with them more Czechs than Germans, particularly when the movement for religious reform assumed a national and social character. Literature, as is understandable, reacted to these forces earlier and more intensively than plastic art and painting. Men of learning, graduates of the University of Paris, such as Vojtěch Raňkův who was an authority on all the problems of contemporary theology, and Matěj of Janov, a preacher of burning eloquence, desired to popularise the reform doctrines which, through the medium of preachers like Jan Milič of Kroměříž and lay writers such as Tomáš of Štítné, spread among the broad masses of the people. This profound interest in religious and moral questions grew, as is well known, into a national Czech movement when Master John Huss entered upon the scene and, taking his place at the head of the revolutionary party, appealed as reformer, preacher and writer first and foremost to the Czech nation. The yearning for a regeneration of life on the basis of the fundamental truths of Christian doctrine then acquired a universal spiritual force that could not but influence even plastic art and painting. Signs of this change we can observe first in the sphere of book illustrations accompanying the texts of the Czech Bibles of the beginning of the XVth century. The change manifested itself, however, rather in a certain freedom from ornamentation than in any change in style or expression of the miniatures themselves. Panel painting reacted, so far as the specimens that have been preserved bear witness, less sensitively to this current. It was not until the period round 1420 and after that it showed any clear signs of a change, when the pathetic aspect of expression was intensified in painting. But this development which might perhaps have prolonged the life of Czech painting, already decaying within, was checked by the outbreak of the Hussite revolution and by the disturbance of the following war years.

From what has been said above it follows that Czech painting in the XIVth century was not middle-class art but Court art, flourishing in the sunny environment of power and wealth, and dependent upon the arbitrary will of the sovereign and of the Court circles that shared his taste in matters of culture. The rapid growth of this dazzling art, the sudden and quick alternation of its plastic tendencies and styles and its rapid decline testify, in fact, to the atmosphere of a hothouse in which it is possible to achieve remarkable results in the transplanting, crossing, growth and flowering of plants so long as the special care of them is maintained. Only in such a way is it possible to explain the successful and fruitful crossing of the influences of Italian and French art with the domestic traditions, and only in such *a manner is it possible* to understand the sudden extinction of styles scarcely mature and their replacement by others often inexplicable from the point of view of traditional development and logic, and only thus is it possible to elucidate the mighty plunges ahead followed by declines and reversions, of which the history of Czech painting in the XIV th century is full. With this is connected a question recently much discussed, namely, whether that art had a distinctive, specifically national character. To apply the present-day criterion of national consciousness to a period long past and pertaining to the intellectual cosmopolitanism of the Middle Ages is nowhere so out of place as in the sphere of Czech plastic art and painting of the XIV th century. The complex personality of Charles IV was one in which German, Czech and French elements combined to form a unified being of almost international culture, and Czech art of his day has something within it which raised the conception of the „Czech" element above one simply of the two nations who formed the population of the lands of the Bohemian Crown. It is not to be denied that in the XIV th century the Germans were here the stronger element from the economic and cultural angle, and it is equally undeniable that in considering Prague as a point of concentration of art forces one must necessarily reckon with the calling in of artists from abroad, for the most part from some part or other of the German Empire. Contemporary records which have come down to us, the registers and lists of members of the Prague guild of painters show that for a fairly long time artists of German origin were in the majority and that it was only towards the close of the XIV th century that there was an increase, among the artists, of master painters of Czech origin. The origin of one artist, whose historical and artistic personality is identifiable among so many anonymous figures, Master Theodoric, is unknown and will probably never be ascertained. Another artist mentioned in a few historical references, but to whom no ascertainable work of art can be attributed is Mikuláš Wurmser who came to Prague from as far afield as Strasbourg. When we bear in mind, however, what a profound influence the far-sighted calling in of the architect and sculptor Peter Parléř to Prague exercised, we must admit that the co-operation of foreigners in the development of painting was notable and fruitful. If we insist that the conception of Bohemian character as applied to the XIV th century is a conception that transcends both nationalities and corresponds to a political, economic and cultural symbiosis of the two nations living and developing side by side in the Bohemian lands, then we may also speak of a Bohemian art of the XIV th century, all the more so as its historical development and character differ from all that Central Europe created in the rest of its national and racial areas. In this sense Bohemian painting is a cultural possession which we have a right to claim as the Czechs' own.

Czech panel painting of the XIV th and the first half of the XV th century forms an extensive whole which has no equal, in quantity and importance of the works that have been preserved, either in Central Europe or in Western Europe. The very number of the panel pictures that have come down to us shows in itself how vast must have been the wealth of works of art of this kind in the Czech lands, since a great proportion of them perished as early as during the Hussite tumults, while it is safe to assume that a by no means inconsiderable number were destroyed in the subsequent centuries, which showed little consideration towards medieval works of art. We know from historical sources that before the Hussite upheavals there were 60 altars in Prague Cathedral alone, that the Týn Church had 24 and that the Collegiate Church at Vyšehrad possessed 32 altars, so we may assume that corresponding numbers were to be found in other Prague churches as well as in the churches of other towns, and that monastery churches, castle chapels and other places of worship possessed works of art in the form of paintings. Relics of this wealth of art treasures found at places often far distant from one another show that artists' work found a clientèle over a very wide area. It is natural that Prague, the residence of the King and Emperor, the head-quarters of the political authority, the economic forces and cultural aspirations of the entire kingdom should have been the centre of all artistic production, that artists should have settled there, that workshops should have sprung up and put forth branches, the output of which won a great reputation far afield, and that the most notable master painters should at Prague produce works which determined the trend and standard of development in the sphere of art. The very existence of a fraternity of painters founded in the year 1348 and the list of its members in the guild register bears eloquent testimony to Prague as an art centre. It may nevertheless be assumed that the excessive number of artists necessitated an exodus of many of them to the provincial towns of Bohemia and Moravia. Flourishing Bohemian towns such as Kutná Hora, Plzeň, and towns of the importance of Brno and Olomouc in Moravia certainly attracted painters, and similarly many a painter found employment in the country in the service of some noble family. In this connection it is necessary to touch upon a question which would appear just recently to have been definitively settled. In the course of their researches it had long been noted by art historians as a remarkable fact that a large number of works of art dating from the XIVth and XVth centuries were preserved in South Bohemia, in particular in the regions owned by the Lords of Rožmberk. A fact to be stressed was that, in additon to panels dating from the first half of the XVth century, the works of two of the greatest masters of the XIVth century were preserved there — fragments of the Vyšší Brod and Třeboň altars. From this it was deduced that South Bohemia played an eminent role in the evolution of Czech painting, and the South-Bohemian school of painting was even spoken of as being a centre responsible for the development of Czech painting. Subsequent new finds of works belonging to all branches of development of XIVth century painting showed, however, that this assumption could not stand. The provenance of these works of art as well as their affinity of style and their inter-connection leads to the conclusion that it was Prague that was the centre of art production in the epoch of Charles and Wenceslas, and that the preservation of a large quantity of works in South Bohemia must be explained otherwise. In this region namely, many art relics of the XIVth and XVth century were preserved because the dominion of the Lords of Rožmberk that included this part of Bohemia was nearly spared the war disasters which elsewhere reduced the plenty of relics of the Middle Ages art, already in the XV century. But if to-day we regard the Vyšší Brod and Třeboň altars as works apparently imported from Prague we must not wholly exclude the possibility of the existence of such a South Bohemian school. The number and the character of the paintings dating from the first half of the XVth century preserved in South Bohemia, showing as they do a certain affinity of style, proves that, at least at the time when political events were shaking Prague and other Czech towns, the painting of panels continued to flourish in South Bohemia, even though it were only in the character of provincial art. Similarly, on the basis of recent finds it may be assumed that panel painting on an intensive scale developed round about the year 1420 in Moravia, linking up with Bohemian painting and raising it, if not to a higher artistic level, at least to a more advanced stage of development.

It has not escaped the notice of those engaged in research work in the sphere of Czech panel painting that among so many preserved specimens there is no work that dates back in its origin to an earlier period than the first half on the XIVth century. This phenomenon has led some investigators to assume that prior to the days of Charles IV there was no panel painting in Bohemia of a high standard, and that the roots of Czech Gothic painting must be sought elsewhere. There are many weighty reasons for the rejection of this view. It is not possible that the older churches at Prague and in the country, as well as the newly-erected town and monastery churches which arose in the first half of the XIVth century in no small numbers at Prague and in the provinces, should not in course of time be filled with altars adorned with pictures in keeping with the expansion of the Gothic style in which the churches had themselves been erected. That such altars did actually exist in the older churches is proved by records which speak of the transfer of altars from old to new churches (for example from a romanesque basilica to the newly erected Church of St. Vitus at Prague) or of the use of older altars in the fitting out of new churches (as, for example, in the case of the Týn Church). Moreover, the expansion and rise of the sister arts of illumination and mural painting in the latter half of the XIVth century prove in themselves that panel painting could not have been a neglected and unfruitful branch of art. If panel painting was able at the period round about 1350 to appear in such perfection of technique and was distinguished by such high quality of work as that demonstrated by the panels that have come down to us, then we must presuppose, at least for the preceding quarter of a century, panel-painting of a considerable level of technique and artistic execution. Investigators in the history of art cannot, of course, resort in such matters to mere unsupported assumptions, and must begin their studies only with works that have been preserved, contenting themselves at the most with a few likely retrospective deductions.

As the oldest of the Bohemian panel paintings of the XIVth century that have come down to us we regard the *Roudnice Predella,* the half-life size figures of which are still dominated by the abstract linear Gothic style which developed from Western impulses in various schools throughout Central Europe in the period following the year 1320. The affinity of the style of this predella with South German and, in particular, with Austrian painting is, indeed, undeniable, but it is not such as makes it necessary to look upon the predella as a work of foreign origin. The fact that the panel came from the episcopal palace at Roudnice, and the affinity of its style with that of relics of book illuminations and mural paintings of the latter half of the XIVth century, permit us to regard the predella as a work of Czech origin. If the Czech book illumination in the manuscripts of Queen Rejčka attain in their iconography and style the full height of which Gothic painting was capable in the period round about 1320, and if works could originate in Bohemia such as the Passional of abbess Kunhuta (among the miniatures of which there are several that in their grandeur, style and artistic value attain the standard of English and northern French art of the first quarter of the XIVth century), we may safely assume for Czech panel painting the like standard of style and artistic expression. The Roudnice predella, then, presents itself to us as a painting in which this older style is dying out and which already displays some traces of the influence of Italian painting that, as may be deduced from contemporary book illuminations, intensified its influence upon Czech painting in all its branches after 1340. This penetration of Italian art into Bohemia was, it is true, as we to-day know, part of a wider current, but nowhere did Italian painting have such a far-reaching effect on the development of Gothic painting as in Bohemia. Book illuminations of the years 1340—1365 give us abundant proof that this influence advanced and intensified until the alien elements were completely assimilated and equality and synthesis in artistic style with the original were attained. From illuminations we can learn approximately how the evolution in panel painting proceeded, even though the specimens of painting that have come down to us are not so abundant as those of book illumination. In one case as probably in the other, Italian pictures were introduced to Bohemia which induced Czech painters to adopt iconographic and compositional motifs, and to imitate even the peculiarities of style of Italian painting. Even if the fundamental achievements of Italian art in the treatment of space and form were not fully understood in Bohemia, none the less these painters did all they could to make their form more plastic and to combine colour more intensely with the line drawing, which till then had been wholly dominant. It was, apparently, mostly copying activities which initiated them into the secrets of Italian form. From the period round about the middle of the XIVth century till well within the XVth century pictures of the Madonna imported from Italy were copied in Bohemia, and the oldest of them, the Most Madonna, proves how an early Czech painter endeavoured to imitate, in both form and colour, the structure of the foreign model. The modelling, intensity of colouring and depth of tone, the painting of shadows and varnish glazes — all these show that the painter aimed at achieving the fulness of form of the painting which he had before his eyes as a model. That he was only partially successful in this endeavour was, of course, merely the consequence of the existing local tradition to which he had been born. The Northerner, a lover of colourfulness, gave through his colours a variety and piquancy to his work unusual in Italy.

The result of course was different when Czech painters who were acquainted with Italian works of art were faced with tasks in which they had to produce pictures in the domestic tradition and were partly or completely unable to turn to foreign models. In such cases there resulted a crossing of the older style with the formal motifs and elements adopted from abroad. At this parting of the ways arose the first artist whose personality scientific research has determined, *the Master of the Vyšší Brod Cycle*. The original destination and arrangement of this cycle remain a mystery to this day. The painter was doubtless a child of the domestic tradition in the form in which it had linked with the current of Central Europe and Gothic, in its turn influenced by the West, but in the course of his artistic career he had come into contact with Italian art. It is probable that this contact had been made in Prague rather than in any foreign environment, if we are to judge from the relation of his work to the whole group of panels of this style and character which will be referred to below. The influence of Italian art on this master was strong and in his case penetrated deeper than in the case of his elder forerunner, the Master of the Klosterneuburg Altar, who, while outwardly adopting Italian motifs, had remained an adherent of Northern Gothic. The Vyšší Brod Master, too, it is true, adopted his subject grouping and composition motifs from Italian art, with more or less understanding of their structural significance, but he also endeavoured to achieve a picture with greater depth of space, with great substantiality and plasticity of forms on the Italian model. In the type of several of the heads one sees the obvious influence of Italian models, an influence which here and there manifests itself in the complexion of the figures. And in other respects the influence of Italian models is to be observed, particularly in the colouring. Here and there the Gothic colourfulness gives way to a striving for harmony of tones; the modelling of the heads and hands is dominated almost throughout by the use of relative intensity of colour as a modelling medium — all in the sense of Italian art. But on the whole the Master of the Vyšší Brod cycle remains a Gothic artist of the northern type. In his work Gothic northern idealism dominates, and even the realistic elements which come to the fore are of the same origin, and answer to the growing realistic tendencies of Gothic painting about the middle of the XIVth century. From the moment when research began to occupy itself more closely with the Vyšší Brod cycle, the lack of uniformity of this work in style and expression was a feature that specially struck art historians. This may be explained partly by the influence of the models or by memories of the works which the painter had seen, and one may also concede the influence of the hand of assistants. But we must not minimise the creative initiative and artistic responsibility of a master whose spirit and intelligence, despite all differences, dominate the whole work. In this cycle the Vyšší Brod Master reveals himself as a calm, yet sensitive narrator of sacred history, as a painter of lyric rather than of epic character who places beauty of form above force of expression. A quiet story-telling mood pervades all his pictures, softening the dramatic intensity of the forms even in the most stirring scenes. Only in the picture of the Descent of the Holy Ghost does there appear another order and rhythm of composition. Perhaps this is the only case in which it would be possible to speak of a contribution by some other hand, obviously that of an assistant whose artistic temperament differed from the master's own. Whether it is possible to regard the achievement of the Descent of the Holy Ghost as a sign of more advanced artistic development or whether it is necessary to explain it as a relic of an older style, is an important question. Upon the answer to it depends how we are to arrange and group other pictures falling within this stage of development and within the circle whose centre is represented by the Master of the Vyšší Brod Cycle. It seems to us that the picture marks indeed a step forward, a step in the direction of strengthening the dynamics of form and thus of intensifying the dramatic character of the picture in the sense of the advancing Gothic tradition, and that the existence here of a negligible number of italianisms must be explained by a gradual emancipation from Italian influences during the process of work on the altar. The picture of the Descent of the Holy Ghost would thus be in point of time one of the last, if not the last, of the pictures of the cycle. That the studio of the Master of Vyšší Brod in the period round 1350 had a central importance, and that from it there issued forces which dominated painting in the Fifties of that century has been an acknowledged fact from the time when the forgotten *Madonna of Veveří* was re-discovered and examined. A recent cleaning of the panel has revealed the whole beauty of form, colour and technique which was the attribute of the studio of the Master of Vyšší Brod. In this picture the borrowed motif of Madonna with bird is treated in a wholly independent fashion and thus, leaving aside the Most Madonna as the copy of an Italian model, forms the first link in the chain of Madonnas of this iconographical type so popular in Bohemia. The attempts at a poetically conceived expression of depth of feeling and beauty of form, which are the distinguishing marks of the art of the Master of Vyšší Brod, achieved their culmination in the *Kladzko Madonna* which is closely related to the Madonna of Veveří, and these marks now remained as permanent features of Czech Madonnas, even when the iconographical types or stylistic genus were different.

The finding and study of the Madonna of Veveří enriched this group by another work, the age of which still remains in doubt. This is *the Strahov Madonna* which, despite the fact that its value has depreciated by repainting, shows close affinity to, if not actual common origin with, the Madonna of Veveří. In contradistinction to the latter the Strahov Madonna reveals the hieratic severity of the Byzantine-Italian Madonnas, and together with it something of the very archaic formal features of the same origin. The decorative freedom of form and a certain lack of facial expression remain, and give an unfavourable impression in comparison with the Madonna of Veveří, but the method and technique of the painting, (in so far as it is possible, in spite of the repainting, to examine it in uncovered places), supports the assumption that the work probably came from the same studio that painted the Madonna of Veveří.

To the group closely connected with the art of the Master of Vyšší Brod belongs also a work that in its extent and its complexity of composition surpasses the Madonna of Veveří and attains the artistic level of that painting. This is the *Kladzko Madonna*, the centre-piece of a lost altar which the Archbishop of Prague, Arnošt of Pardubice, presented to the church of the Monastery of the Augustinian Order at Kladzko. In this work the one-sided dependence on Italian painting has been overcome, even though the striking similarity in the motif of the Child with that of the Most Madonna shows that the painter grew up among admirers of Italian art. In the entire structure of the composition and form the features of northern Gothic again assert themselves, this time in the refinement of form, answering to an environment and an epoch which laid emphasis upon grace and elegance of form. A certain French accent in the whole and in individual parts is undeniable, but the nationalisation of the type of Czech Madonna has here advanced a step further, pointing the way to painters of pictures of the Madonna towards an increasingly humanised conception of the Queen of Heaven.

If we regard this growing trend in favour of Gothic as a sign of liberation from dependence upon Italian painting, and pictures carrying these features as products of a further stage of development, of which we are convinced, then the small panel of *Kaufmann's 'Crucifixion'* is seen as a work having its origin in the wider circle of painting that developed around the art of the Master of the Vyšší Brod Cycle, and subsequent to him. The teaching which Czech painters had gained from Italian art was in this case not forgotten, but the painter applied all this acquired knowledge in a free and independent manner. Complexity of composition and compactness of the groups, the dramatic tension and eloquence of expression of the individual figures is not a sign of dependence upon the old Gothic style but the manifestation of a reaction to the earlier italianisation of artistic form, and a sign of the growing influence of Western Gothic which reveals itself also in the colourful saturation of the local tones which is also a striking feature of the Kladzko Madonna.

From this group, linked with the cycle of the Vyšší Brod Master, two works, showing close affinity with each other, diverge. They are the *Wroclaw 'Holy Trinity'* and the Košátky picture entitled the *Death of the Virgin Mary* which were apparently painted by the same artist. These pictures, too, are permeated with italianism, and they display several features of style of the same kind as do the pictures emanating from the Vyšší Brod master's circle, but in addition we observe a whole series of characteristics which bear witness to the work of an artist of considerable independence of style and initiative in composition. At a period when the dependence on models of Italian art had already declined, the painter of the two panels made abundant use of Italian patterns, especially those of Siena, having a better understanding of Italian motifs and more freedom in dealing with them than the Vyšší Brod Master. In the picture of the Holy Trinity, which shows an affinity to the traditional scheme of composition, this well-defined personality of the painter is not so prominent, but in the picture of the Death of the Virgin Mary, which is perhaps a later work than the picture of the Holy Trinity, the creative initiative of the artist finds full vent. In the complex structure of its composition, in the skilful and logical construction of architectural space as well as in the dramatic vitality of the figures and their personal characterisation this picture represents the greatest achievement in that sphere of Czech painting which was influenced by Italian art. That it was from highly developed and artistically outstanding models that the artist took his inspiration is proved by the complex architecture, which is a direct derivation from the architectural motifs of the frescoes in the Lower Church of Assisi; and how well he grasped the sense of space of the adapted motifs is shown by the faultless construction, from the visual angle, of the tripartite arcade. A wholly personal feature, however, is the dramatic pathos of the group with its figure types sharply defined in physiognomy and expression, and the range of feeling and thought shown by the gestures of faces and hands. The unusually realistic talent of the painter contributed to this intensively expressive character of the picture. The expressiveness of the heads, fundamentally still true to the prevailing type, is enhanced by realistic features drawn from the artist's visual experience, but his talent for observation stands out most prominently in the drawing and foreshortening of the hands. In this work the artist overcame the contemporary schematism in such a radical fashion that not only in all the preceding but also in all the subsequent development do we find no analogy to such realism, such prepossession with fidelity to form.

In the picture of the Death of the Virgin Mary was attained the most complete assimilation of Italian influences with the northern Gothic tradition, and everything goes to prove that in the period round about 1360 the influence of Italian art began to decline and once again a traditional Gothic sentiment gained the upper hand, and that with it the creative capacity of Czech painting grew in scope and quality. Illuminated manuscripts bearing dates from the early Sixties of the XIVth century show in most instructive fashion that in addition to the studios in which painting was still carried on under the strong influence of Italian patterns (such as the studio of Arnošt of Pardubice) there developed others which had already replaced imitative activities by independent effort and by an output that surpassed aesthetically all that had gone before (among them the workshop of Jan of Středa). In no way different was the development of panel painting, which had also begun to emancipate itself from dependence on alien models and to seek out a path of development of its own. What had been gained by contact with Italian art was not forgotten; on the contrary, Czech painters, ceasing to cling to the borrowed elements of Italian painting, began to penetrate to the fundamental meaning of that art in the structure of space and plastic form. In the panel painting of the Sixties of the XIVth century, just as in book illumination, there was a striking increase of careful attention to depth of space and three-dimensional corporeal volume, while at the same time the modelling of light dominated over expression of form by line. This new tendency appears for the first time in the Budějovice picture of the *Madonna with St. Catherine and St. Margaret*. The artist who painted it belonged already to that section who had emancipated themselves from one-sided dependence on Italian art and had reverted to the traditional roots of northern art. Contact with the art of the new plastic orientation, apparently with French art, had prompted him to fill out his draft sketch with light and shade which modelled the forms and made the local colours fluid.

To this section belongs a work whose age until recently was in doubt, but whose perfectly executed restoration has revealed one of the most significant works of art of this period, *the Zbraslav Madonna*. This, too, is one of the type of Madonna and Child where the Child plays with a bird, but it is a work so independent and mature in its style and artistic execution that we must regard it as the product of the hand of a master eminent in that circle of artists who combined Italian features of style with Western elements, possibly direct French elements.

This turn in development finds confirmation in a number of pictures dating from the period round 1360 in which an advance in plastic outlook can be observed in many of the individual variations. To this category belongs the small *Vienna diptych* carrying pictures of the Madonna and the Man of Sorrows, in which a painter of this transitional period elaborated two iconographical Byzantine-Italian types. Despite the fact that he adopted the composition fairly faithfully from his model, he nevertheless interpreted the forms in his own way in the spirit of the domestic tradition, strengthened by a return to the spiritual basis of northern Gothic, and he found new artistic modes of expression in light and shade and in the structure of form by means of colour. With the Vienna diptych is associated the small picture of *the Rome Madonna*, (after the Madonna of Veveří) a further specimen of the Madonna type known as the Madonna of Zbraslav which is merely a revised motif of the Madonna with Child and Bird. But it is a new style of painting. The suppression of line, the intensification of the plastic tendency, the filling out of the drawing by an energetic under-painting of the figures — all this corresponds to the new plastic sentiment which, at the beginning of the Seventies of the XIVth century, is manifested in book illumination (Liber Viaticus). It is more difficult to place in point of time the picture of the *Vyšehrad Madonna*, which is closely allied to Italian variations on the Byzantine theme of the Galaktotrophusa. It is undoubtedly a copy of an Italian model. It was at one time a disputed question, whether the Czech picture had its origin in the schools which supported the Italian trend in art after the middle of the XIVth century, or whether it was a later copy. After a fresh study of the problem we are inclined to place the date after 1360, although we are well aware that the last word in the matter cannot be spoken until the many patches of repainting done in 1911, which distort the picture, have been removed.

After the comprehensive discussion which has taken place as to where *the small panel from the Morgan Library*, with pictures of the Adoration of the Three Kings and the Death of the Virgin Mary, is to be placed as regards origin and style, it is no longer necessary to doubt the Czech origin of this work of art, so outstanding in its development. The trend towards the mellow style of painting of the Sixties and Seventies has here made considerable advance, apparently more than may be surmised from the badly worn picture. The pictures are still permeated with strong Italian influences, the form still displays something of the drawing style of the older painting marked by Italian trends; but the simple articulation and the imposing plastic fulness of the figures already correspond entirely to the artistic views of the Sixties which modelled figures by means of intensifying the highlights on places in higher relief, and displayed a fondness for softly merged transitions in the modelling of the draperies. This stage of development is represented by the style of *the Boston Madonna* which marks a fresh step ahead in the gradual abandonment of the hieratic, and in the humanising of the image of the Mother of God.

The origin and the rise of the realistically, indeed naturalistically oriented style of art of the close of the Sixties which is closely connected with the person of the Court painter *Theodoric* and his great work in the Chapel of the Holy Cross has raised one of the most outstanding questions of Czech painting in the XIVth century, the more so since even the Karlštejn panels themselves are problematical in both their origin and their age. The rise of this new style cannot be explained by anything in the development of Czech panel painting before about 1360, since the new features which appear in the pictures of the transitional group of which we have spoken above, are rather the reflection of an already existing new style than of its precursor. The most weighty objection to the assumption of an immediate connection in development between the two groups is that the art of the new style rejected practically all the achievements of the older Italian-oriented art, that it abandoned its structural efforts in the delineation of space and form, its pregnancy of form and its firmness of character. In the elucidation of this new style it is not enough to assume that Theodoric's art derived from book illumination-though in this we can indeed also trace a gradual liberation of form from the domination of line, by the introduction of solidity of form, by emphasizing the slightness of the articulation of corporeal bulk, and by softly graded modelling produced by subduing the local tones and adding light to them. But we cannot for many reasons regard book illumination as the branch of painting in which this sudden change took place. On the contrary, all the inferences to be drawn from analysing the appropriate book-illumination material, as well as considerations of a general character, lead to the conclusion that book illumination here merely followed and imitated the style of panel painting. Nor does the assumption that a deeper insight into the problems of Italian painting brought about this turn of affairs altogether suffice to clear up the mystery. Not even in its greatest freedom of form, as we meet it in the work of illuminators, did Italian painting advance to such a breaking-up of compositional form as that to which this new style attained. If the master painter Theodoric was its adherent, its representative or even its author (as we assume on good grounds), then this style must have existed at least in principle even before the year 1359, when, as documentary evidence proves, Theodoric was already living in Prague in the capacity, moreover, of Court painter. That the phenomenon of Theodoric could be explained by a gradual evolution from the older italianising art is in conflict with the psychology of the medieval artist. The style which distinguishes Theodoric has no analogy in any European art of the time except for a striking affinity with the art of the Hamburg master Bertram. This has up to now been explained, not without objections, by assuming some connection between Bertram's schooling and Master Theodoric. It is doubtful whether one can say that the art of Theodoric has no foreign roots whatsoever, and perhaps Bertram's art does proceed from the same source as that of Theodoric. Knowing, as we do to-day, that the liberation of Gothic form from abstract linear conceptions was a thing of Western art, too, and that even the impetuous impulses towards naturalism were a feature of contemporary French and Dutch painting (for example, the portrait of King Jean le Bon in the Louvre, and the epitaph of Hendrik van Rijn in the Antwerp Museum), we cannot exclude the possibility that Theodoric might have been a foreigner, called to Prague in the Fifties from somewhere in the West. It is true that we even meet in Italy with a work which displays the like features of style as the art of Theodoric, namely the frescoes on the vaults of the chancel of San Francesco at Treviso, but these paintings are to-day regarded by Italian experts on the art of the trecento as the works of a painter of non-Italian, trans-Alpine origin.

Another open question is that of the paintings decorating the Chapel of the Holy Cross. The painter of these, according to a Charles IV charter of the year 1367, was Master Theodoric. The question is whether the paintings, a great system of panels depicting in half-life-size figures the celestial soldiers of Christ, scenes of the Crucifixion and a triptych of the 'Man of Sorrows', are an original work by Theodoric or whether they are later copies of originals. From the moment when authorities on art history began to occupy themselves with the Karlštejn panels they were struck by the peculiarly formal character of these paintings. In the Romantic period, which concerned itself with the question of the origin and rise of oil-painting, the cause of the difference in the panels of the Chapel of the Holy Cross was thought to lie in the painting technique. Even then historians were struck by the soft, free, broad manner of painting which was never attained in the traditional tempera of the Middle Ages. Later, when a knowledge of the relics of Czech painting of the XIVth century was well advanced and when questions of form had already begun to be the object of interest to experts, the question of the Karlštejn panels was one of the main problems of Czech Gothic painting. For a time it seemed that the assumption of a later painting-over of the panels could be supported by the special character of their style, but a systematically executed restoration and scrutiny of the panels in our own day has shown that this assumption is erroneous. It was found that both the wood and the painting, except in the picture of the Crucifixion and some gusseted panels, were in a remarkable state of preservation, that apart from some slight retouches in oil colour the paintings had not been substantially affected by restoration, and that the pictures had darkened only because of the decay of the varnish surfaces. On the removal of the darkening coats of varnish the original brilliant colouring of the pictures was revealed. At the same time the special stylistic features of the painting itself came all the more to the front. In the relevant section of our catalogue the reader will find observations, studies and conclusions on the latest researches connected with the Karlštejn panels. Here only the main points of this complicated problem will be touched upon.

The first question is one of chronology. It is a matter of deciding whether the origin of the paintings is to be placed between the dates of the first and the second consecration of the Chapel of the Holy Cross, that is, between the years 1357 and 1365, or between 1365 and 1367, that is, between the year of the second consecration of the Chapel and the year when Theodoric was rewarded by the Emperor for his work on the decoration of the Chapel. Since two dates of consecration of a church mean as a rule that there have been two stages in the process of building, or more or less fundamental and extensive changes in adjustment and finishing, it may be assumed that the second arrangement of the Chapel of the Holy Cross was completed in the year 1365. The question remains whether the chapel was decorated by Theodoric's panels at that time, or not until after 1365, and whether the substitute panels were not set in the walls in place of the original ones (which were perhaps decayed or unsuitable for mural decoration). The assumption that the panels may have replaced the actual original mural paintings is supported by a number of observations made in the course of a study of these panels. In addition, the mature style which the panels reveal is itself an argument for placing them rather in the late Sixties than in the period just after 1357 when we still presuppose the existence of a style of an older and different character. Another question is whether the panels that have been preserved are really the work of Theodoric and whether they were painted in the Sixties. The opinion had been advanced that the panels are perhaps later copies of Theodoric's original paintings, whether mural or panel paintings. The main reason for doubt lay in their style and the technique of the execution which seemed to be beyond the stage of development of painting in the XIVth century. After a fresh re-examination of the material and in particular after a fresh study of the Mulhouse Altar, which represents a late and extreme link in the development of Theodoric's style, we incline to-day to the opinion that not only the panels but also the paintings in the window recesses of the Chapel of the Holy Cross at Karlštejn are the original work of Theodoric, though we do not wholly dismiss the possibility of their being later copies. The final answer to the question is a matter of further research.

A striking feature of Theodoric's art is his indifference to the constructive problems of space with which artists in the preceding period occupied themselves so much. The concentrated attention on corporeal form revealed in the Karlštejn panels, whether in the narrative scenes, in the Crucifixion, in the Man of Sorrows or the three women, might be explained by the decorative tendencies of the embellishment of the Chapel of the Holy Cross, but the pictures painted on the wall in the window recesses show, despite their complexity of composition, that the plastic programme of painters of the generation that preceded him was alien to Theodoric. The artist's whole interest was concentrated on the human form, and its development in the sphere of plastics and painting. He applies in his figures the canon of proportion, emphasising the physical solidity and dimension of the human body. A stocky trunk, a large thick head on a short neck, full fleshy face and hands are characteristic features of the artist's proportions. In the development of his bodily forms Theodoric found scope for his inclination to materialism, and in a manner at that time unprecedented throughout Europe. It would be possible to speak of an attempt at a designed individualisation of figures if it were not for several fundamental types in the whole group of saint figures, and if the entire mass of the figures of the celestial army of Christ could not be reduced to a masculine and feminine prototype. An endeavour to rise above the traditional idealism of Gothic faces is everywhere apparent, but this endeavour is not enough — comprehensibly enough in a painter of the XVIth century — to achieve the actual form of skull and hands, the real structure of sinews and muscles, or to attain optical foreshortening in harmony with the position of the head or hand. It is only a certain number of individual realistic details which give vitality to the surface of the faces and hands, but they surprise us with their expressive and lifelike character.

The naturalistic character of Theodoric's Karlštejn pictures is substantially heightened by his method and technique. The painter, emphasizing the cohesion of corporeal bulk and intent on plasticity of form wraps his figures in sack-like, little-articulated folds of only slightly undulating drapery. The outline is merely a working aid for him which, as his work progresses, he covers with his paint, producing forms with soft colour darkening in the shadows and growing brighter in the light. Intensity of local tone is employed in every imaginable degree, and the quality of the colour too is brought to a perfection till then unknown. It is remarkable what manifold variations of colour there is in the complexions of the men and women, and how completely in harmony with the complexions is the colouring of the shading by means of various tints of pigment. Theodoric's passion for colourfulness, however, runs riot particularly in the draperies where sometimes two different qualities of colour are brought together in the same material, without any essential motivation but merely for reasons of colouring. The soft process employed by Theodoric, reminiscent of oil technique was made possible by new binding media which prevented a rapid drying of the painting and permitted work with a soft and broad brush. It would seem that the whole was painted alla prima with the exception of a little enamel which mostly perished in time. All this proves that the Court painter was a personality both inventive and bold. Probably this method and technique of painting were evoked by the necessity of mastering so extensive a task in such a short space of time.

It is a question whether Theodoric could have accomplished such a great task with the usual help afforded by a medieval art workshop. A formal analysis of the panels enables us to see that the entire cycle was painted by the hands of two painters who have left clear traces of their work. If more painters were engaged in the work their share was of minor importance, one of mere assistants. The first group of panels is roughly that of the part of the chapel containing the altar and separated from the rest by iron railings, the second group covers the greater part of the walls at the entrance The pictures of the first group exhibit alike the same canon of proportion, massiveness of body, large heads and soft grading of forms from the basic colours — these are the common features of this group. In the other group we note considerable changes in proportion: the heads are usually smaller in proportion to the body, the faces are more finely articulated and the physiognomy more expressive, the modelling is carried out with greater energy, thanks to the use of dark tones in the shading. From all this it can be assumed that the work was divided up between a master painter who painted the more important first part and his assistant who worked on the second part. This assistant was of course one of the master's pupils and kept to the master's intentions with the fidelity of a disciple, but with enough individuality of his own as to impress some personal features upon the work of collaboration from the workshop.

The number of works that have been preserved in which there are direct evidences of the inspiration and influence of Master Theodoric is smaller than we should have expected in the case of a painter of his importance. The most closely allied to his style is the *Votive picture of Jan Očko of Vlašim*, ordered by the Archbishop of Prague some time after the year 1370 for the new chapel of the episcopal palace at Roudnice. The original gold background, fragments of which were disclosed during a recent restoration, brought into prominence the magnificence of the local colours, and the figures were presented in all their naturalness without detracting from the monumental effect and ceremonial pathos of the picture. The figures of the Emperor, of his son and of the archbishop, are no longer the small figures representative of the donor but are on the same scale as the figures of the saints, reduced merely by their kneeling posture. The modelling of the faces is done in dark colours, but the relief of the magnificently plaited folds of the robes is brought into prominent contrast to the intense local colour mainly by means of white. All this corresponds to the method and technique of painting adopted by Theodoric, whose pupil the painter apparently was, but the efforts he made to give the heads of the historical personages the character of portraits derive from some other source. The painter was obviously influenced in this matter by the artist responsible for the royal mural portraits in the Church of St. Mary, Karlštejn, who kept to the realistic tendency of contemporary French portrait painting.

While the painter of the votive picture of Očko belongs to the circle of Theodoric's workshop, the panel of the *Crucifixion from the Emmaus Monastery* in Prague pertains to the circle of wider influence of the Master. In a composition of none too great skill the artist, making use of densely packed groups of women and soldiers under a super-dimensioned Crucified Christ, applies Theodoric's principles of composition, but in his figures slenderness and suppleness of form triumph over the stockiness of Theodoric's figures.

That the influence of Theodoric's art was felt in Czech painting more frequently and for a longer time than we might judge from the number of works that have come down to us, is evidenced by the first dated work and the first completely preserved, winged altar of Bohemian origin, the Mulhouse Altar of the year 1385. In the hands of a painter of but little talent, and a slipshod worker who tried in the main face of the open altar to produce all that he was capable of with the figures of Ss. Wenceslas, Vitus and Sigismund, the decomposition of form into colour proceeded far, most of all in the roughly executed remaining panels where the artist worked with conventional lines and with a drawing which at times was sketchy. All the greater, however, is the effect of the altar in its expression, for the haphazard manner of painting intensifies the dramatic expression of the scenes of the passion. In this work which was on a level with bourgeois art we feel distinctly the reflection of the growth of piety and ardent yearning to experience in spirit the sacrifice of the Redeemer, which had sunk deep and spread far and wide at the close of the century. The last work, apparently a late one, which proclaims its affinity to the art of Theodoric is the small Brno picture depicting *the Death of the Virgin Mary*. In this, however, one notes a number of other features of form and technique more advanced in style.

Theodoric's art deviated too sharply from the line of previous development and aimed too radically at naturalism as the goal of art, and adopted too boldly the fusing of form in colour and light to be able to develop further in this direction. It would seem that Theodoric's style came to an end with the group of his immediate pupils and followers. Nor was the echo of his work either great or lasting outside Bohemia. A lack of surviving examples of panel painting does not, it is true, permit us to know in what direction the development of panel painting tended in the Seventies of the XIVth century, but the mural paintings in the transept of the Church of Emmaus are eloquent proof of what different tendencies in art, what new influences continually penetrating from the South and the West made their presence felt in the works of art produced in that decade, and what artists of creative personality were engaged in that work. In this Church we find complex narrative pictures displaying extensive and deep sectors of space and already dominated by an advanced perspective projection of three-dimensional form on to the plane of the picture. The Biblical scenes are interpreted by the artist in complex figure groups, the figures acquiring an unprecedented vivacity by the variety of their different positions, postures and motions. Although there is much to indicate borrowings from Italian, French and possibly even Dutch art, the final synthesis none the less shows a creative will working at high tension and a plastic talent surpassing all that the development of art had hitherto displayed. Growing realism, vivid eloquence of form and a keen eye for actuality give abundant support to a fondness for realistic motifs carrying moral lessons. All this, however, does not in any way weaken the spiritual pathos of the typological grouping of the Emmaus cycle. Never before had the depicting of sacred history attained such spiritual sensibility and depth of expression as wells forth from the pictures of the Emmaus cycle. This intensified spirituality of the art of the Seventies was equally a reaction against the naturalism of Theodoric and a result of the deepening of the religious sentiment of the day, still profoundly concerned with the questions of redemption and salvation. It reached its culminating expression in the work of *the Master of the Třeboň altar*, of which there remain only three panels, with pictures of Christ on Mount Olivet, the Resurrection and the Laying in the Sepulchre on the front, and figures of male and female saints on the back. This Master's activities, as has now been proved after extensive discussion, are to be placed in the period round about 1380. Several features of his style point to some connection between the early stages of his development and the art of the close of the Sixties and of the Seventies (the cycle of the Apocalypse in St. Mary's Church at Karlštejn and the cycle in the transept of the Monastery of Emmaus), but alongside elements which the master adopted from the preceding development there are obviously new features here of a type so little based on previous development that we must reckon with the personal genius of the master as a factor of fundamental importance. The elements on which the artist builds up his space belong to the older inventory of Gothic landscape. They are coulisses extended vertically and foreshortening into depth, in the intervening spaces of which are placed figures on much the same scale as the surrounding landscape. The painter here strove for visual unity of space and form with a structural logic which surpasses the abstract graphic character and symbolism of Gothic space. The painter succeeds in giving depth to this space even for objects in perspective (the sarcophagus in the picture of the Resurrection) and in grouping the figures in a natural and lively three-dimensional whole. In his conception of the human figure the Třeboň master owes, it is true, something to the naturalism of his predecessors, but he revives the traditional Gothic canon both in his slender, supple bodies and the flexible movement of the limbs. He enriches the conventional type of head by an expressive and realistic characterisation of his own and does not hesitate to sharpen the caricature-like features of the faces of his figures appearing in the Passion scene. On the other hand he never succumbs to the seductions of naturalism so far as to sacrifice to it the spiritual content or the sense of the picture either as a whole or in its parts. The spiritualism with which the Třeboň master was imbued did not permit his desire for realism in the facial features to extend to the other parts of the body (the hands and feet, for example, which are practically schematic) nor to allow of the drapery being a faithful representation of actual robes and garments. His group of soldiers shows with what exactitude, almost moralising in its effect, the master succeeded in presenting the vulgar types of human figures, how successful he was in employing the features of contemporary clothing and weapons for vitalising and giving picturesqueness to the Passion scenes, and yet the main characters, in spite of all the realism of the heads, remain in the realm of a spiritual vision which insisted upon a fanciful outline of body and head and upon an idealistic sweep of folds. Even though something here is due to the achievements of the mellow style of painting of the preceding period, the conventionalising Gothic line once more lays claim to its rights. The drapery is again dominated by a system of curves and loops, the linear design of which is merely screened by the artist's execution of bulk and form. That the linear articulation of the drapery was thus subdued by colour, out of regard for the unity and integral character of the Passion pictures, is proved by the figures of the male and female saints on the reverse of the panels. There, where th, figures are conceived as isolated presentations and designed to have the effect of polychrome statuese the Třeboň master arranged the drapery in skilful systems of folds which already anticipate the views and taste of the coming period which created the so-called beautiful style in sculpture and painting.

The Třeboň master was able to carry out his aim to fashion a picture visually complete in all its elements by a method whose existence at this point is a real mystery. His pictures are based on an atmosphere which shrouds the space in semi-darkness, into which falls light from some magic, supernatural source sharply illuminating only the main features. This light is so absorbed by the dusky space that the outlines practically disappear altogether. How conscious is this reliance upon some definite source of light is shown in the picture of the Resurrection where the artist has painted a cast shadow behind the figures of Christ and the soldier. The artist has achieved this chiaroscuro by a consistent ground-painting of all his figures in dark-brown pigment, which robs the local tones of their intensity of colour and unites all the colours in a uniform basic tone. This method of painting and technique was, it is true, initiated to a certain extent in the style of the Theodoric period, which could modulate the local tone through decoloration by means of light impinging from above and darkening it in the depths, but this method of painting cannot be explained merely as the result of such development. Nor can the method be deduced either from French or Italian painting, even though some preliminary bases for this style came into being there. There is nothing left but to assume in this case a touch of genius on the part of the artist who, long before the time when chiaroscuro became an inevitable feature in the development of art, anticipated its method and technique. The study made up to now of the work of the Třeboň master proves that the artist grew up in the tradition of Czech painting of the XIVth century, to become its consummator. But it remains a disputed point whether it is possible to place all the greatness of his art to the credit of his creative initiative. The fact is that in almost all the phases of development of Czech Gothic painting, including those in which the dominance of Italian art is undeniable, French art, and at the close of the century Franco-Flemish art, too, influenced that development, and this prompts the assumption that even the Třeboň master owes more to the West than it has yet been possible to show. The lack of surviving specimens of French and Dutch painting of the second quarter of the XIVth century prevents us from fixing the extent of these influences upon the art of the Master of Třeboň, but attention may be drawn to the Passion Altar in the Besançon Museum dating from about 1370, which in the parts that have not been repainted and in those from which the later painting has been removed, reveals in some sectors features of a cognate art, albeit of an older development.

It is comprehensible that the art of a painter who was able to give such life and wealth to the traditional formulae of picture-painting and who could give voice to his artistic sentiments and experiences in such an expressive and eloquent form, should have a profound influence not only upon his own immediate environment but also upon a circle wider than that of any of his predecessors. Of his pupils obviously the most talented was the assistant whose co-operation has been ascertained in the picture of the Laying in the Sepulchre, and in the figures of the saints on the reverse of the panel. This man was also the one who actually continued the master's work in the synthesis of idealism and realism which aimed already at the 'beautiful' style to which Czech sculpture and painting clung towards the close of the century. The master's principle of light was understood, it is true, in substance by his pupil, the modelling of the faces is oval and soft, but in the Laying in the Sepulchre we note a return to a greater lightness of the tones and a renewal of the significance of local colours. Another individual touch closely connected with the workshop of the Třeboň master is to be seen in the Crucifixion panel *from the chapel at Sv. Barbora* near Třeboň, a picture which perhaps formed, together with the panel of the Adoration of Christ discussed below, part of the second Třeboň altar. The compositional and typological affinity of the picture to the Emmaus Crucifixion is considerable, but this does not justify the conclusion that we are concerned here with the work of some predecessor of the Třeboň master or of some work of the master's of an earlier date. The colour structure of the picture and the technique of painting show that the picture was painted by an artist independent of the painter of the Třeboň altar, one who had possibly some sort of connection, perhaps in the early stages of his career, with the art of the older generation. To some other hand among the circle of the Třeboň master must probably be ascribed the panel depicting *the Adoration of Christ* preserved at Hluboká Castle, a work of art noteworthy in many respects. In its iconography and typology this picture is a proof of how Franco-Flemish influences increased at the close of the century. The complex form of the cottage is borrowed from the West (cf. the Adoration in the Public Collection of Art in Basle) but the perspective construction was not understood by the Czech painter and was distorted. The realistic figures of the herdsmen, too, correspond to the typology of contemporary Western painting. The seriously damaged picture shows in the parts that have been somewhat better preserved, that in its colouring and expression it forms a link in the chain which already unites the school of the Třeboň master to the painting of the beginning of the XVth century. A very close connection with the workshop of the Třeboň master is shown in the frame pictures of the panel depicting *the Madonna Aracoeli*, itself a copy of the Byzantine type of the Mother of God Agiosoritissa, venerated in the Aracoeli Church in Rome. The frame figures of female saints are in all their typological and colour structure derived from the art of the Třeboň master, although some formal features point to the later advanced period in which a reaction against the style of painting of the master had already set in.

A wholly special place in the sphere of influence of the Třeboň master is occupied by *the Vyšší Brod Crucifixion*, the painter of which had already estranged himself considerably from the ideals of the art of the Třeboň master. What above all impresses the beholder as a new feature is the emotional, pathetic expression of the composition as a whole, and of the separate figures, an effect coming from the mobile lines of the figures and the mimicry of the postures. Here for the first time is raised the voice of an epoch which regards with a perturbed mind the mystery of the redemption, here the mystical spirituality of the Třeboň master acquires a sharp dramatic tone which has already something in it of the pathetic sentiment of Late Gothic. Certain reminiscences of the art of the oldest generation of Czech painting are a sign of return to the motifs of the Italianising style such as we more frequently observe in painting round about and after 1400. Among the specimens of Czech panel painting of the period round about 1400 there is no work which would display in its expression traits similar to those of the Vyšší Brod Crucifixion. A single work which answers to the style of the dying influence of the school of the Třeboň master, a much repainted panel with a picture of *the*

Madonna with Ss. Bartholomew and Margaret preserved in Hluboká Castle, displays on the contrary traces of the view of art which came into being at the close of the XIVth century as a reaction to the expressive tendency and artistic form of the Třeboň master. In this picture it gained the upper hand over considerations expressive of care and purity and beauty of form; here manifested themselves the first signs of a decorative formalism which subsequently dominated painting in the first two and a half decades of the XVth century.

That the Třeboň master found none to continue his work and that even painters belonging to his circle were carried away by reactionary currents inimical to the master's art, bears witness to the fact that this master was an exceptional genius who was born before his time, and that the development of Czech art followed an unsteady course. This phenomenon is all the more striking since, by contrast, the influence of the Třeboň master abroad was considerable and fruitful both in style and execution. Frankish art received from this source important impulses in its development, the influence of the Třeboň master was felt in Austrian art, too, and more than one of his pupils carried his style far afield to the North, to Poland and East Prussia (the altar at Grudziadz). Not until round about the year 1420 did many elements pass from the art of the Třeboň master into the general contemporary style. Only then did the art of this great Czech artist acquire an actual influence upon subsequent development.

Contrary to all expectations there occurred, as has already been mentioned, a sudden change in development at the close of the XIVth century. Czech painting turned aside from expressive realism and from the interpretation of form by colour and light, and reverted to the traditional poetic idealism, and with it, to linear and plastic abstraction of form. Round about the year 1400 form again appears as tangibly firm, articulated in outline and drawing; modelling is again dominated by abstract light and shade. Rich articulation of the draperies, and with it a flexible plasticity of the folds, had its origin here apparently under the influence of contemporary sculpture, which also affected painting by its aestheticism of form culminating in the group of 'beautiful' Madonnas. Painting, too, succumbed to this aesthetic movement which was connected with early humanism. The fragility, elegance, grace of movement and delicate mimicry of figure which we meet with in sculpture, in panel painting, in book illumination and the mural painting of this period, corresponds to the refined character of the Court culture of the reign of Wenceslas, into which the strengthened influence of French art had again penetrated. Alongside novelties in form, however, we observe a certain retrospective tendency. The painting of this epoch seems glad to revert to the schematic of composition and the motifs of the old Italianising generation, and it elaborated on eclectic lines many of the typological achievements of the development up to that day. An inclination to calligraphic form grew with the time, and there already appear signs even of mannerism, leading away from a solution of the fundamental problems of plastic art and painting.

The epitaph of Jan of Jeřeň which is dated 1395 is evidence of the development of a new style which had already reached an advanced stage. The beginnings of this style, however, we can observe in the sphere of book illumination round about the year 1390, of course in a weaker reflection. The slender, pliant forms on the epitaph, robed in folded draperies which pay scant respect to the body, are already dominated by a kind of style that shows a fondness for sharply outlined and flexibly modelled shapes. Light, it is true, still dissolves the local coloured form, but colour already returns again to its old role as a medium of expression. That the development tended rapidly towards a decorative simplicity of drapery is proved by a picture related to the epitaph in style but much more conservative in form, *the Dubeček Votive Panel*, with its figures of the patron saints of Bohemia and the donor, a canon. The draperies show the decorative tendencies of the new style and the formalism of the system of folds. In the heads, too, which are merely a revised version of the types created by the Theodoric school and given greater depth of expression by the Třeboň master, the efforts towards greater delicacy of form and refinement of expression, which were a commanding feature of the 'beautiful' style, continued their course. On this new level of style, however, realism would not be denied and also played a part, in the increased wealth of detail and greater expressiveness of the faces. This is evidenced by the *Cirkvice Mater Dolorosa* whose face is full of detail, almost individualising the conventional type of Madonna. All the features of the 'beautiful' style, however, appear in a work of an artistic quality equal to that of the contemporary statues of 'beautiful' Madonnas and influenced by them — *the Madonna of St. Vitus Cathedral*. This represents a new elaboration of type in the line of variations which go back to the Strahov Madonna. The grave hieratic expression of the faces of both Mary and Christ appear here as the last relic of the old iconic type, but the humanising of the figures, the charm of the lineaments of the Mother and the delightful naturalness of the little head and body of the Child come from a sentiment which is able to combine the new realism of detail with the idealising tendencies of the 'beautiful' style. That contemporary sculpture directly influenced painters is shown by the realistic feature where Mary's hand is pressed into the body of the child, a feature that appears in the "beautiful" Madonnas and which could have its rise solely in sculpture. This type of Madonna was frequently copied (the oldest copy is possibly *the Lnáře Madonna*) and became common later under the name of the miracle-working *Zlatá Koruna Madonna*. This last-named appears to us to-day like a replica of the St. Vitus Madonna or some other model of the same type. It is the work of a painter not of first rank, who often failed to grasp what his model had to tell him about form, and who, as a colourist, contented himself with coarse effects. That the basic likeness for this type may have been the full-length figure of Mary is evidenced by the small panel of the seated Madonna of *Jindřichův Hradec*, painted with the delicacy of technique of miniature painting and artistically of the same quality as a master-piece of the 'beautiful' style of the beginning of the XVth century. In this picture a unity of expression of Mother and Child has been achieved, while both figures became intensely human through touches that are realistic but are enhanced on the formal side by the adoption of the 'beautiful' style. This picture is a proof that Czech painting, like Czech sculpture at this period, was imbued with the creative ideal of Renaissance art. *The Berlin Crucifixion* among these panels issuing from the 'beautiful' style forms a special link. It is an example of this style in its ultimate development, manifesting as it does certain traits of mannerism in its form, but not displaying any closer affinity with any of the preserved panels of this class. In contemporary book miniatures we find, however, reflections of the same style, with its affectation of form and expression, which produced this picture in some workshop from which no other work has come down to us.

At the outset of the XVth century there appeared among the Madonnas which repeat or modify the St. Vitus type of Madonna, variations of the traditional Mary motif, distinguished from the hitherto prevailing half-life-sizes by turning the figure of Mary from left to right and by changing the position of the Child. It is a type which from old times has taken its title from the Miraculous Madonna of Vyšší Brod, although this one is not itself the oldest preserved specimen of the type. The oldest, and from the point of view of art the most valuable representative of this type is *the Roudnice Madonna*, the importance and beauty of which was only recently revealed by the removal of a clumsy Baroque retouching and a complete restoration of the picture. In the Madonna of this new type the last traces of the icon-like fixed gaze ahead of Mother and Child disappear. Mary's eyes are cast down to gaze at the Child whose eyes look up to her. This substantially intensifies the spiritual bond between Mother and Child to which the development of the portrayal of Mary tended. The form-structure of the Roudnice Madonna shows that this final humanising of the motif of the Madonna was achieved within the scope of the 'beautiful' style. Closely connected with the Roudnice Madonna is *the Madonna of the Church of the Holy Trinity* at České Budějovice, the oldest of the copies and a variation of this popular type. The decorative calligraphy of the 'beautiful' style manifests itself here especially in the frame pictures, though with somewhat lessened expression. To the Holy Trinity Madonna which, despite the fact that it has been preserved in a South Bohemian town, is not a work of provincial origin, is quite closely related *the Veraicon of the Cathedral of St. Vitus* with its face of Christ, which is an elaboration of the Byzantine-Italian prototype in the spirit of an art aiming at beauty of form. The frame figures of saints, too, still adhere to the form of the 'beautiful' style, even though they already display some formal features suggesting another origin.

That Byzantine and iconographical motifs lost nothing of their attractiveness as time went on is proved by the extensive, though incomplete, *Cycle of Heads at the Capuchin Church*, Prague, in which appears the pattern of Byzantine Deésis in its Czech version, showing traces of Eastern typology only in the heads of Christ and the Madonna. All the other heads are a revised version of the typical Czech types in which, ever since the time of Theodoric, efforts were made to strengthen the individualist characteristics of the heads of the saints and apostles. Only the penetrating gaze of their eyes has in it something taken from some Byzantine, or, more probably, Byzantine-Italian model. These pictures are painted with meticulous technique and purity and beauty of form and pertain to the sphere of the 'beautiful' style, although in this case the painter by his efforts at expression went beyond the psychological scope of that style. The Capuchin cycle is closely connected, as has been previously observed, to the Ambrass sketch-book, whose artist based his work on the beautiful style and possibly came directly from the workshop in which the Capuchin cycle originated, and sketched a series of heads as models for painting. A typological echo of the heads of the apostles as delineated in the 'beautiful' style is to be found in the Nuremberg picture of *the Death of the Virgin Mary*, which, however, displays no close affinity with any of the relics of that style; it shows rather some joint characteristics with book illumination round about the year 1410.

With *the Roudnice Altar* we come to the stage of development in the predella which divides the epoch of the 'beautiful' style from the painting which derived from it, but which had already other aims of form and expression. In the heads of the principal figures we find, it is true, practically all the traditional types as given ultimate shape round about the year 1400, while in the flowing, trailing folds of the draperies, too, is still to be seen the calligraphic tendency of the 'beautiful' style, but the figures have neither the beauty of form achieved by the preceding period of art, nor the power of expression to which painting rapidly achieved in the period after 1420 when it was desired to overcome the mannerisms which had remained as a heritage from the beautiful style. The composition of the Death of the Virgin shows clearly how the aesthetic sense of the painting of this period had declined, how the painters borrowed, in eclectic fashion and without a deeper understanding of fundamental problems, from the treasures of older art and how in expression, which had already begun to be a matter of contemporary interest, nothing more for the moment could be attained than what the hand of an assistant succeeded in imprinting on the outer pictures of the wings.

If this analysis of style, upon which alone we can rely in a study of the art of this period, does not deceive, Czech painting after the year 1410 showed a great expansion of output in all its branches, spreading far and wide throughout all the Czech provinces and regions. Although the number of works of art that have been preserved is considerable and though these works are distinguished by unity of a contemporary style, it is nevertheless difficult to classify them chronologically and to recognise the ties of affinity between them. The artistic standard of these works that have been preserved is not for the most part very high, manifestations of creative individuality are few and far between, while old and new forms intermingle in an eclectic medley. At the same time it is a disadvantage that research work up to now has been but little occupied with this material and that it was not until quite recent times that the most notable specimens have attracted attention. What we have to say in the following sector of this volume is merely an attempt to create some sort of order in this material. As we are summarising the results of our investigations in the Catalogue, we shall content ourselves with giving in this introductory survey merely an outline of the probable development. The task of arriving at final conclusions in this matter must be left to further research.

The state of affairs round about the year 1420 is documented by what is artistically the most important work of this last epoch of Czech painting — *the Rajhrad Altar* with its cycle of panels depicting scenes of the Passion. The style of the pictures undoubtedly corresponds on the whole to the stage of development which followed the Roudnice Altar. But despite all the unity of fundamental stylistic characteristics in the Rajhrad Altar, it displays differences in form and execution which point to the work of a number of hands in a common production. The most striking difference lies in the fact that several parts of the pictures are based on the principle of subduing local colour by chiaroscuro modelling on a strong ground colour, a principle which dates back as far as to the Master of Třeboň, whereas other parts are painted in the hard plastic style of the period which showed a fondness for the full play of local colour. From this it may be deduced that work on the altar was done on the one hand by a painter who was acquainted with the art of the Třeboň master and imitated it, and on the other hand by painters who worked in the contemporary style indifferent to such reminiscences. This divergence is most noticeable in the light and brightly coloured scene of the Resurrection. It may thus be assumed that the painter who had got his inspiration from the master of Třeboň was the head of a workshop in which the rest of the work was divided up among his helpers who followed the contemporary style. While noting these differences in the method and technique of painting we see however that we are concerned with a group of painters who are wholly at one in their view of space construction and rules of composition. The landscape and architectural space show that this workshop had not advanced beyond the achievements attained in previous development, and that the structure of its figures, though it might be richer in motifs, had not attained a higher organic character of composition. Nor does the realism visible in the characterisation of the heads show any substantial advance upon the old type-conception, although in those parts in which we believe we see the hand of the master the facial characteristics attain an almost naturalistic expression in which even the traits of Gothic conventionalism disappear—although otherwise this still finds frequent application. From the fact that the panels of the Rajhrad Altar were all preserved in Moravia, and that other later works closely associated with the workshop in which the Altar was painted are of Moravian origin, it may be assumed that this workshop was in operation in one or other of the larger towns of Moravia.

Despite traits which indicate that different hands were at work upon it, the Rajhrad Altar displays a common tendency of style in the disposition of the draperies, a tendency which puts an end to the formal dominance of clothing over the human form, and develops from a richly decorative articulation of robes and from a plastic multiplicity of folds to a simpler and quieter system of drapery. The garment again clings more to the outline of the body, it is more closely fastened, and by a quieter outline the folds lose their plastic hollowness, the borders of the draperies undulate in a softer rhythm and their lappets are shorter. In the figures, conceived with a moralising purpose, simple folds merging into each other are a prominent feature. All this is the outcome of a revolution which set in, as dated specimens of illuminated books show, in the second decade of the XVth century as a natural reaction to the 'beautiful' style.

The new tendency did not, however, penetrate into Czech painting of the second decade of the century at one stroke, the reason probably being that except for the workshop in which the Rajhrad Altar originated there existed no centres of any considerable importance to influence the direction of painting of that day. It is a striking circumstance that among the works that have come down to us there is no painting which could possibly be regarded as the product of any important Prague workshop. On the contrary, many of these panels are of provincial origin. The not inconsiderable number of panel pictures preserved in South Bohemia or coming from that area proves that artists were at work there whose output was marked by a fairly uniform contemporary style. The panels are not, as their nuances of style and the differences of the handiwork show, the product of some independent school, nor are they bound to a common workshop tradition, but they are never-theless united with each other by something which we may call a common artistic atmosphere. All these pictures display basically the creative view of the 'beautiful' style, though of course not all to a like intensity or equal quality of work. A rich arrangement of draperies, a graceful rhythm of folds and a lyrical sweetness in the expression of the figures constitute a common feature of them all.

In this category we must include *the Panel of the Church of St. Thomas* with its Madonna of the St. Vitus type, the reverse of which displays the traditional Veraicon. Despite the loss in parts of its enamel, this panel bears witness to an endeavour to achieve fulness and splendour of coloured form in the sense of the 'beautiful' style. To this category belongs also the České Budějovice panel with the picture of *the Adoration of Christ* which on the reverse has a picture of Christ on the Mount of Olives. This panel, however, displays notable new features both in its content and in its composition and style. Although in its construction of space and figures it links up with the older patterns in vogue in the school of the Master of the Třeboň Altar, it must none the less be regarded as a sign of progress that the space in the Adoration is extended to a greater depth, and that in the Garden of Olives the impression made by the landscape is enhanced by several realistic features, drawn probably from West-European art.

These works of average quality of Southern Bohemian origin are, however, surpassed by a group of pictures which came into being probably as early as the period immediately following 1420 and which are closely related to each other. Behind this group we may assume the personality of a painter whose activities gave a definite direction to art production over a wider circle than that of a workshop and who profoundly influenced the development of Southern Bohemian painting in the second quarter of the XVth century. In this group, too, the system of the folds domi-nated the drapery as in the preceding period, both in the wealth of articulation of the robes (albeit bereft by then of systematic character) and in the calligraphic disposition of the borders. The stiffening of plastic form, however, which had already manifested itself in the Rajhrad Altar here advanced a step further. A prominent feature here is the broken contour of the borders, the blunt endings of the lappets of the robes as if cut off as they touch the ground and the dark, massive colouring of the draperies. In this group of pictures which arose in all probability after the year 1420 the personality of a leading master is clearly evident, the master from whose hand we have *the Vyšší Brod Madonna*. In that work the dying fold-system of the 'beautiful' style is still in evidence, and in the heads, the types of the bygone period are also still to be seen, but realism has already put forward its claim, the realism that we have already observed in the Rajhrad Altar as a force disintegrating the conven-tionalism of the 'beautiful' style. This realistic tendency reveals itself most strikingly in the figure of the donor on the frame of the Vyšší Brod Madonna, where the system of folds on the rochet is studied in detail from actual life. These individual traits reach their full development, however, in pictures in which the principles of a new style are plainly outlined. One of these is the tripartite *Altar with the Crucifixion* in the centre, in all probability the work of the master and workshop producing the Vyšší Brod Madonna. But the superficiality with which the majority of the pictures of this altar were painted proves that the assistants' share in the work was considerable. The Crucifixion indicates a revaluation of the old system of composition under the stress of a growing sense of personal experience of the scenes of the redemption. In the representation of space and in the structure of the figures there is, it is true, nothing substantially new, but the dramatic character of the scene is intensified in the close-ranked crowds and densely packed figures. This increase in the dramatic element has been achieved by greater vitality in the individual figures and by the intensive emphasizing of the marks of physical suffering on the bodies and heads of the crucified. In the groups of figures assembled under the cross we note manifold degrees and nuances of spiritual participation in the death of Christ.

A painter of superior talent and greater maturity than the author of the Vyšší Brod Madonna was the painter who gave us the *Wroclaw Madonna*. A plastic fulness of form, the dynamic articulation of the folds of the robes, the vitality of expression and beauty of the painting place this master close alongside the painter of the *Náměšť Panel* which has on both sides scenes from the martyrdom of Ss. Apollonia and Catherine. Both these masters probably came from the same workshop as the Master of the Vyšší Brod Madonna, but the painter of the Náměšť panel was of a personality rare in Czech painting round about 1420. It is possible that he was actually a pupil of the Master of the Rajhrad altar. Affinities in composition, and similarities in the drawing, painting and ornamentation of the aureoles are at least so striking that we may assume that such was the origin of the painter. In both the pictures we find the fundamental marks of style which we have ascertained to be peculiar to the South Bohemian group of specimens that have come down to us, but they are out of all proportion superior in artistic execution. Here, as there, a fondness is displayed for crowding a shallow space with large-scale figures, and condensing fractional motifs of composition into a single entity; here, as there, we observe an attempt to get rid of calligraphic folds and to intensify the expressiveness of the figures by a racial elaboration of the heads. But all this now comes to the fore as a consciously designed piece of work directed by an artist of individuality who commands methods and techniques inaccessible to painters of the former group. Without substantially altering the fundamentals of space and figure-structure therein, the realistic tendency in the conception and expression of the figures was unusually strengthened. The legendary subjects in these pictures necessarily encouraged the characterisation in moral-depicting fashion of the actors in the legendary scenes. The traditional saintly types lost their significance in this environment as creators of style. In the figures of Ss. Catherine and Apollonia the decoratively developed drapery is an anachronism, for on all the other figures a system of folds is applied which pays due regard to the natural possibilities of folded material, whether in the case of robes falling freely in lengthy folds running one into the other, or in the case of a robe or portions of a dress somewhat crumpled by the movement of the body or by dropping to the ground. Much here issues from the more realistically directed imagination of the painter, but some of the motifs of the folds are the result of direct observation of real life and developed in harmony with the material, form and cut of the garment. Not only in the draperies but also in the heads of the figures the individualistic and realistic tendencies triumph over traditional adherence to figural type. The female figures still retain the fanciful, ideal character of the older typology, but in the male figures an individualisation of traditional types emerges to such an extent that their unity with the female figures practically disappears. Caricaturing realism, which had already appeared in the painting of the XIVth century in the depicting of originators and perpetrators of crime, manifested itself here in a new form in which the artist availed himself abundantly of realistic observation and used it to intensify the expression of these heads. The pictures of the Náměšť panel, however, owe their plastic communicativeness not only to these new elements of form but also to the method and technique of painting which rises high above the contemporary South Bohemian standard of production. The technique of under-painting the forms is pursued here consistently and thoroughly so as to build up form in a suffused scattered twilight by a soft rise and fall of relief, tempering and uniting the local colours, in themselves none too vivid, into a harmonious whole. How carefully and in what detail this under-painting is carried out is shown by heads from which the enamel is worn away and the under-painting exposed. This method has no analogy in the works which we have up to now reviewed, but a similar method is seen in several of the pictures of the Rajhrad altar, which moreover is connected with the Náměšť panel not only by the fact that both are of Moravian provenance, but also by many common features of fundamental style. This affinity is so organic that it is necessary to assume that the Náměšť panel and the Rajhrad Altar issued from one and the same workshop, the Náměšť panel being the earlier in time and development. We here come to the question of the connection between South Bohemian painting and this Moravian workshop; whether it was one of direct dependence or whether it was a matter of mere coincidence, arising from the parallel development of two independent spheres which had only their starting point in common. The question is further complicated by the fact that at this stage of development the influence of contemporary Austrian painting began to be felt in South Bohemian painting.

The striving to intensify dramatic expression which manifests itself as a new feature of Czech painting round about the year 1430, was assuredly a general tendency. We observe it also in pictures far below the standard of the pictures of the Náměšť panel, and it occurs too with an insistence which is all the greater in cases in which minor artists were the painters. This trend towards the dramatic reached the stage of almost pathetic expressiveness in the *Crucifixion* panel of the *Zátoň altar ;* not by new constructions or attitudes but by a deliberate application of the accents of expression. In the structure of the space and in the figures that fill it we observe a fondness for overcrowding spaces, whether open or closed, with large-scale figures. This too is the outcome of an attempt to strengthen the expressive effect of the scenes depicted, an endeavour which is very observable in the pictures on the wings of the Zátoň altar depicting the life and death of St. John the Baptist. It, too, is a sign of the fondness for dramatic biography which transfers the pathos of martyrdom from Christ to his saintly followers.

The fertility of the South Bohemian workshops in the period round 1430 was by no means inconsiderable. From this period are preserved fragments of several altars, the rest of which is lost in each case, painted by the hands of painters who were independent of each other. One of these fragments originating from České Budějovice carries a picture of the *Visitation of the Virgin Mary* with a severed figure of Christ in the Garden on the back of the panel. Another is a picture of the *Mater Dolorosa* with fragments of the figures of Ss. Peter and Paul on the reverse.

Among these fragments there are three panels which form the remnant of an altar whose painter was a personality of no common talent and skill. We designate him, after his most finely executed picture, *the Master of the Carrying of the Cross* and regard him, if not as the author, at least as the head of the workshop in which the altar together with the preserved panels of the *Visitation of the Virgin Mary* and the *Adoration of the Child* (Budapest) originated. In these pictures the style towards which painting tended round about 1430 is seen in full maturity. The dress falls in heavy continuous folds, the material is broken or lies crinkled on the ground in simple forms. The heads acquire a new stereotyped character, a feature which is not, however, restricted to South Bohemian painting but had its analogy also in contemporary Austrian art. Another nuance of form of this art appears in the Vyšší Brod panel with its picture of the *Annunciation*, which in style is closely associated with the preceding pictures and were it not for a difference in the dimensions of the panels could well be regarded as another part of the same altar.

With the advance of Austrian influences the specifically independent evolution of Czech painting came to an end, and with it ceased, too, the connection of the South Bohemian school with the workshop which had turned out the Rajhrad Altar and the Náměšť Panel. Here we may now come back to the question posed above, that is, what was the connection between the South Bohemian school and the Moravian workshop? We are of the opinion that it was a direct connection, whether of permanent character or only for a brief period. The Rajhrad altar, in several panels of which we have noted a strong reflection of the art of the Třeboň master, apparently marks the starting point of this style about 1420—1430, a style which developed parallel in South Bohemian painting and in the work of the Moravian workshop. It is possible, however, to admit a mutual exchange of artistic achievements between the two circles, and even an exchange of artists between South Bohemia and Moravia. In this way might be explained the variations in style and execution within the scope of an allied view of art, which we find in the Rajhrad Altar and in the output of South Bohemia, as also at a later date the common features which accompany the work of the two circles in the course of their subsequent development after the year 1420. In the Thirties this connection, it would seem, came to an end, and the work in the two schools, as is proved by the specimens that have been preserved, continued to develop along independent lines. In South Bohemia painting afterwards showed a steady decline, despite the fact that it received a few fresh impulses from neighbouring Austria. *The Skalice Crucifixion* provides us with a proof of its incapacity to avail itself of new impulses in order to attain a higher artistic level.

All that was still being produced in South Bohemia in the period round about 1440 is represented by works of but little artistic value, such as the panel of *the Madonna of Doudleby* with its scene of the Adoration of Christ on the reverse. In the depiction of the landscape there is still something of the older attempt at realism, but the rustic character of the style and technique of the painting is already conspicuous. These features appear also in the last altar of South Bohemian origin, *the Altar from Sv. Majdalena* which in all probability originally adorned the Church of St. Giles at Třeboň. It is not impossible that this altar was a product of the workshop in which the Madonna of Doudleby originated. On the other hand, Moravia succeeded even at this late epoch in reacting briskly to foreign influences, thanks probably to the tradition which had been established by the leading Master of the Rajhrad Altar. This tradition is indeed still observable in the extensive cycle of the *Altar at St. James's* but in a stage of later development. In this case the old workshop had either passed into the hands of younger painters or it was a matter of a new workshop formed by a breakaway from the old. The cycle of the St. James's Altar was the work of a number of hands, just as was the Rajhrad Altar, but their work points to two trends. While they observed the same fundamental view of plastic execution, none the less they differed in respect of style. The St. Mary cycle is connected in parts of its pictures with the older tradition, and in the typology of its figures, its system of drapery folds and its colouring, shows a manifest connection with the workshop which produced the Rajhrad Altar, and more particularly with the decorative style of the Rajhrad Resurrection. The reversion to older models proceeds, however, in some cases still further as in the Adoration of the Three Kings where the painter links up with the Želnava Adoration. In the architectural constructions, however, the spirit of later art already manifests itself and influences the figure-system in several pictures, most of all in the Visitation picture which is dominated by a system of lengthy folds broken as they reach the ground. On the other hand, the St. James's cycle of legends corresponds in its overall fundamental constitution to the tendency which manifested itself in the Náměšť panel. All the desire of the artist for expressiveness comes into full play, filling the figures with dramatic emotion, carrying the beholder away with realistic movement of body and limbs. The caricatural realism of the heads intensifies the austere expressiveness of the saintly figures, while motifs taken from contemporary costumes are adapted to several systems of folds which appear side by side with one another in the various pictures of the cycle. Despite their considerable artistic level the pictures of the St. James's Altar are the fruit of the eclecticism which dominated Czech painting in the second quarter of the XVth century, and an indication of the crisis in which medieval painting of this period found itself on the eve of its great swing-over to Late Gothic. Owing to the cultural exhaustion which prevailed as the aftermath of the Hussite period it was no longer given to Czech painting to free itself from this confusion and to make a determined effort to attain new aims in the sphere of creative art.

The development of Czech painting never advanced beyond the level attained by the St. James's

Altar. On the contrary, almost everything that has come down to us from that epoch reveals a very considerably retrospective tendency, even when here and there some features of a younger style alternate with the formal features of the older art. In this complex sphere, which displayed such inequalities in artistic value, and in which many works came into being as late as after the middle of the XVth century, worthy of mention is *the Madonna of H. M. the King of England*, a work which probably originated in the same style, if not directly in the circle, of the master of the St. James's Altar. At this stage several other pictures of Madonnas originated in which the older Czech types of St. Mary were repeated. *The Madonna at St. Stephen's*, like *the Lanna Madonna* which is allied to it, copies the popular type of the Roudnice Madonna. The first of these, in its frame pictures uses the older composition scheme. In this last stage of development of Czech Gothic painting, however, a new type of Mary suddenly appears. This is in the likeness of the Assumpta standing on a crescent in a flowering bush. The *Lanna Assumpta*, very closely related in its style to the Lanna Madonna is the last attempt to preserve that idealism of form and expression which gave birth to the 'beautiful' Czech Madonnas round about the year 1400. In other respects, however, all that could prolong the life of the old types of the Virgin was already lost by the middle of the XVth century. To what extent even the conception of the miraculous pictures of Mary had changed is proved by a picture of such large dimensions as *the Assumpta of the White Mountain,* which is a mere shadow of the delicate beauty of the older Czech Madonnas. The Assumpta at Deštná also still reveals something of the idealism of the „beautiful' style. But here the features of late Gothic naturalism already manifest themselves not only in the figures of the donors but also in the drawing of the background. For the first time we here meet with indications of the system of broken folds. This picture probably originated in South Bohemia, most likely in the circle of painters who produced the *Madonna of the České Budějovice Museum* and perhaps the *Visitation of the Virgin Mary* of Český Krumlov. Several further panels constitute the last group in the series of Czech pictures of the Madonna. They are: *The Brussels Madonna* (in the M. van Gelder Collection), *the Madonna of Jindřichův Hradec* and *the Vienna Madonna* with Veraicon on the back of the panel. All these, however, are but soulless replicas from the period after the middle of the XVth century, and they breathe as it were beauty of form and expression by mere mechanical repetition.

The time had already come when Czech painting, having exhausted the impulses with which Austrian painting provided it in the second quarter of the XVth century, began to turn with curiosity to the south-West, in order to acquire in the Franconian area some knowledge of the new style which had taken root there and was spreading under the influence of Dutch painting. Round about the year 1470 Czech painting in its turn entered the field of Late Gothic, but then merely in dependence upon German art.

BIBLIOGRAPHY

T. Pešina z Čechorodu, Phosphorus septicornis. Pragae 1673.

Vincencius a Guilelmo, Nová záře mariánská (Rukopis Nár. musea I F 26). Praha 1687.

Wilhelm Gumpenberg, Marianischer Atlas oder Beschreibung des Marianischen Gnadenbildes durch die ganze Christenwelt (Vyd. podle Gumpenberga upravil P. Augustinus Sartorius). Prag 1717.

Florian Hammerschmid, Prodromus gloriae Pragenae. Pragae 1733.

Chr. von Mechel, Verzeichnis der Gemälde der k. k. Bilder-Gallerie in Wien. Wien 1783.

Jar. Schaller, Topographie des Königreichs Böhmen VII. Berauner Kreis. Prag 1788.

Jar. Schaller Beschreibung der Königl. Haupt- u. Residenzstadt Prag. IV. Prag 1797.

Jar. Schaller, Topographie des Königreichs Böhmen XIII. Budweiser Kreis Prag. 1797.

A. G. Meissner, Historisch-malerische Darstellungen aus Böhmen. Prag 1798.

Jos. Schiffner, Gallerie der interessantesten und merkwürdigsten Personen Böhmens nebst der Beschreibung merkwürdiger böhmischen Landesseltenheiten alter und neuer Zeiten, aus den besten u. bewährtesten böhmischen Geschichtschreibern historisch-chronologisch abgefasst I.—V. Prag 1802—1804.

Jos. Schiffner, Gallerie, aneb Vyobrazenost nejslovutnějších a nejznamenitějších osob země České, spolu s vypsáním důležitých pamětních věcí. I.—II. Praha 1803-9.

Franz Auge, Beschreibung der kaiserlichen königlichen Burg Karlstein in Böhmen. Prag 1804, 2. vyd. 1819.

Fr. Schlegel, Schloss Karlstein bei Prag (Das Deutsche Museum II.). Wien 1812.

G. J. Dlabacz, Allgemeines historisches Künstler-Lexikon für Böhmen und zum Theil auch für Mähren u. Schlesien. Prag 1815.

J. D. Fiorillo, Geschichte der zeichnenden Künste in Deutschland u. den vereinigten Niederlanden I. Hannover 1815.

V. F. Welleba, Beschreibung der Burg Karlstein (Hyllos I., 2). Prag 1819.

Fr. Schlegel, Schloss Karlstein bei Prag (Sämtliche Werke IV.). Wien 1823.

Die Burg Karlstein (Hormayrs Taschenbuch V.). München 1824.

Alois Primisser, Über die alten Gemälde auf dem Schlosse Karlstein bei Prag. (Jahrbücher der Litteratur XXVII.). Wien 1824.

A. Hirt, Kunstbemerkungen auf einer Reise über Wittenberg u. Maissen nach Dresden u. Prag. Berlin 1830.

J. M. Schottky, Die Burg Karlstein nebst ihren Umgebungen. Prag 1831.

K. G. Grüneisen, Übersichtliche Beschreibung älterer Werke der Malerei in Schwaben. Sendschreiben an Herrn Prof. Dr. Franz Kugler in Berlin (Cottas Kunstblatt 1840, No 96). Stuttgart 1840.

A. F. M. Honsatko, Die k. k. dann des Koenigreichs Boehmen Haupt- u. Metropolitan Kirche zu St. Veit ob dem Prager Schlosse. Prag 1833.

Schildereien der böhmischen Königsburg Karlstein in Böhmen. (Hormayrs Taschenbuch für die vaterländische Geschichte, Neue Folge V.) München 1834.

Die Heiligenbilder in Karlstein (Bohemia, No 92—4) Prag 1839.

Restauration des tableaux de saints, conservés à Carlstein en Bohême depuis le XIVe siècle. (Carro, Alman. de Carlsbad). Carlsbad 1840.

F. Auge-Ferd. Jitschinsky, Beschreibung der kaiserlichen königlichen Burg Karlstein in Böhmen. Prag 1841.

Ant. Jar. Beck, Starožitnosti w jižných Čechách (Časopis Českého Museum XVII., strana 415—425). Praha 1843.

J. D. G. Memminger, Denkmale des Altertums und der alten Kunst im Königreich Württemberg, zusammengestellt von dem kgl. statistisch-topographischen Bureau (Württ. Jahrbücher 1841). Württemberg 1843.

Franz Al. Heber, Böhmens Burgen, Vesten und Bergschlösser I. (Pilsner u. Klattauer Kreis). Prag 1844.

G. F. Waagen, Kunstwerke und Künstler in Deutschland II. Wien 1845

J. E. Wocel, Grundzüge der böhmischen Alterthumskunde. Prag 1845.

J. E. Wocel, O starožitnostech Českých a o potřebě chrániti je před zkázau (Časopis Českého Musea, XIX., str. 649—82). Praha 1845.

Alexandr Popow, O starobylé české malbě (Časopis Českého Museum XX., str. 501—16; 627—37). Praha 1846.

Fr. Auge-Ferd. Jitschinsky, Beschreibung der kaiserlichen königlichen Burg Karlstein in Böhmen (4. vyd.). Prag 1847.

F. X. Fernbach, Bemerkungen auf einer Reise nach Schwaben (Cottas Kunstblatt 1847). Stuttgart 1847.

Fr. Kugler-Jacob Burckhardt, Handbuch der Geschichte der Malerei seit Constantin dem Grossen. I. Berlin 1847.

G. F. Waagen, Nachträge zur zweiten Auflage von Kugler's Handbuch. (Deutsches Kunstblatt I). Leipzig 1850.

E. Foerster, Geschichte der deutschen Kunst I. München 1851.

G. Th. Legis Glückselig, Das Königsaaler Gnadenbild (Illustrierte Chronik von Böhmen I., str. 30—32; 566—7). Prag 1852.

G. Th. Legis Glückselig, Die böhmische Künstlerbruderschaft von 1348 (Illustrierte Chronik von Böhmen II, str. 696—705). Prag 1852.

G. Th. Legis Glückselig, Kronveste Karlstein u. deren Kunstdenkmäler (Illustrierte Chronik von Böhmen I., str. 306—12; 363—77). Prag 1852.

Franz Kugler, Flüchtige Reisenotizen vom Jahr 1844 (Kleine Schriften u. Studien zur Kunstgeschichte II., str. 494—8). Stuttgart 1854.

G. Th. Legis Glückselig, Böhmische Kunstalterthümer im Auslande. Die Gemälde zu Mühlhausen am Neckar v. Jahre 1380. (Illustrierte Chronik von Böhmen II., str. 564—7). Prag 1854.

C. Heideloff-Fr. Müller, Die Kunst des Mittelalters in Schwaben. Stuttgart 1855.

K. Vl. Zap, Zbraslav (Památky archaeologické a místopisné I., str. 71—84; 117—25). Praha 1855.

J. D. Passavant, Über die mittelalterliche Kunst in Böhmen und Mähren. (Zeitschrift für christliche Archäologie und Kunst I). Leipzig 1856.

Gregor Wolný, Kirchliche Topographie von Mähren II. Abtlg. I. Brünn 1856.

Jul. Körner, Die Burg Karlstein, ihre Kirchen und Capellen. Prag 1857.

Hugo Toman, Archeologické procházky po jižních Čechách (Památky archaeologické a místopisné II., str. 319—24; 358 až 362). Praha 1857.

Aug. Ambros, Der Dom zu Prag. Prag 1858.

Ferd. B. Mikowec, Das Cistercienserstift Hohenfurth in Böhmen. Wien-Olmütz 1858.

Ferd. B. Mikowec, Die königliche Burg Karlstein in Böhmen, Wien-Olmütz 1858.

J. E. Wocel, Bericht über eine Kunstarchäologische Reise in Böhmen und Mähren (Mitteilungen der k. k. Central-Commission etc. III., str. 144—9; 169—180). Wien 1858.

Fr. Isidor Proschko, Das Cistercienser-Stift Hohenfurth in Böhmen. Linz 1859.

J. E. Wocel, Relací o opravě hradu Karlštejna od r. 1597 (Památky archaeologické a místopisné, III., str. 67—74). Praha 1859.

K. V. Zap, Kaple sv. Kříže a sv. Kateřiny na Karlštejně (Památky archaeologické a místopisné, III., str. 75—80). Praha 1859.

Ferd. B. Mikowec, Alterthümer und Denkwürdigkeiten Böhmens I. Pr g 1860.

Ferd. B. Mikowec, Malerisch-historische Skizzen aus Böhmen. Wien-Olmütz 1860.

Ferd. B. Mikowec, Starožitnosti a památky země České I. Praha 1860.

A. Essenwein, Die archäologische Ausstellung des Vereines Arcadia in Prag (Mittheilungen der k. k. Central-Commission zur Erforschung u. Erhaltung der Baudenkmale, VI., str. 277 až 284). Wien 1861.

Franz Bock, Schloss Karlstein in Böhmen (Mittheilungen der k. k. Central-Commission zur Erforschung u. Erhaltung der Baudenkmale, VII., str. 69—78; 90—99). Wien 1862 (zvl. otisk z téhož roku).

G. Th. Legis Glückselig, Christus-Archäologie, Prag 1862.

Ferd. B. Mikowec, Fotografisches Album böhmischer Alterthümer aus der im September 1861 auf dem altstädter Rathause zu Prag veranstalteten ersten archäologischen Ausstellung des Vereines Arcadia. Prag 1862.

Joh. Trajer, Historisch-statistische Beschreibung der Diöcese Budweis. Budweis 1862.

G. F. Waagen, Handbuch der deutschen und niederländischen Malerschulen. Stuttgart 1862.

Burg Karlstein und ihre Sehenswürdigkeiten. Ein treuer Führer für deren Besucher. Prag 1863.

Karlův Týn a veškeré jeho části s přehledem dějepisným. Praha 1863.

J. E. Wocel, Starožitné obrazy v proboštském chrámu roudnickém. (Památky. Časopis Musea království Českého pro dějepis hlavně český, V., str. 185—6). Praha 1863.

A. W. Ambros, Die Burg Karlstein u. ihre Restaurierung (Mittheilungen der k. k. Central-Commission zur Erforschung u. Erhaltung der Baudenkmale, X., str. 43—56). Wien 1865 (zvl. otisk z téhož roku).

Fr. Beneš, Obrazy, jež p. Šťulík z Budějovic v museu vystavil (Památky archaeologické a místopisné, VI., str. 311—312). Praha 1865.

Ferd. B. Mikowec, Alterthümer u. Denkwürdigkeiten Böhmens II. Prag 1865.

Ferd. B. Mikowec, Starožitnosti a památky země České II. Praha 1865.

A. R. v. Perger, Über das Herkommen verschiedener Gemälde in der k. k. Gemäldegallerie im Belvedere (Mittheilungen der k. k. Central-Commission zur Erforschung u. Erhaltung der Baudenkmale, X., str. 205—36). Wien 1865.

A. D. Výšek, Mistra Jetřicha tabulové obrazy na Karlšteině (Památky archaeologické a místopisné, VI., str. 161—3). Praha 1865.

Alwin Schultz, Urkundliche Geschichte der Breslauer Maler-Innung. Breslau 1866.

A. D. Výšek, O středověkém malířství v Čechách. (Časopis musea království Českého, XL., str. 142—54.) Praha 1866.

G. F. Waagen, Die vornehmsten Kunstdenkmäler in Wien I. Wien 1866.

Bernh. Grueber, Die Herren von Rosenberg als Förderer der Künste (Mittheilungen des Vereines für Geschichte der Deutschen in Böhmen V., str. 19—26). Prag 1867.

Fr. Kugler-Jacob Burckhardt, Handbuch der Geschichte der Malerei seit Constantin dem Grossen I. (3. vyd.) Leipzig 1867.

J. E. Wocel, Tré obrazův Karlšteinských. (Památky archaeologické a místopisné VII., str. 65—8). Praha 1868.

F. Beneš, Kaple sv. Kříže na Karlštejně (Světozor IV. str. 222). Praha 1870.

Alwin Schultz, Schlesiens Kunstleben im dreizehnten und vierzehnten Jahrhundert. Breslau 1870.

Afred Michiels, Origines de la peinture allemande. École de Bohême (Gazette des Beaux-arts, XV année, IIe période, VII., str. 146—52). Paris 1873.

Carl Schnaase, Geschichte der bildenden Künste im Mittelalter VI. (Die Spätzeit des Mittelalters bis zur Blüthe der Eyck'schen Schule.) Düsseldorf 1874.

J. Vladyka z Marianova, Arcichrám na hradě Pražském s dějinami království Českého. Budějovice 1876.

Bernh. Grueber, Die Kunst des Mittelalters in Böhmen III. Wien 1877.

Mat. Pangerl—Alfr. Woltmann, Das Buch der Malerzeche in Prag (Quellenschriften für Kunstgeschichte und Kunsttechnik des Mittelalters und der Renaissance, XIII.). Wien 1878.

Ad. Patera—Ferd. Tadra, Das Buch der Prager Malerzeche. (Kniha bratrstva malířského v Praze) 1348—1527. Prag 1878.

Bernh. Grueber, Die Kunst des Mittelalters in Böhmen IV. (Die Spät-Gothik, 1437 bis cca 1600.) Wien 1879.

Alf. Woltmann, Geschichte der Malerei I. Leipzig 1879.

Karel Chytil, Obrazy Karlšteinské v Belvedere vídeňském. (Památky archaeologické a místopisné XI., str. 265—270). Praha 1881.

P. Raphael Pavel, Führer durch die sehenswerten Räumlichkeiten des Stiftes Hohenfurt. Graz 1882.

Frant. Ekert, Posvátná místa král. hl. města Prahy I. Praha 1883.

K. B. Mádl, Vera-ikon (Ruch V., str. 208). Praha 1883.

Frant. Ekert, Posvátná místa král. hl. města Prahy II. Praha 1884.

Aug. Sedláček, Hrady, zámky a tvrze v království Českém III. Praha 1884.

J. E. Wessely, Klassiker der Malerei. Deutsche Schule I. (Klassiker-Bibliothek der bildenden Künste). Leipzig 1884.

Hulakovský, Staré obrazy nalezené v kostele sv. Maří Magdaleny u Třeboně (Světozor XIX., č. 14, str. 222—3). Praha 1885.

K. B. Mádl, Mutina a Dětřich (Ruch VII., str. 15—16; 33—4; 52—3; 67—8). Praha 1885.

Joseph Neuwirth, Zur Geschichte der Tafelmalerei in Böhmen (Repertorium für Kunstwissenschaft, VIII., str. 58—79). Berlin 1885.

Aug. Sedláček, Zprávy a drobnosti (Památky archaeologické a místopisné XIII., str. 41—2). Praha 1886.

K. Chytil, Über einige Madonnen-Bilder Böhmens aus dem 14. u. 15. Jahrhundert (Mittheilungen der k. k. Central-Commission zur Erforschung u. Erhaltung der Kunst- u. historischen Denkmale. Neue Folge XIII., str. XIX.—XXV.). Wien 1887.

Viktor Barvitius, Katalog obrazárny v domě umělců Rudolfinum v Praze. Praha 1889.

H. Janitschek, Geschichte der deutschen Malerei (Geschichte der Deutschen Kunst III.). Berlin 1890.

Katalog retrospektivní výstavy (Skup. XXV.). Praha 1891.

K. B. Mádl, O pokladu dómu Svatovítského v Praze (Zlatá Praha VIII., str. 547—9; 559—62; 567—70; 579—82). Praha 1891.

Jos. Neuwirth, Böhmens Kunstleben unter Karl IV. (Sammlung gemeinnütziger Vorträge, Nr. 153). Prag 1891.

Aug. Sedláček, Hrady, zámky a tvrze království Českého VIII. Praha 1891.

Henry Thode, Die Malerschule von Nürnberg im XIV. u. XV. Jahrhundert in ihrer Entwickelung bis auf Dürer. Frankfurt a. M. 1891.

K. Chytil, Mistr Oswald a jeho účastenství při výzdobě chrámu Svatovítského (Památky archaeologické a místopisné XV., str. 26—30). Praha 1892.

K. Chytil, Retrospektivní výstava. Malířství drobné a tabulové (Památky archaeologické a místopisné XV., str. 607—12). Praha 1892.

Josef Braniš, Dějiny středověkého umění v Čechách II. Praha 1893.

Joseph Neuwirth, Karlstein in Böhmen und Runkelstein in Tirol, zwei Burgen (Albert Ilg's Kunstgeschichtliche Charakterbilder aus Österreich-Ungarn, str. 110—22). Wien-Prag-Leipzig 1893.

Josef Neuwirth, Die Junker von Prag (Studien zur Geschichte der Gothik in Böhmen III.). Prag 1894.

Franz von Reber, Abhandlung über die Stillentwicklung der schwäbischen Tafelmalerei im 14. und 15. Jahrhundert (Sitzungsberichte der philosophisch-philolog. und der hist. Klasse der kgl. bayr. Akad. d. Wiss. 1894, Heft III.) München 1894.

Z. Winter—Č. Zíbrt, Dějiny kroje v zemích českých II. Praha 1894.

Karel Eichler, Kaple Matky Boží u hradu Veveří ve farnosti Veversko-Bytyšské (Method XXI., str. 53—6; 62—6). Praha 1895.

Václav Kocián, Rodička Boží Svatoštěpánská v Praze. Praha 1895.

K. B. Mádl, Varia z dějin umění. Madona staroboleslavská (Památky archaeologické a místopisné, XVI., str. 478—9). Praha 1896.

Joseph Neuwirth, Malerei und Plastik im Mittelalter (Die Österreichisch-ungarische Monarchie in Wort und Bild. Böhmen 2. Abt., str. 347—63). Wien 1896.

Joseph Neuwirth, Mittelalterliche Wandgemälde und Tafelbilder der Burg Karlstein in Böhmen (Forschungen zur Kunstgeschichte Böhmens I.). Prag 1896.

Ed. Šittler-Ant. Podlaha, Národopisná výstava českoslovanská v Praze r. 1895, III. Sbírka staročeských obrazů a soch Marianských (Vlasť XII., str. 775—82; 876—85; 1001—11; 1091—96; 1174—85). Praha 1896.

K. Chytil, Karlštejn (Čechy IX., str. 326—47). Praha 1897.

Ant. Podlaha-Ed. Šittler, Deskový obraz „Ukřižování" ze XIV. stol. v klášteře Emauzském (Method XXIII., str. 19—21). Praha 1897.

Ant. Podlaha-Ed. Šittler, Album svatovojtěšské. Praha 1897.

Boh. Matějka, Soupis památek historických a uměleckých v politickém okresu soudnickém. I. (Soupis památek historických a uměleckých v království Českém IV.) Praha 1898.

Max Dvořák, K dějinám malířství českého doby Karlovy (Český časopis historický V., str. 238—48). Praha 1899.

Josef Braniš, Soupis památek historických a uměleckých v politickém okresu českobudějovickém (Soupis památek historických a uměleckých v království Českém VIII). Praha 1900.

Frant. Mareš—Jan Sedláček, Soupis památek historických a uměleckých v politickém okresu třeboňském (Soupis památek historických a uměleckých v království Českém X.). Praha 1900.

Max Dvořák, Die Illuminatorem des Johann von Neumarkt (Jahrbuch der kunsthistorischen Sammlungen in Wien XXII., str. 35—126). Wien 1901.

K. B. Mádl, Z Vídně na Karlštejn (Národní Listy z 15. 9. 1901). Praha 1901.

Jos. Novák, Soupis památek historických a uměleckých v politickém okresu jindřichohradeckém (Soupis památek historických a uměleckých v království Českém XIV.). Praha 1901.

Vinc. Smolík, Karlštejn (Národní Listy č. 11). Praha 1901.

Eugen Gradmann, Geschichte der christlichen Kunst. Stuttgart 1902.

Jos. Alex. Freiherr von Helfert, Die Wiederherstellung der Burg Karlstein in Böhmen (Mittheilungen der k. k. Central-Commission für Erforschung u. Erhaltung der kunst- u. historischen Denkmale. XXVIII., Neue Folge, str. 1—17) Wien 1902.

Julius von Schlosser, Vademecum eines fahrenden Malergesellen (Jahrbuch der kunsthistorischen Sammlungen des allerhöchsten Kaiserhauses, XXIII., str. 314—26). Wien 1902.

K. Chytil, O Junkerech pražských. Praha 1903.

J. Košnář, Poutnická místa a posvátné svatyně v Čechách. Praha 1903.

Josef Lintner, Kostel sv. Víta v Soběslavi (Sborník Musejního spolku v Soběslavi VI., str. 3—13). Soběslav 1903.

Ant. Podlaha—Ed. Šittler, Chrámový poklad u sv. Víta v Praze. Praha 1903.

Ant. Podlaha—Ed. Šittler, Poklad svatovítský (Soupis památek historických a uměleckých v království Českém). Praha 1903.

Josef Soukup, Soupis památek historických a uměleckých v politickém okresu pelhřimovském (Soupis památek historických a uměleckých v království Českém XVIII.). Praha 1903.

Exposition des Primitifs Français au Palais du Louvre et à la Bibliothèque Nationale. Catalogue. Paris 1904.

Ant. Podlaha, Obrazy marianské v Čechách ze stol. XIV.—XVI. Praha 1904.

Aug. Prokop, Die Markgrafschaft Mähren in kunstgeschichtlicher Beziehung II. Das Zeitalter der gotischen Kunst. Wien 1904.

Jan Kř. Roškot, Listiny týkající se založení děkanství a kapituly na hradě Karlštejně. Praha 1904.

Frant. Bareš, Soupis památek historických a uměleckých v politickém okresu mladoboleslavském (Soupis památek historických a uměleckých v království Českém XXI.). Praha 1905.

H. Bergner, Handbuch der kirchlichen Kunstaltertümer. 1905.

Ant. Podlaha, Almanach mariánský. Praha 1905.

K. Chytil, Malířstvo pražské XV. a XVI. věku a jeho cechovní kniha staroměstská z let 1490—1582. Praha 1906.

Exhibition of early German Art. Burlington Fine Arts Club. London 1906.

Konrad Lange, Das Altarwerk von Mühlhausen am Neckar (Studien aus Kunst und Geschichte. Friedrich Schneider zum siebzigsten Geburstage gewidmet von seinen Freunden und Verehrern, str. 419—52). Freiburg im Breisgau 1906.

Jos. Braniš, Svatá Koruna, bývalý klášter cistercienský. Praha 1907.

K. Chytil, Das Madonnenbild des Prager Erzbischofes Ernst im Kaiser-Friedrichs-Museum (Jahrbuch der königlich preuszischen Kunstsammlungen XXVIII., str. 131—49). Berlín 1907.

Ant. Podlaha, Posvátná místa království českého I. Praha 1907.

A. Venturi, Storia dell' arte italiana. V. (La pittura del trecento e le sue origini, str. 961—2). Milano 1907.

A. Hrdlička, Topografie diecese brněnské. Brno 1908.

Carl Gebhardt, Anfänge der Tafelmalerei in Nürnberg. Strassburg 1908.

Boh. Lukavský, Chrámové inventáře děkanství karlštejnského ze XVII. a XVIII. stol. (Památky archaeologické a místopisné XXII., str. 567—76). Praha 1908.

K. Chytil, v ref. o Schlesiens Vorzeit im Bild und Schrift, Neue Folge V. 1909 (Památky archaeologické a místopisné XXIII., str. 603—5). Praha 1909.

Joseph Jungnitz, Zwei Tafelbilder aus der böhmischen Malerschule des 14. Jahrhunderts in Breslauer Diözesan-Museum (Schlesiens Vorzeit im Bild und Schrift, Neue Folge V.: Jahrbuch des schlesischen Museums für Kunstgewerbe u. Altertümer V., str. 71—6). Breslau 1909.

Ant. Podlaha, Posvátná místa království českého III. Praha 1909.

Hans Posse, Die Gemäldegalerie des Kaiser-Friedrich-Museums (Vollständiger beschreibender Katalog mit Abbildungen sämtlicher Gemälde). Berlin 1911.

Pavel Bergner, Katalog obrazárny v domě umělců Rudolfínum v Praze. Praha 1912.

Rich. Ernst, Beiträge zur Kenntnis der Tafelmalerei Böhmens im XIV. u. am Anfang des XV. Jahrhunderts (Forschungen zur Kunstgeschichte Böhmens VI.). Prag 1912.

Joseph Neuwirth, Prag (Berühmte Kunststätten, No. 8). Leipzig 1912.

Fritz Burger, Die deutsche Malerei vom ausgehenden Mittelalter bis zum Ende der Renaissance. I. Berlin-Neubabelsberg 1913.

Ernst Heidrich, Recense Ernstových Beiträge (Monatshefte für Kunstwissenschaft VI., str. 333—6). Leipzig 1913.

J. Leisching, Das Erzherzog Rainer-Museum für Kunst u. Gewerbe in Brünn. Wien 1913.

Ant. Matějček, Český mistr (?) Vyšehradská Madonna, t. ř. dešťová (Umělecké poklady Čech, I., str. 64—5). Praha 1913.

Ant. Matějček, Český mistr, Madonna (Lannova) (Umělecké poklady Čech I., str. 36—7). Praha 1913.

Ant. Matějček, Čeští patroni. (Umělecké poklady Čech I., str. 28—9). Praha 1913.

Ant. Matějček, Galerie v Rudolfíně (Zlatoroh. Sbírka illustrovaných monografií, sv. XIX—XXI). Praha 1913.

Ant. Matějček, Votivní obraz pražského arcibiskupa Očka z Vlašimě (Umělecké poklady Čech I., str. 12—13). Praha 1913.

Curt Glaser, Italienische Bildmotive in der altdeutschen Malerei (Zeitschrift für bildende Kunst, Neue Folge XXV., str. 145—58). Leipzig 1914.

K. Guth, Recense práce Ernstovy a Burgrovy (Český Časopis Historický, XXI., str. 85—91). Praha 1915.

Ant. Matějček, Části bývalého oltáře třeboňského (Umělecké poklady Čech II., str. 63—4). Praha 1915.

Ant. Matějček, Český mistr, zevní strana oltářního křídla (Umělecké poklady Čech II., str. 3). Praha 1915.

V. V. Štech, Ukřižovaný (Umělecké poklady Čech II., str. 8—9). Praha 1915.

Z. Wirth, Křídlový obraz kostela sv. Jana Kř. ve Výtoni. (Umělecké poklady Čech II., str. 35). Praha 1915.

Curt Glaser, Zwei Jahrhunderte deutscher Malerei. München 1916.

Hans Heubach, Die Hamburger Malerei unter Meister Bertram und ihre Beziehungen zu Böhmen (Jahrbuch des kunsthistorischen Institutes der k. k. Zentralkommission für Denkmalpflege X., str. 101—170). Wien 1916.

Jar. Pečírka, Navštívení P. Marie švamberské (Umělecké poklady Čech III., str. 2—3). Praha 1916.

Rich. Ernst, Die Krummauer Madonna der k. k. Staatsgallerie (Jahrbuch des kunsthistorischen Institutes der k. k. Zentralkommission für Denkmalpflege XI., str. 109—31). Wien 1917.

Max. Dvořák, Idealismus u. Naturalismus in der gotischen Skulptur u. Malerei. München-Berlin 1918.

Carl G. Heise, Norddeutsche Malerei. Studien zu ihrer Entwicklungsgeschichte im 15. Jahrhundert von Köln bis Hamburg. Leipzig 1918.

K. Chytil, Tabulové obrazy ve sbírkách Zemského musea (Památky archaeologické, XXX., str. 16—26). Praha 1918.

F. Mareš-J. Sedláček, Soupis památek historických a uměleckých v politickém okresu krumlovském (Soupis památek historických a uměleckých v království Českém, XLI.). Praha 1918.

Joseph Neuwirth, Die Beziehungen des Graudenzer Altarwerkes der Marienburg zur alt-böhmischen Malerei (Studien zur Geschichte der Gotik in Böhmen, VI.). Prag 1918.

K. Chytil, O založení kláštera na Zbraslavi a Madoně zbraslavské (Ročenka Kruhu pro pěstování dějin umění za rok 1918, str. 48—50). Praha 1919.

Hermann Ehrenberg, Deutsche Malerei u. Plastik von 1350—1450. Bonn-Leipzig 1920.

Walter Mannowsky, Ein deutsches Tafelbild des XIV. Jahrhunderts und seine Beziehung zu Giotto (Berliner Museenberichte aus den preuszischen Kunstsammlungen. XLII., str. 81—7). Berlin 1920—1921.

Ant. Cechner, Soupis památek historických a uměleckých v politickém okresu kaplickém (Soupis památek historických a uměleckých v království Českém XLII.). Praha 1921.

Ant. Matějček, Die böhmische Malerei des XIV. Jahrhunderts (Bibliothek der Kunstgeschichte, Bd. 12). Leipzig 1921.

Ant. Matějček, Mistr vyšebrodský a mistr třeboňský (Volné Směry XXI., str. 98—107). Praha 1921—22.

L. Baldass, Die altösterreichischen Tafelbilder der Wiener Gemäldegalerie (Wiener Jahrbuch für bildende Künste V., str. 67—70). Wien 1922.

Katalog Výstavy starých obrazů z místního majetku Městského musea v Č. Budějovicích. Č. Budějovice 1922.

Ant. Matějček, O českém malířství XIV. stol. (Ročenka Kruhu pro pěstování dějin umění za rok 1920—21, str. 24—34). Praha 1922.

E. Dostál, Vyšehradská Madona (Časopis Matice Moravské, XLVII., str. 1—14). Brno 1923 (zvl. otisk tamže).

Vinc. Kramář, Archa zátoňská (Život III., str. 15—19). Praha 1923.

R. Kuchynka, Obraz smrti P. Marie v Košátkách (Památky archeologické XXXIII., str. 148—9). Praha 1923.

Ant. Matějček, Příspěvky k dějinám deskového malířství českého (Památky archeologické XXXIII., str. 231—42). Praha 1923.

Ant. Matějček, Vyšehradská Madona (Kritika článku E. Dostála z ČMM XLVII. Památky archeologické XXXIII., str. 364 až 365). Praha 1923.

Wilhelm Pinder, Zum Problem der „Schönen Madonnen" um 1400 (Jahrbuch der preuszischen Kunstsammlungen XLIV., str. 147—71). Berlin 1923.

Výroční zpráva Městského musea v Č. Budějovicích za rok 1922 až 23. České Budějovice 1923.

Erich Wiese, Schlesische Plastik vom Beginn des XIV. bis zur Mitte des XV. Jahrhundert. Leipzig 1923.

K. Chytil, K datování maleb karlštejnských (Ročenka Kruhu pro pěstování dějin umění za rok 1923, str. 26—40). Praha 1924.

Betty Kurth, Aus dem Kreise des Meisters von Wittingau (Belvedere V., Forum, str. 73—5). Wien 1924.

Ant. Matějček, Dějepis umění II. Praha 1924.

Ant. Matějček, L'école tchèque de peinture au XIVe siècle (Actes du Congrès d'Histoire de l'Art II. sec. Ière Partie. Str. 233—8). Paris 1924.

Térey Gábor, Az O. M. Szépművészeti Múzeum Régi Képtárának katalógusa V. Budapest 1924.

Wilh. Worringer, Die Anfänge der Tafelmalerei. Leipzig 1924.

Berth. Haendcke, Die Madonna in Königsberg Pr. von etwa 1340 u. der böhmische Einfluss (Repertorium für Kunstwissenschaft, XLVI., str. 212—25). Berlin-Leipzig 1925.

K. Chytil, Madona svatoštěpánská a její poměr k typu Madony vyšebrodské a k české malbě 15. stol. (Památky archeologické XXXIV., str. 41—73). Praha 1925.

Franz Kieslinger, Nachklänge zum Werke des Verduner Meisters in der Wiener Kunst des 14. Jahrhunderts (Belvedere VIII., Forum, str. 102—16). Wien 1925.

Feliks Kopera, Średniowieczne malarstwo w Polsce (Dzieje malarstwa w Polsce I.). Kraków 1925.

Jos. Opitz, Von altböhmischer Malerei (Sudetendeutsches Jahrbuch I., str. 51—3). Augsburg 1925.

A. Podlaha, Ilustrovaný průvodce metropolitním chrámem svatého Víta v Praze. Praha 1925. IV. vydání.

J. Röder, Geschichte der Vorstadt-Pfarrkirche SS Ap. Philipi et Jacobi in Olmütz-Neustift. Olmütz 1925.

E. Dostál, Iluminované rukopisy svatojakubské knihovny v Brně (Časopis Matice Moravské L., str. 276—404). Brno 1926.

Katalog der Ausstellung „Gotik in Österreich". Wien 1926.

Hans Karlinger, Die Kunst der Gotik (Propyläen-Kunstgeschichte VII.). Berlin 1926.

Ernst Kloss, Schlesische Kunst des Mittelalters auf der Ausstellung Breslau-Scheitnig (Cicerone XVIII., str. 589—605). Leipzig 1926.

Franz Landsberger, Breslau (Berühmte Kunststätten, Bd. 75). Leipzig 1926.

Ant. Podlaha, Český slovník bohovědný III. Praha 1926.

Wilhelm Suida, Österreichs Malerei in der Zeit Erzherzog Ernst des Eisernen und König Albrecht II. Wien 1926.

Ernst Buchner, Schlesische Malerei und Plastik des Mittelalters (Zeitschrift für bildende Kunst, LX., str. 184—93). Leipzig 1926—7.

Franz Landsberger, Ein Kapitel schlesischer Malerei (Die Kunst in Schlesien, str. 199—253). Berlin 1927.

Erwin Panofsky, „Imago Pietatis" (Festschrift für Max J. Friedländer zum 60. Geburtstage, str. 261—308). Leipzig 1927.

Luise Strauss-Ernst, Die Ausstellung mittelalterlicher Kunst aus Kölner Privatbesitz (Cicerone XIX., str. 735—9). Leipzig 1927.

E. Winkler, Archa z kaple svatováclavské ve Znojmě (Památky archeologické XXXV., str. 398—402). Praha 1927.

E. Dostál, Umělecké památky Brna. Praha 1928.

Katalog der Gemäldegalerie (Führer durch die kunsthistorischen Sammlungen in Wien). Wien 1928.

Fr. Kieslinger, Gotische Glasmalerei in Österreich bis 1450. Zürich-Leipzig-Wien 1928.

Vinc. Kramář, La peinture et la sculpture du XIVe siècle en Bohême (L'Art vivant 1928, 202—215). Paris 1928.

Jos. Opitz, Gotische Malerei und Plastik Nordwestböhmens (Katalog der Ausstellung in Brüx-Komotau 1928). Brüx 1928.

Jos. Opitz, Zwei Jahrhunderte gotischer Malerei und Plastik Nordwestböhmens (Witiko, I., str. 265—75). Eger 1928.

Erich Wiese, Gotische Malerei und Plastik Nordwestböhmens (Kunstchronik u. Kunstliteratur. Beilage zur Zeitschrift für bildende Kunst LXII., str. 89—90). Leipzig 1928—9.

H. Braune-E. Wiese, Schlesische Malerei u. Plastik des Mittelalters (Kritischer Katalog der Ausstellung in Breslau 1926). Leipzig 1928.

Josef Cibulka, Korunovaná Assumpta na půlměsíci (Sborník k sedmdesátým narozeninám K. B. Mádla, str. 80—127). Praha 1929.

Genthon v Archaeologiai Értesítő XLIII., str. 161. Budapest 1929.

K. Chytil, Umění české na počátku 15. stol. II. Malířství a plastika (Umění II., str. 263—86; 331—52; 359—76). Praha 1929 (zvl. otisk 1930).

Betty Kurth, Die Wiener Tafelmalerei in der ersten Hälfte des 14. Jahrhunderts und ihre Ausstrahlungen nach Franken und Bayern (Jahrbuch der kunsthistorischen Sammlungen in Wien, Neue Folge III., str. 25—55). Wien 1929.

Bella Martens, Meister Francke. Hamburg 1929.

Ant. Matějček, Výstavy gotického malířství a sochařství severozápadních Čech (Umění II, str. 94). Praha 1929.

Jos. Opitz, Gotické malířství a plastika severozápadních Čech na výstavách v Mostu a Duchcově 1928 (Umění II., str. 561 až 76). Praha 1929. (Zvl. otisk 1930).

Otto Pächt, Österreichische Tafelmalerei der Gotik. Augsburg 1929.

Otto Benesch, Grenzprobleme der österreichischen Tafelmalerei (Wallraf-Richartz-Jahrbuch, Neue Folge I., str. 66—99). Frankfurt a/M. 1930.

P. Dominik Kaindl, Geschichte des Zisterzienserstiftes Hohenfurt in Böhmen. Böhm. Krumau 1930.

Vinc. Kramář, České středověké malby z majetku čs. státní obrazárny. (Národní Osvobození VII., č. 53, 60, 63, 67, 87). Praha 1930.

Ant. Matějček, Votivní obraz rytíře z Všechlap (Od pravěku k dnešku. I. K 60tým narozeninám J. Pekaře, str. 314—28). Praha 1930.

Ant. Matějček, Výstava obrazů a plastik zakoupených státem v letech 1919—1930 (Umění III., str. 223—38). Praha 1930.

Ed. Šittler, Místopis svatováclavský (Časopis katolického duchovenstva LXXI. (XCVI) str. 71—9; 279—99), Praha 1930 (zvl. otisk tamže).

Výstava obrazů a plastik zakoupených státem. (Březen 1930 v Ústř. knih. hl. m. Prahy). Praha 1930.

Beschreibendes Verzeichnis der Gemälde im Kaiser-Friedrich-Museum und Deutschen Museum. 9. Aufl. Berlin 1931.

Katalog der Staatsgalerie zu Stuttgart. Stuttgart 1931.

Curt Glaser, Les peintres primitifs Allemands du milieu du XIVe siècle à la fin du XVe. Paris 1931.

Katalog der Ausstellung der Nürnberger Malerei in Nürnberg. Nürnberg 1931.

Ant. Matějček, Malířství. (Dějepis výtvarného umění v Čechách I. Středověk, str. 240—379). Praha 1931.

Ant. Matějček, Strahovská obrazárna v Praze. Praha 1931.

Ant. Matějček, Theodorikovy malby v kapli sv. Kříže na Karlštejně (Umění IV., str. 395—402). Praha 1931.

Wolfg. Stechow, Zur Datierung des „dritten böhmischen Stils" (Repertorium für Kunstwissenschaft LII., str. 70—3). Berlin-Leipzig 1931.

H. Weinberg v Bamberger Blätter für fränkische Kunst und Geschichte. VIII. Nr. 9. Bamberg 1931.

L. Baldass, Nürnberger Tafelbilder aus dem zweiten Viertel des 15. Jahrhunderts. Ein Nachwort zur Nürnberger Ausstellung von 1931 (Städel-Jahrbuch, VII.—VIII., str. 62—73). Frankfurt a/M. 1932.

Eug. Dostál, Eine neue böhmische Madonna (Prager Presse, XII., Nr. 352). Praha 1932.

Genthon, A régi magyar festőművészet. Vác 1932.

Vinc. Kramář, V poslední hodině (Národní Listy LXXII., č. 45). Praha 1932.

Ant. Matějček, Madona na trůně ve Stát. galerii v Praze (Umění V., str. 77—8) Praha 1932.

L. H. Labande, Les primitifs français. Peintres et peintres-verriers de la Provence Occidentale. Marseille 1932.

Ant. Matějček, Gotická deska česká s obrazem Zasnoubení sv. Kateřiny (Umění V., str. 309—12). Praha 1932.

Alfons Nowack, Führer durch das Erzbischöfl. Diözesanmuseum in Breslau. Breslau 1932.

A. Péter, Magyar Müvészet VIII. str. 322, Budapest 1932.

Boh. Slánský, Konservace tabulového obrazu „Madony na trůně" z poč. 15. stol. (Umění V., str. 433—5). Praha 1932.

E. Heinrich Zimmermann, Nürnberger Malerei 1350—1450. B. Die Tafelmalerei (Anzeiger des Germanischen Nationalmuseums, 1930—1, str. 23—48). Nürnberg 1932.

Hermann Beenken, Zu den Malereien des Hochaltars von St. Jakob in Nürnberg (Zeitschrift für Kunstgeschichte, II., str. 323 až 33). Berlin-Leipzig 1933.

Otto Kletzl, Studien zur böhmischen Buchmalerei (Marburger Jahrbuch für Kunstwissenschaft VII., str. 1—76). Marburg 1933.

Ant. Matějček, Strahovská Madona (Kniha o Praze IV., str. 21—5) Praha 1933.

L. Baldass, Das Ende des weichen Stiles in der österreichischen Tafelmalerei (Pantheon XIV., str. 373—381). München 1934.

L. Baldass, Österreichische Tafelmalerei der Spätgotik 1400 až 1525. Wien 1934.

Ant. Friedl, Pasionál mistrů vyšebrodských. Praha 1934.

F. A. Martens, Wann ist der Wittingauer Altar entstanden? Ein Beitrag zur böhmischen Frage (Zeitschrift des deutschen Vereines für Kunstwissenschaft I., str. 176—93). Berlin 1934.

Alf. Stange, Deutsche Malerei der Gotik I. Berlin 1934.

L. Baldass, Eine südböhmische Malerwerkstatt um 1420 (Zeitschrift für Kunstgeschichte IV., str. 301—19). Berlin-Leipzig 1935.

O. J. Blažíček, K výstavě Madony, církevního malířství a sochařství doby 1350—1550 (Dílo XXVI., str. 172—80). Praha 1935.

G. H. Edgell, Madonna of the school of Avignon (Bulletin of the Museum of Fine Arts XXXII., str. 32—6). Boston 1935.

Alois Elsen, Der Kreuzaltar der Münchner Augustinerkirche (Pantheon XVI., str. 171—5). München 1935.

Emil Filla, Úvod k románské plastice. (Volné Směry XXXI. str. 214—31). Praha 1935.

Gotické umění Městského musea v Českých Budějovicích. (Katalog výstavy pořádané Uměleckou Besedou v Praze 8.—28. října 1935). Praha 1935.

Vinc. Kramář, Bolestný Kristus (Volné Směry XXXI., str. 73 až 81). Praha 1935.

Vinc. Kramář, O restauraci Madony českobudějovického musea a práci dílny SVPU pro krajinské sbírky (Život XIV., str. 48—51). Praha 1935.

Vinc. Kramář, Výstava nových prací restaurátorské dílny obrazárny Společnosti VPU. (Národní Osvobození XII., č. 223; 225; 230). Praha 1935.

A. Kutal, Gotické umění Moravy a Slezska na výstavě Zemského musea v Brně (Lidové Noviny z 24. listopadu 1935). Brno 1935.

A. Liška, Nález fresky z doby Václava IV. v Praze I. (Za starou Prahu XIX., str. 33—5). Praha 1935.

Madona. Církevní malířství a sochařství doby 1350—1550 (Katalog výstavy pořádané u příležitosti prvního celostátního sjezdu katolíků v ČSR v Praze, 8. června až 7. července 1935 v domě JVU v Praze). Praha 1935.

Ant. Matějček, Malířství. (Československá vlastivěda VIII., Umění, gotické umění, str. 52—70). Praha 1935 (zvl. otisk tamže).

Vl. Novotný, Recense díla Friedlova (Volné Směry XXXI., str. 242—6). Praha 1935.

K. Oettinger, Der Meister von Wittingau u. die böhmische Malerei des späteren XIV. Jahrhunderts (Zeitschrift des deutschen Vereines für Kunstwissenschaft II., str. 293—307). Berlin 1935.

K. Oettinger, Neue Beiträge zur Kenntnis der böhmischen Malerei u. Skulptur um die Wende des 14. Jahrhunderts (Wiener Jahrbuch für Kunstgeschichte X., str. 5—23). Baden bei Wien 1935.

Boh. Slánský, Oprava obrazů z hradu Karlštejna (Volné Směry XXXI, str. 205—10). Praha 1935.

Výstava gotického umění na Moravě a ve Slezsku (Zemské museum v Brně 27./10. 1935—15./1. 1936). Brno 1935.

Vl. Denkstein, Jihočeská gotika (Život XIV., str. 45—6). Praha 1935—1936.

D. Csánky, Magyar Művészet XII., str. 244. Budapest 1936.

Zoroslava Drobná, Výstava gotického umění na Moravě a ve Slezsku (Volné Směry XXXII., str. 146—8). Praha 1936.

Zoroslava Drobná, Brněnská kresba evangelisty (Volné Směry XXXII., str. 161—2). Praha 1936.

Jar. Dřímal, Referát o M. Steifově: Weg u. Hinweis zur Identifizierung des Meisters von Raigern (Naše věda XVII., str. 89—92, 226—8). Praha 1936.

A. Kutal, Poznámky k výstavě gotického umění na Moravě a ve

Slezsku v obrazárně Zemského musea v Brně (Akord. Umění str. 6—10). Brno 1936.

A. Kutal, Ukřižování novosadské (Volné Směry XXXII., str. 67—74). Praha 1936.

Ant. Matějček, Brněnská výstava gotického umění na Moravě a ve Slezsku I. Deskové malířství 14. a první čtvrtiny 15. století (Umění IX., str. 405—10). Praha 1936.

Ant. Matějček, Mistr rajhradský, Kritické poznámky k výstavě brněnské (Volné Směry XXXII., str. 213—24). Praha 1936.

K. Oettinger, Zur Malerei um 1400 in Österreich (Jahrbuch der kunsthistorischen Sammlungen in Wien, Neue Folge X., str. 59—87). Wien 1936.

Jos. Opitz, Výstava „Madonna" v Praze (Umění IX., str. 43—4). Praha 1936.

Jar. Pečírka, Výstava gotického umění z Městského musea v Českých Budějovicích (Umění IX., str. 10—13). Praha 1936.

Jar. Pešina, Výstava gotického umění Městského musea v Českých Budějovicích (Volné Směry XXXII., str. 48—50). Praha 1936.

Alf. Stange, Deutsche Malerei der Gotik. II. (Die Zeit von 1350 bis 1400). Berlin 1936.

Max. Steif, Weg u. Hinweis zur Identifizierung des Meisters von Raigern (Die Internationale Kunstwelt III., str. 7—12; 72—7). Praha 1936.

Stručný průvodce obrazárnou Společnosti vlasteneckých přátel umění v Čechách. Praha 1936.

Eb. Wiegand, Die böhmischen Gnadenbilder. Würzburg 1936.

Frant. Žákavec, Obraz Ukřižování od Konráda ze Straubingen (Umění IX., str. 112—13). Praha 1936.

Frant. Žákavec, Referát o článku A. Elsena v Pantheonu XVI., 1935 (Umění IX., str. 271—5). Praha 1936.

Tad. Dobrowolski, Rzeźba i malarstwo gotyckie w województwie Śląskim. Katowice 1937.

Alex. Dorner, Meister Bertram von Minden. Berlin 1937.

Herbert v. Einem, Recense A. Stange, Deutsche Malerei der Gotik II. (Zeitschrift für Kunstgeschichte VI., str. 388—91). Berlin 1937.

Ant. Friedl, Tabulový obraz Madony typu zlatokorunského ve Lnářích. (Zprávy památkové péče I., seš. 7., str. 7). Praha 1937.

Die Gemälde des 13. bis. 16. Jahrhunderts (Kataloge des Germanischen Nationalmuseums zu Nürnberg I. až II.). Leipzig 1937.

W. Güttel—G. Grundmann, Breslau. Berlin 1937 (2. vyd.).

Č. Chyský, Narození Páně (Letem světem XII., č. 11). Praha 1937.

H. Jerchel, Das Hasenburgische Missale von 1409, die Wenzels-werkstatt u. die Mettener Malereien von 1414 (Zeitschrift des deutschen Vereines für Kunstwissenschaft IV., str. 218 až 241). Berlin 1937.

Vinc. Kramář, Madona se sv. Kateřinou a Markétou Městského musea v Č. Budějovicích. Praha 1937.

Vinc. Kramář, Narození Páně v české gotické malbě (Národní Politika, Vánoční zábavná a poučná příloha č. 353, str. 4). Praha 1937.

Vinc. Kramář, Práce restaurátorské dílny obrazárny SVPU pro Městské museum v Č. Budějovicích (Zprávy památkové péče I., seš. 6, str. 15—16). Praha 1937.

Vinc. Kramář, Restaurátorská dílna obrazárny Společnosti vlasteneckých přátel umění v roce 1936 (Zprávy památkové péče I., seš. 1, str. 18—19). Praha 1937.

Ant. Matějček—J. Myslivec, České Madony gotické byzantských typů (Památky archaeologické XXXX., Nové řady IV.—V., str. 1—24). Praha 1937.

Ant. Matějček, Mistr třeboňský (Prameny sv. 13). Praha 1937.

Ant. Matějček, Podíl Čech na vzniku portrétu ve 14. století (Umění X., str. 65—74). Praha 1937.

K. Oettinger, Altböhmische Malerei (Zeitschrift für Kunstgeschichte, VI., str. 397—406). Berlin 1937.

Országos Magyar, Szépművészeti Múzeum. A Régi képtár kata-lógusa. Budapest 1937.

Jar. Pešina, Ukřižování třeboňské (Památky archaeologické XXXX., str. 95—8), Praha 1937.

W. Pinder, Die Kunst der ersten Bürgerzeit bis zum Mitte des 15. Jahrhunderts (II. Vom Wesen u. Werden deutscher Formen). Leipzig 1937.

Karl M. Swoboda, Zum deutschen Anteil an der Kunst der Sudeten-länder. Brünn-Prag-Leipzig 1937.

Heinz Thiele, Die Landschaftsszenerie des Mittelalters in der deutschen Malerei des 14. u. bis zur Mitte des 15. Jahrhunderts. Berlin 1937.

Česká malba gotická. Deskové malířství 1350—1450. Zpracoval Ústav pro dějiny umění university Karlovy v Praze. Práce vedl a úvodní stať napsal prof. dr. *Antonín Matějček*. Praha 1938.

Eugen Dostál, Obraz ,,Ukřižování" z Kaufmannovy sbírky v Berlíně. (Umění XI., str. 353—361). Praha 1938.

Vincenc Kramář, Nová instalace Státní sbírky starého umění. (Zprávy památkové péče II., str. 142 a n.) Praha 1938.

Jan Loriš, Mistr Theodorik (Prameny, sv. 24). Praha 1938.

Jan Loriš, Problém Theodorikových desek na Karlštejně (Volné Směry XXXIV., str. 152—66). Praha 1938.

Postavy českých dějin (Katalog výstavy pořádané SVU Mánes v Praze ve dnech 27. května—28. srpna 1938). Praha 1938.

Boh. Slánský, Oprava tabulových obrazů v kapli sv. Kříže na hradě Karlštejně (Zprávy památkové péče II., str. 24—7). Praha 1938.

Stručný průvodce po sbírce jihočeského umění gotického. Č. Budějovice 1938.

Stručný průvodce Státní sbírkou starého umění. Praha 1938.

E. Wiegand, Beiträge zur südostdeutschen Kunst um 1400. (Jahrbuch der preuszischen Kunstsammlungen LIX., str. 67—82). Berlin 1938.

Christel Hansen, Die Wandmalereien des Kapitelhauses der Westminster-Abtei in London. (Beiträge zur Kunstgeschichte und Archaeologie, Heft 2). Würzburg-Aumühle 1939.

Pavel Kropáček, Bolestná P. Maria církvická (Zprávy památkové péče III., str. 52—53). Praha 1939.

Vlad. Novotný, Moderní methody při studiu a restauraci obrazů (Národní Noviny, č. 44 z 13. II. 1939).

Pavel Kropáček, Madona zbraslavská. (Volné Směry XXXV., str. 8—10). Praha 1938—40.

Jan Květ, Česká malba gotická. (Český Časopis Historický XLV. str. 300—305). Praha 1939. (Recense na knihu Česká malba gotická, Praha 1938).

Kurzer Führer durch die Staatliche Sammlung alter Kunst in Prag. Praha 1939.

Výstava přírůstků. (Katalog výstavy, uspořádané Státní sbírkou starého umění v Praze; též německý). Praha 1939.

Josef Cibulka, Pacino di Bonaguida a mistr Theodorik. (Umění XII., str. 3—4). Praha 1939—40.

J. Cibulka, J. Loriš a V. Novotný, Výstava přírůstků ve Státní sbírce starého umění v Praze (Umění XII., str. 153—163 a separát). Praha 1939—40.

Jaroslav Pešina, Dvě nová bohemica v cizině (Umění XII., str. 127—130). Praha 1939—40.

Boh. Slánský, Konservace středověkých obrazů z kláštera kapucínského v Praze (Umění XII., str. 285—290). Praha 1939—40.

Jitka Cuřínová, Obraz Madony dešťové v kostele na Vyšehradě (Památky archaeologické VI.—VIII. (XXXXI.), str. 53—67). Praha 1940.

Werner R. Deusch, Deutsche Malerei des dreizehnten und vierzehnten Jahrbunderts. Berlin 1940.

Jar. Pešina, Pozdně gotické deskové malířství v Čechách. Praha 1940.

Bohumil Ryba, Svatojakubská legenda (Věda a život VII., str. 62—67). Praha 1941.

Friedrich Winkler, Altdeutsche Tafelmalerei. München 1941.

Alois Elsen, Der Wittingauer Meister und Kaiser Karl IV. (Pantheon XXIX., str. 1—8). München 1942.

Otto Fischer, Geschichte der deutschen Malerei. München 1942.

Karl Oettinger, Altdeutsche Maler der Ostmark. Wien 1942.

Albert Kutal, O české malbě gotické (Časopis Matice Moravské LXV., str. 168—175). Brno 1943 (Recense na knihu Česká malba gotická, Praha 1938).

Katalog vybraných děl 14.—20. stol. (Katalog výstavy, uspořádané Národní galerií v Praze). Praha 1945.

Pavel Kropáček, Malířství doby husitské. Praha 1946.

Výstava tří obrazů (Katalog výstavy, uspořádané Národní galerií v Praze). Praha 1946.

Jaromír Neuman, Výstava tří obrazů v Národní galerii. (Život XX., str. 174—5). Praha 1946—7.

Jar. Pešina, Doplňky a opravy ke knize Pozdně gotické deskové malířství v Čechách (Památky archaeologické XLII., str. 101—109). Praha 1946.

Jar. Pešina, Ukřižování soběslavské. (Jubil. sborník Měsst. musea v Soběslavi 1897—1947, str. 26—8). Soběslav 1947.

Jar. Pešina, Výstava tří obrazů v Národní galerii (Umění XVII., str. 211—13). Praha 1945—7.

CATALOGUE

---

1.   THE ROUDNICE PREDELLA. — Before 1350.   Plates 1.—2.

Prague, National Gallery, Inv. No. O 2715.

Lime-wood, canvas-covered, gesso ground, tempera. — Height 40, width 90.5 cm. Preserved only in a fragment of the left part. The painting is in a good state of preservation, the repaintings, particularly those in the backgrounds, were removed after 1898.

This is part of the unpreserved altar of Roudnice, the country seat of the Prague bishops and archbishops. Since 1898 deposited at the Museum of Bohemia in Prague, since 1920 on loan

to the National Gallery in Prague; purchased in 1925.

The character of the painting (particularly of the heads) is in the spirit of the linear style so typical of the XIVth century. The plasticity of the cloak already shows Italian influences. The stylistic connection with the embroidered antipendium of Pirna offers proof of the Czech origin of the Predella, the kinship of which with the school of the Klosterneuburg altar is only a general one.

---

2.   THE MOST MADONNA. — Before 1350.   Plate 3.

Most, Capuchin Monastery church.

Poplar-wood, canvas-covered, gesso ground with incised drawing, tempera. — Height 53, width 40 cm. Cut down, baroque style, at top. Repaintings dating from the XVIIth and XVIIIth centuries removed in 1937—1938. The history of the painting may be traced right back to the second half of the XVIth century, when it used to hang above the entrance to the parish priest's house at Most. Both conographically and stylistically this painting derives

from the Byzantine-Italian model, which the painter followed in the covering of the head with a maphorion without crown and in the types of the faces. It is most probably the prototype of the Madonna with Child Holding a Goldfinch, which makes its appearance for the first time in Czech painting on the Rajhrad breviary of Queen Rejčka in the period before 1323. It is at the same time the oldest painting of the Czech Miraculous Madonna type.

3.—11.   THE MASTER OF THE VYŠŠÍ BROD CYCLE: NINE PANELS   Plates 4.—25.
DEPICTING SCENES FROM THE LIFE AND SUFFERINGS OF CHRIST. — About 1350.

Prague, National Gallery.

3. Plate 4. Annunciation of the Virgin Mary. 4. Plates 5.—7. Birth of our Lord. 5. Plates 8.—9. Adoration of the Three Kings. 6. Plates 10.—13. Christ on Mount Olivet. 7. Plate 14. The Crucifixion. 8. Plates 15.—16. Lament for Christ. 9. Plates 17.—20. The Resurrection. 10. Plate 21. The Ascension. 11. Plates 22.—25. Descent of the Holy Ghost.

Lime-wood on oaken base, canvas-covered, gesso ground with incised drawing traced out in black, tempera. Each panel consists of three 13—16 mm thick boards, glued together. — Height 95, width 85.5 cm. State of preservation. In the year 1940 the work of restoring the Cycle was

started at the National Gallery in Prague with the panel bearing the Descent of the Holy Ghost. The warped panel, which had broken apart into three pieces, was reinforced by the insertion of a movable grid, the new gold in the background was removed and the heads of the apostles and of the Virgin Mary were cleaned of retouchings and repaintings. The original gold and original painting were found in good condition. No further work could be done in Prague on the removal of the repainting from the other pictures; the work of restoration was continued in Germany. From three the more recent gilding was removed. On the Annunciation panel, the original gold was found in an almost entirely ruined state altogether upon being laid bare, on the Birth of our Lord panel about one third ruined, and only on the Crucifixion panel is it in a better state. On the remaining five pictures, the gold was left in its former, i. e. re-gilt state. The wood of the panels underwent restoration in the case of the Annunciation, Birth of Christ and Resurrection pictures. The paraffin coating was removed, the parts which had dropped apart were joined with each other again by means of vertically running, new strips of wood. These panels are not provided with grids and are warped. The wood of the remaining panels was left unrestored. The retouching and re-painting was removed (though only partly) from seven panels. On the Resurrection panel, about one third of the whole painting was cleaned. The uncovered, original painting is in a bad condition. On the Ascension picture the top left part of the picture was cleaned. Here, too, the condition of the original painting is not good. On the Christ on Mount Olivet picture, cleaning was effected of the apostle next to the left border of the picture. The original painting in this place appears greatly damaged. On the Crucifixion panel, the retouching was removed from the whole of the painting. Some parts of it appear well preserved, whilst others are nearly wholly ruined (the head of St. John, the head of the Virgin Mary and the feet of Christ). A similar state of things also exists in the case of the Birth of our Lord picture. The cleaned paint of the Birth and Annunciation pictures is in a fairly good state. The work of repairing the Adoration and Lament for Christ panels has not started at all so far.

The panels were kept from times immemorial at the Cistercian Monastery in Vyšší Brod, Southern Bohemia. They were put in safe deposit by the Prague National Gallery in 1938; on being returned to the Monastery in 1940, they were carried off by the occupants to Germany, whence they were restituted in 1946. At present, the whole Cycle is once more deposited at the National Gallery in Prague.

Who commissioned the painting of these panels, and for whom they were intended, cannot be safely ascertained. The only safe assumption is that they were ordered by and painted for some monastery within the territory of the Rožmberk estates.

They apparently represent what remained of a dismantled altar from which several panels would seem to be missing, as attempts so far to reconstruct the ensemble have proved unsatisfactory. The absence of further panels could well be explained on external and iconographic grounds.

The Vyšší Brod Cycle is a synthesis of Northern tradition and Italian influences which were made use of in a compilative manner and, in some cases,

without adequate understanding. It is not possible to determine for certain the exact Italian stylistic basis, but some rather conspicuous points of agreement (the Birth of our Lord and the same theme in the Capella dell' Arena at Padua) bear witness to a direct contact with Italian art, of which, besides the Tuscan school, the main influence was probably exerted by the Siena school on both form and expression. Italian ideas are here put into practice primarily in the colouring and modelling, but also in the conception and building up of space do new ideas of the trecento clearly come to the fore. Particularly the architecture of the thrones, presented stereoscopically and as an independent problem of space, points by its optical construction (duality of lower parts seen from above and upper parts from below) and its form to lessons learned from Italian patterns; these must be looked for in the pictorial architecture of monumental Italian painting rather than in the architecture of thrones in panel painting. Their importance also lies in that they by their illusive space-creating motifs (and this likewise applies to the other panel paintings of this group) anticipate in many ways the space problems of the mural cycles at Karlštejn Castle. The undeniable kinship with the paintings of the Klosterneuburg altar can be satisfactorily explained by a style common to both, but not by a direct dependence on each other. There is all the less reason, therefore, to consider Austria as the homeland of the Vyšší Brod master. The considerable differences in style between the various pictures of the cycle need not be attributed to a work divided amongst several painters. These differences are mainly due to the use made of different models, and to the effort on the part of the painter to reconcile, on the one hand, the traditional Northern usages (scantiness of space, sense of natural reality, rhythmic line, multi-coloured local tones) and, on the other, with the new creative currents of Italian origin (construction, plastic modelling and the chiaroscuro painting method). — The Vyšší Brod cycle is the work of only one artist, though in the case of the last panel, the Descent of the Holy Ghost, the speculation is admissible that some assistant may have collaborated who possessed an artistic personality differing in his form and expression and whose development was also more progressive. As to the whereabouts of the Vyšší Brod master's workshop, no proof is available. It may have been — and most probably was — in Prague, the centre of the country's arts, but the possibility may also not be excluded that it was situated in the Southern Bohemian domain of the Rožmberks. It was, viewed from every angle, about 1350 that these pictures in all probability were created.

THE MADONNA OF VEVEŘÍ. — About 1350.

Plate 26.

Prague, National Gallery, Inv. No. DO 235.

Pine-wood, canvas-covered, gesso ground with incised and black-traced drawing, tempera. — Height 79, width 63 cm, with the original, plainly moulded, 6 cm wide frame. The painting is in very good condition. The repaintings dating from the XVIIIth century were removed during the 1937—1938 restoration.

The picture came from the cemetery chapel of Mary's Ascension at Veveří Castle in Moravia. Since 1938 it is deposited at the National Gallery in Prague.

Compared with the Madonna of Most, the Veveří Madonna represents the second type of miraculous picture, in this case with the Child Jesus sitting upright on the right forearm of the Virgin Mother. Some Byzantine-Italian traces notwithstanding, the painting shows a further step in the assimilation of Italian influences, which are adapted in an individually and stylistically balanced manner. In style, the picture belongs to the school of the Vyšší Brod Cycle, in which it shows a close relationship to the Kladzko and Strahov Madonnas.

THE MADONNA OF STRAHOV. — About 1350.

Plate 27.

Prague, National Gallery, Inv. No. DO 247.

Wooden panel, canvas-covered, gesso ground, tempera. Height 94, width 84 cm. Top part cut down in baroque manner, with arcuate finish. Considerably repainted during the Baroque period. Only the left and top parts of Mary's halo, Christ's halo, the covering that flows from Mary's head and the wrapping of the Infant Jesus are in the original state. The remaining parts of the background were renovated. The heads were entirely repainted. Retouchings appear on the body of the Infant Jesus, on Mary's hands and the folds of her robe.

The painting was acquired in the second half of the XIXth century for the picture gallery of the Strahov Monastery in Prague, whence it was loaned to the Prague National Gallery in 1938.

Although the Strahov Madonna shows more archaisms (due to an Italian model) than the Madonna of Veveří, both these pictures have so many points of contact with each other that it may be presumed they come from one and the same workshop. On account of its uncommonly large and, in the Czech panel painting of the XIVth century most unusual dimensions — apart from other reasons — the painting was formerly regarded as a later copy of a lost original. In view of the loosening in composition the origin of the picture can be advanced, in contrast to the Veveří Madonna, to a period slightly less remote.

THE MADONNA OF KLADZKO: MIDDLE PART OF
A DISMANTLED WING ALTAR. — About 1350.

Berlin, Deutsches Museum, Cat. No. 1624. (Since 1945 temporarily in the USA.)

Poplar-wood, canvas-covered, gesso ground, with incised and black-traced drawing, tempera. — Height 186, width 95 cm. In good state of preservation. Small retouchings on the Madonna's face along the join of the panel, and on the heads of the angels in the upper part of the painting.

The panel represents the middle part of an altar, the wings of which were formed by panels not now preserved and depicting the Birth, the Circumcision, the Flight from Egypt and the twelve years old Jesus in the Temple. The donor of the altar was Arnošt of Pardubic, Archbishop of Prague, depicted in the left-hand bottom part of the panel. Arnošt of Pardubic was a devoted propagator of the Marian cult. He was also a well-known benefactor of the town of Kladzko (Glatz) where he had spent the years of his childhood and where he also had himself buried in the local parish church. It was at Kladzko that in 1350 he founded an Augustinian monastery, with a church of the Annunciation of the Virgin Mary, and where he also donated the altar of which our panel is a remnant that remained in Kladzko until 1904, when it was bought for the Deutsches Museum in Berlin.

On the iconographical side the painting represents, certain archaic motifs notwithstanding, a further chapter in an evolution that sought to humanise and render more ardent the relationship between the

Mother and the Child, and strove for a sensual, poetic permeation of the theme and the acclimatisation of the Italo-Byzantine type. Tradition is preserved in the type of the queen of heaven enthroned on high surrounded by angels and the lions of King Solomon's throne; there are some novel features which spring from an interest in realistic detail.

The Kladzko Madonna appears as the supreme product of Marian pictures created in the wider circle of the Vyšší Brod master's school. Its master was indubitably an independently creative persona-lity who, in the construction of his painting, was more progressive than the Vyšší Brod master, being an artist who worked in the spirit of a reviving northern tradition and in the spirit of Gothicism (as evidenced by the proportional canon and Gothic elements in the architecture of the throne) which here meet with Italian influences. In the architecture of the throne there appear anew ideas of Italian origin, which are subsequently used on a large scale in monumental Czech paintings (Karlštejn). The accents of a French style are doubtlessly present here.

15. THE CRUCIFIXION (Kaufmann). — After 1350. Plates 33.—36.
Berlin, Deutsches Museum, Cat. No. 1833.

Originally on wooden, canvas-covered panel with gesso ground and incised drawing, black-traced tempera. In 1918 the painting was lifted from the panel and given a new, adhesive canvas backing. H. 67, w. 29.5 cm. Upper part triangularly cut down, top horizontally lopped off. State of preservation very good, restoration effected in 1918. Small retouchings of gold in the background.

Probably the middle portion of a small, folding altar. Acquired in 1918 for the Berlin Gallery from the Kaufmann Collection in Berlin.

The picture still falls easily into the school of the Vyšší Brod cycle, but Italian influences are here lived through and worked up with great individuality, and with full understanding and great formal culture. The dramatic depiction, the more intense expression, mellowness and mobility of the figures and diversity of the local tones are proof of the increasing importance of the northern type of Gothic. For this reason as also on account of the more independent relation to Italian themes, the painter of Kaufmann's Crucifixion must be regarded as representing the more progressive group working probably contemporaneously with the more conservative group of the Vyšší Brod master. The opinions that were voiced on the relations of this picture to Austrian painting would seem to be amply substantiated, albeit with the reservations expressed about the Vyšší Brod cycle in general.

16. THE HOLY TRINITY OF VRATISLAV. — After 1350. Plate 37.
Wroclaw, Archiepiscopal Diocesan Museum, Cat. No. 124 (of 1932).

Oak-wood, canvas-covered, gesso ground with incised and black-traced drawing, tempera. H. 56, w. 39 cm. Painting well preserved. Retouchings on figures of angels. Restored in Berlin, 1904.

Openings in the right-hand moulding of the frame justify the surmise that this panel formed at one time the left wing of a small folding altar, perhaps a diptych. The origin of the picture is unknown. It was discovered in 1898 in the rectory of Schönau, whence it was handed over to the Diocesan Museum at Wroclaw. — This picture can be attributed to the followers of the Vyšší Brod master, in whose work a combination of Byzantine-Italian influences and traditional northern feelings rises to a perfect comprehension of all components of expression. Characteristic of the work of these disciples is the strict compositional structure, accurate drawing and a new stressing of the beauty of line which not even the soft modelling of forms can suppress.

17. DEATH OF THE VIRGIN MARY OF KOŠÁTKY. — After 1350. Plates 38.—41.
Prague, owned by Mr. J. Kolowrat-Krakowský.

Oak-wood, canvas-covered, gesso ground with incised and black-traced drawing, tempera. H. 100, w. 71 cm, cut down at sides and lower end. The painting is well preserved, though the panel is cracked vertically in the middle portion and shows partial traces of repainting. A new grid was provided and the painting cleaned in 1934.

The picture was found in 1922 in the Mater Dei

Chapel of Košátky Castle near Mladá Boleslav, from where it was loaned by its owner to the National Gallery in 1923. It was returned to the owner in 1939. The provenance of the picture is unknown. The figure of the kneeling priest in the right-hand bottom part may be regarded as that of the unknown donor.

The Košátky panel represents a synthesis of the northern tradition and the influences of Sienese painting, which show here more than anywhere else. The architectural frame work of the scene — the first picture of inner space to appear in Czech panel painting — was taken over completely, from the mural painting of „The twelve-year old Jesus in the Temple" in the Lower Church of St. Francis of Assisi, albeit with northern reservations (lack of perspective, the inner space not tallying with the picture surface, steeper under-views). This derivation bears witness to a direct contact with progressive Italian art. The painter, in his attempt to create an optically inter-connected architectural space thus sets out directly from the contemporary Italian endeavours to arrive at a new organization of space, but at the same time he also adheres to his northern background with the dramatic compactness of his grouping, the sensuous expression of his figures and his able drawing. His personal contribution to art is an uncommon realism in the drawing of hands, which, both in earlier and later Czech painting, has no equal. Common features, down to the closest detail, with the Vratislav Holy Trinity point to a workshop common to both.

18. THE MADONNA BETWEEN ST. CATHERINE AND   Plates 42.—44.
ST. MARGARET. — MIDDLE PART OF A WING ALTAR. — About 1360.

České Budějovice, Municipal Museum, Inv. No. I. 12.

Pine-wood, canvas-covered, thick gesso ground with incised drawing, tempera. H. 95, w. 101,5 cm. The panel is cut down on both its vertical sides. The gold of the background is worn off in places, the pattern of the rug covering the throne is almost destroyed, the enamel in its major part is rubbed off.

Restoration took place in Prague in 1936. In the course of repairs the 8—10 cm wide extensions were removed, the paint was fixed, the holes were stopped and the painting was lightly cleaned.

The picture represents the centre portion of a folding altar. According to tradition it comes from Zlatá Koruna in Southern Bohemia. Purchased in the Eighties of the last century from private owners in Český Krumlov for the Municipal Museum in České Budějovice.

The picture is the product of a workshop which, rather than seeking inspiration from an Italian art the structural sense of which the painter could no longer grasp (note the deformation in the architecture of the throne, disruption of the optical cohesion of the plans), set out from the northern tradition, with which it falteringly coupled new formal ideas from the end of the Fifties of the XIVth century (increased function of light).

19. THE ZBRASLAV MADONNA. — About 1360.   Plate 45.

Zbraslav Parish Church, formerly Monastery Church of St. James.

Lime-wood, gesso ground with incised and black-traced drawing, tempera. H. 89, w. 59,5 cm. The panel of the picture has buckled concavely and cracked in two places. The holes and mechanically damaged places on the painting were covered by retouchings which assumed the character of repainting along the whole figure of the Child Jesus, and most materially so on the left cheek of the Madonna and her entire neck. The top layer of the painting on the part of the Madonna's face that had not been repainted appeared to be worn through. The background was regilt. The stones and pearls studding the crown, the haloes, the hem of the robe and the buckle of the mantle were set into position at a later date. Originally they were painted on and the drawing of the crown embossed. The work of restoring the picture, done in Prague and completed in 1945, included the removal of varnish, of retouchings, repaintings and old putty from the painting and stopping the holes and mechanically damaged places.

The provenance of the picture is unknown. The first news of it appeared in 1646, when it was already kept at the Zbraslav Monastery which King Wenceslas II of Bohemia founded toward the end of the XIIIth century and which at that time served as the burial place of Bohemia's rulers.

The Zbraslav Madonna, preserved in countless

baroque copies which bore witness to the fame and immense esteem it enjoyed as a miracle-working picture was itself almost unanimously believed to be a later copy. The repairs in recent years have restored to it its age and real importance. Iconographically, the Zbraslav Madonna most nearly approximates to the Rome Madonna, representing a further variant and not, as used to be formerly thought, the prototype of a Madonna with Child holding in His hand a goldfinch. — There is no direct connection between the Zbraslav Madonna and the group of the Vyšší Brod master. Italian motifs find here their last, faint echoes and, in so far as any archaisms — such as the facial types — are here discernible, they are due to the byzantinising pattern. For a later age of origin speak such features as the more Gothic proportions of both the figures, a great effort at modelling, the displacing of drawing by valeur and an advanced realism of the jointing of the fingers on the Madonna's hands. By these signs as well as by the positioning of the Child's feet and ear the Zbraslav Madonna closely approaches the Madonna of Rome, which it outstrips in size, richness of form and quality of workmanship.

20.—21.   THE VIENNA DIPTYCH. — About 1360.   Plates 46.—47.

Vienna, in private possession.

20. Plate 46. Madonna with Child. 21. Plate 47. The Man of Sorrows.

Small wooden panels, canvas-covered, gesso ground with incised and black-traced drawing, tempera. H. 20, w. 14,5 cm. The painting in in good condition. The two small panels form a diptych, most probably a miniature travelling altar. Of unknown provenance.

Both these pictures are linked with Byzantine-Italian patterns (as regards the Madonna, with the „Pelagonitissa" type) which, however, has here already undergone a certain transformation by the individual stylistic feelings of the artist who, under the influence of the Marian cult of the time, sought for a more intimate conception of the theme. Stylistically, this diptych seems to signify a passing to a further evolutionary stage around 1360.

22.   THE ROME MADONNA. — About 1360.   Plate 48.

Prague, National Gallery, Inv. No. O 1439.

Beechwood, canvas-covered, gesso ground with incised drawing, tempera. — H. 22, w. 16,5 cm. Fairly well preserved.

Originally most probably one of the parts of a diptych, the left part of which has gone astray. Discovered in private possession in Rome and bought for the Prague National Gallery in 1927.

The Rome Madonna is a further miniaturely treated variant and simplified version of the type of Madonna with Child and Bird. With its suppression of drawing, strengthening of plasticity and heightened importance of light it comes already near the group of the „soft style". It probably sprang from the same workshop as the Vienna diptych.

23.   THE VYŠEHRAD MADONNA OF THE RAINS. — About 1360.   Plate 49.—50.

Prague VI., Collegiate Church of Ss. Peter and Paul, third chapel of the southern nave.

Canvas-covered wood, gesso ground, tempera. H. 58, w. 43 cm. Cut down top and bottom.

The picture was repainted several times. Damaged places appear retouched and entire portions of the painting repainted (the covering, body, face of Jesus, the face and hands of the Madonna). During repairs to the panel in 1911 the additions and baroque repaintings were removed. The designation „Our Lady of the Rains" was given to this Madonna by processions who addressed their prayers for rain to the picture in times of drought.

The picture would seem to emanate from the Church of S. Maria de humilitate at Vyšehrad, founded by Archbishop Jan Očko of Vlašim before the year 1364.

Iconographically the panel is the solitary specimen in Bohemia of the suckling Madonna, the so-called 'Galaktotrophusa' type which passed from Coptic art into Byzantine and thence into Italian painting. It became commonly familiar in Italy in the XIVth century under the name 'Madonna dell'Umiltà' (Our Lady of Humility) which, as far as is known, first appears in the picture by the Genoese painter Bartolomeo da Camogli of 1346 (Palermo, Museo Nazionale). With this, too, the Vyšehrad Madonna shows close similarities. The North Italian origin of the other pictures of this type which are more or less akin to our panel, tends to prove that the model for the Czech panel came from those parts. Whilst certain stylistic connections with Czech works of the Italianizing schools exist beyond any doubt, our panel does not appear to be directly related to any of them. It is therefore somewhat difficult to link it up firmly with the evolutionary whole. The chronological placing of the Vyšehrad Madonna, leaning — inter alia — for support on the dated Italian pictures of this type, too, has settled on the period round about 1360.

24. THE BOSTON MADONNA. — About 1360. Plate 51.

Boston, Museum of Fine Arts.

Small, canvas-covered wooden panel, gesso ground, tempera. H. 8,5, w. 6 cm, with original frame. Good state of preservation. Most probably the right wing of a miniature altar. Discovered in 1932 at an exhibition of French Primitives at Burlington House, London. Acquired in the same year from the owner, a Berlin art dealer, for the Boston Museum. Actual provenance unknown.

The basic compositional theme of the Kladzko Madonna is here recreated in accordance with the formal ideas of the „soft style" by the simplification of the outline, the more massive conception of shapes and the soft modelling. Close relation in figure type to the miniatures of the breviary of Jan of Středa (Liber viaticus) from the period before 1364.

25.—26. THE MORGAN PANELS. — About 1360. Plates 52.—53.

New York, Pierpont Morgan Library.

25. Plate 52. The Adoration of Three Kings.
26. Plate 53. The Death of Virgin Mary.
Small, canvas-covered wooden panels, gesso ground with incised drawing, tempera. H. 29, w. 18,5 cm. Considerably damaged, painting in many places scaled off and bared right down to ground. The panels apparently used to form a whole, perhaps a diptych. Provenance not known. At the beginning of the present century in the possession of Mr. Dowdeswell of London, in 1904 shown at the Paris Exhibition of Primitives as the property of Mrs. M. Lippmann of Berlin, from where they passed into the Pierpont Morgan Collection in New York.

The panels were for a long time held to be of French workmanship. To-day they are re-attributed to Czech painting, into which they fit as a link closely approaching the „soft style" which connects with master Theodoric. They belong there with their indifference to problems of space, their plasticity of form in stressed relief, typicality of the figures, the soft, loose modelling of the garments and the lightness of the pigments used. There is a close stylistic kinship with the Boston Madonna.

27.—155. MASTER THEODORIC: THE CRUCIFIXION, THE MAN OF Plates 54.—73.
SORROWS AND 127 PANELS WITH HALF-LIFE-SIZE FIGURES OF MALE AND FEMALE
SAINTS, ANGELS AND PROPHETS. — 1357—1367 and 1365—1367 respectively.

Karlštejn, Holy Cross Chapel and Prague, National Gallery, Inv. Nos. DO 1880—1883.

Wooden panels without canvas covering, double basic coating, brush-drawing, tempera. Pictures of unequal dimensions, the largest being the Crucifixion, h. 221,5, w. 175 cm. The rest can be divided into three groups according to size and form, but the dimensions do not tally in any two cases; into the first group may be placed 97 panels in all, the dimensions of which are in the vicinity of a height of 114 and width of 90 cm (with frames 9 to 10,5 cm wide). Twelve of the panels, placed in the lowest rows, have one vertical side cut down in bow shape to conform with the frontal arches of the vaulted ceiling. The second group is formed by three smaller pictures, placed under the Crucifixion, depicting two angels, the Man of Sorrows and three women; h. 79, w. 44 and 55 cm respectively.

Twenty-eight panels, with pictures of angels and prophets, have only one vertical and bottom horizontal side of a rectangle each, whilst the opposite side of the panels is cut down to bow shape. The frames are mostly the original ones, many of them bearing traces of recesses in which relics of saints used to be deposited. The state of the pictures is unequal; some are well-preserved, whilst on others the painting appears worn off down to the ground. Comparatively few appear to have been repainted. The greatest damage was suffered by the Crucifixion picture. It appears probable that the pictures underwent repairs as far back as in the Late Renaissance. The first provable restoration of all the panels, carried out in the years 1839 to 1841, confined itself to the preservation of the pictures from the ravages of the death-watch beetle, the fixing of the peeling-off gesso layer, the varnishing of the pictures and their bracing with wooden struts. From 1927 to 1930, twenty-four more of the panels were newly repaired, and additional panels are being gradually repaired.

The position of the panels on the walls of the Holy Cross Chapel is the original one. The pictures are arranged in three and four rows over each other on the walls of the chapel, and in two rows in four window recesses. The grouping follows a plan. The altar wall is covered with pictures representing the mystery to the commemoration of which the chapel was consecrated, the figures of those who witnessed the consecration, and the apostles. On the right-hand walls there are depicted saintly fighters, in the window recesses holy virgins, widows, bishops and Benedictine abbots. A part of the left wall (behind the grille) and its recess is filled with pictures of bishop-saints. On the other half of this wall (in front of the grille) there are placed the pictures of the Holy Lamb and saintly Benedictines, bishops and kings. On the wall facing the altar (entrance wall) there are pictures of saintly hermits, popes and kings. In the recess are four ecclesiasts. The corner panels on all the walls represent angels, seraphim and prophets. Only a few of the saints can be safely recognised by their respective attributes, for the majority of them are merely marked by a book, a crozier, and the like. In 1780 the pictures of the Crucifixion, Ss. Augustine and Ambrose were transferred to Vienna, where they were kept in the Belvedere Gallery until 1901, when they were returned to their former place. The picture of St. Thomas was from 1780 to 1783 in the hands of Professor Ehemant in Prague, from where it was handed over to the Prague University Library, to be finally returned to Karlštejn Castle in 1842. In 1945 the pictures of St. Vitus, St. Matthew, a pope-saint and St. Elizabeth were loaned to the Prague National Gallery.

According to documentary sources, the origin of the decoration of the Holy Cross Chapel may be placed in the years between 1357 and 1367. The first consecration of the chapel took place on March 27th, 1357, the second on February 9th, 1365, and its creator was rewarded by Charles IV on April 28, 1367.

Master Theodoric (Dittrich, Dětřich, Jetřich) is named in the imperial rescript of Charles IV, dated April 28, 1367 as the creator of the decoration of the Holy Cross Chapel, the Emperor expressing laudatory appreciation of his work and exempting the Master's Mořina estate near Karlštejn from tax payments by way of reward. Other reports on Theodoric are rather fragmentary. In 1359 he had a town house on Hradčany in Prague and was the Emperor's painter. About 1365 is the probable date of the entry in the guild book of the Prague fraternity of painters, telling of the payment by him of the customary annual guild fee. The town records of Hradčany again mention his house in 1368. The origin of Master Theodoric is not known. There are disputes about it, some saying he came from a Czech family, others that he was raised by a German family who had settled down in Prague, whilst still others suggest that he was called to this country from foreign parts.

The question of the decoration of the Holy Cross Chapel involves many problems, but the examination of the panels has not yet advanced to a stage where a satisfactory conclusion can be drawn. The manner in which the chapel was decorated was most probably influenced by Italy, in which country a whole series of polyptychs with half-life-size figures of saints have been preserved of which many in their composition remind us of Theodoric's panels — as witnessed, for example, by three panels by Pacino da Bonaguida in the Florence Academy; their composition scheme shows a remarkable affinity — making allowance, of course, for a different stylistic conception — and it is quite possible that such pictures were known to Theodoric. It is not unlikely that the original decoration of the chapel, with which could be coupled the first consecration, consisted of mural paintings which were soon destroyed by damp and were replaced by the present decoration which can be linked with the second consecration and with the date of which its stylistic character would appear far better to tally. It is possible that this decoration set out from the system and manner of the original painting. There are certain indications of this, for example in the manner in which the painting is extended to the surface of the frame. But there is hardly any question of copies from a later period (the XVIth century) as surmised in some quarters, although it is a striking fact that the detailed chronicles of the concluding years of the XVIth century, commenting on large-scale repairs of the castle and its equipment (which by then was already in a state of considerable dilapidation) make no mention of the pictures, although the state of the wood and the painting itself is unbelievably good and shows hardly any repainting whatever. The origin of Master Theodoric's style cannot be traced back to either Southern or Western art. True enough, there are some points of contact in the realisation of form with the art of Italy and in the growing naturalism with Franco-Flemish painting, but they are only basic ideas which in the work of Theodoric subsequently grew into independent expression which cannot be compared with anything that was created in European art during the second half of the XIVth century. Only the work of Bertram, the Hamburg master, appears to some extent stylistically related to the art of Theodoric, yet in spite of all the efforts which research has made in this question, the problem is still not solved in a satisfactory manner. But neither do we find in Czech panel painting any works which throw a sufficient light on the evolution from the Italianising, architectonically strict painting of the middle of the XIVth century to the formlessly soft style of Theodoric who, in this genre of painting, suddenly and seemingly without any preparation grows into a masterly personality. On the other hand, almost the whole evolution can be found in Czech book paintings (miniatures from the period about 1360, inserted into the Rajhrad Breviary of 1342 and the Evangel of Jan of Opava, 1368), but it remains an open question whether Theodoric's style may be explained as having set out from book-painting, as some researchers have suggested. From the technical angle, too (energetic application of impasto, colouring of complexion, sketchy rendering of hair and beard, free brush technique, and, most of all, the manner of painting alla prima) Theodoric's pictures differ fundamentally from all previous development as well as from all that was created in European painting of those times. It would seem that the decoration of the chapel is the work of at least two painters — master and assistant — which must be conceded as feasible in view of the magnitude of the task. The former, with his superior creative power, is characterised by the general modelling of shapes in rounded, almost jointless forms, with the complexions modelled in greyish tones and the colouring subdued and broken, whilst the latter, qualitatively inferior, is characterised by his striving for a more detailed elaboration of the faces, more angular forms, yellow to reddish-brown flesh-tint with olive-brown modelling and lighter colouring in the garments. If Master Theodoric is held to have painted all the panels in the front part of the chapel, the supposed assistant must have done a certain part of the panels at the back.

156. VOTIVE PICTURE OF JAN OČKO OF VLAŠIM. — After 1370. Plates 74.—80.

Prague, National Gallery, Inv. No. O 84.

Lime-wood, smoothed down by thin gesso ground, tempera, H. 181, w. 96 cm. State of the panel prior to repair: Wood badly damaged by death-watch beetles, breaking apart in places. The whole surface shows retouchings and repaintings, particularly in portions of the cloaks. Worst damage suffered by the cloak of St. Vitus through the rubbing off of the enamel. On the other hand, all the heads are in good condition. The background appears repainted all over with a dark brown pigment, reddish in some places. All the haloes and the wings of angels were found to be regilt with an oil gilding. The work of restoring this picture, carried out in 1942—1943, included fixing the wood and reinforcing the panel with a grid, removing repaintings from the background and the more recent gilding, removing retouches and repaintings in general, filling in and touching up the damaged surfaces, completing the gilding and painting in the damaged part of the face of Charles IV (left eye). The picture in all probability was painted for the main altar of the chapel inside the tower of Roudnice Castle, which was consecrated on June 15th, 1371 and dedicated to the glory of the Virgin Mary and the saints of St. Vitus Cathedral, Wenceslas, Adalbert and Sigismund, by the second Archbishop of Prague, Jan Očko of Vlašim (died 1380). It was transferred to Roudnice Abbey in 1776, loaned to the Prague Gallery in 1826 and purchased for the National Gallery in Prague in 1926.

The panel depicts on its upper half the Madonna with Child Jesus, sitting on a throne between St. Sigismund and Emperor Charles IV, St. Wenceslas and Prince Wenceslas (subsequently Charles IV), on its lower half the kneeling donor of the picture, Archbishop Jan Očko surrounded by Ss. Prokop, Adalbert, Vitus and Ludmila. The picture is typical of a representative painting, the scheme of which is determined by tradition. The figures of the Madonna and the saints on the one hand and the figures of persons mundane on the other, are so proportioned as to bring out their relative importance; this rendering springs from the pre-humanistic individualism which pervades the entire spiritual life of that time (the portrait busts in the triforium of St. Vitus Cathedral in Prague, dating from the period after 1378). In the heads of the contemporaries shown there manifests itself an effort at portraiture which is a direct echo of the portrait naturalism of the master hand that painted the royal likenesses in the Church of Mary the Virgin and the St. Catherine Chapel of Karlštejn Castle. This is most apparent in the case of the Archbishop's head, whose portrait features were still more enhanced by the repairing of the panel; it is less observable on the head of Charles IV, which adheres to the established official iconography of the emperor-king. The re-discovery of the original gilt background, formerly hidden beneath a repainting which used to be considered as the original work, has given to the picture its authentic apearance and signifies a revaluation of the qualities and importance of the work. The picture was thereby given back its intended transcendental, supersensual atmosphere, its Gothic colourfulness

and immateriality of figures. Many of its features seem to suggest a connection of the picture with Master Theodoric: lack of interest in space, typicality of the figures, style of folds, suppression of drawing, soft modelling and colourfulness. As against these, some innovations, such as a lessening of naturalism in the drawing of the hands, the more abstract conception of the garments, the heightened function of light and the more advanced breaking-down of solid form, slenderer proportions of the figures and a certain effort to refine the faces, point to a younger pupil of Master Theodoric. Some peculiarities, such as the prodigal employment of costly colours and gold and the almost complete filling in of the picture surface, indicate that the painter was familiar with the technique of book-painting with which it shows not only a considerable kinship from the point of view of style (for example in the Evangel of Jan of Opava of 1368 and the Pontifical of Albert of Šternberk of 1376) but also that he has been schooled in such technique. (The Plate No. 75 was made before the restoration, the other reproductions show the state after restoration).

157.   THE CRUCIFIXION FROM THE EMMAUS MONASTERY. —   Plates 81.—83.
Before 1380.

Prague, National Gallery, Inv. No. O 1252.

Pine-wood, canvas-covered, gesso ground, tempera. H. 132, w. 98 cm. Except for the pigments having darkened by the passage of time, the picture is well preserved. In its main part unrestored, only local retouchings. Probably the centre picture of the altar, which in all likelihood used to stand in the Prague Monastery of Emmaus. Since 1900 in the repository of the National Museum in Prague, whence it was loaned to and exhibited at the National Gallery in Prague. Purchased by the National Gallery in 1937. The picture is still linked up with Theodoric's

style with its spacelessness, figure types and fold motives, although the soft, undulating movement which permeates the composition, the more slender proportions of the figures and the refinement of their faces (that of Mary) as well as the lyricising of expression are marks of difference and progressiveness which do not permit of ascribing the painting to Theodoric himself, and advance its origin to a time near the year 1380. Both by its spirit and form the Emmaus Crucifixion would therefore form a close approach to the art of the Master of the Třeboň Altar.

158.   DEATH OF THE VIRGIN MARY. — About 1390.   Plate 84.

Brno, Moravian Provincial Museum, Inv. No. A 507.

Alder-wood with gesso ground, tempera. H. 33.8, w. 24 cm. Figures not repainted, only the background coarsely covered with a dense bronze coating which partly even impinged on the outlines of the figures. The haloes were gilded over, and also repainted was the cover of Mary's couch. The painting with its ground became in parts detached from the wood. Partial, small retouchings on Christ's cloak, on the head of St. Peter and the vessel in his hand. Last restored in 1925.

Formerly in private possession at Rajhrad. Pur-

chased for the Moravian Provincial Museum in Brno in 1925.

In its spaceless conception of composition, typical figures with their amplitude, the plastic modelling and baggy treatment of the garments, the picture is still closely related to the art of Theodoric, yet it moves away from Theodoric with its strongly accentuated contouring line. The picture must be regarded as a provincial variant of Theodoric's style originating in some Moravian workshop in the relatively late period around the year 1390.

ALTAR WITH THE PICTURE OF SS. VITUS. WENCESLAS AND SIGISMUND IN THE CENTRE.
About 1385.

Stuttgart, State Gallery, No. 1038.

Fir-wood with oak inserts, canvas-covered, gesso ground in front, tempera. — Quinquepartite wing altar consisting of fixed centre picture, two fixed and two movable wings, painted on both sides. Original frame 7.5 cm wide. The ensemble with frame is as nigh as it is wide, namely 233.5 cm. The centre picture without frame is 188 cm high and 51 cm wide, both the fixed and the movable wings measure 204 cm in height and 51 cm in width (without frame). The front part is well preserved except for places where the paint and numerous retouchings have peeled off. The gilt background and the haloes show traces of having been repaired. The reverse side, painted with gouache on a thin gesso ground is badly damaged, the left half of the centre picture being almost entirely rubbed off; the figures of the donors appear slightly better preserved. Restored in 1852 and again in the years 1875—1880. In 1902 the repaintings applied during the first restoration were removed. Last repaired in 1930—1931.

Originally the altar stood in the little church of St. Vitus at Mulhouse-on-Neckar, near Cannstatt in Wurttenberg, built by the Prague burgher Reinhart, a native of Mulhouse, who also donated this altar. Acquired in 1902 by the State Gallery in Stuttgart. When open, the altar shows St. Wenceslas in the centre, St. Vitus on the left and St. Sigismund on the right. When shut it shows: top centre the Coronation of Virgin Mary and below the Annunciation, top left the Man of Sorrows, below the kneeling donor, on the right the Crucifixion. On the reverse side the Crucifixion in the centre, on the sides the kneeling donor (left) and his brother (right). Besides the Latin inscriptions (repaired, but wording left unaltered) which refer to the figures of the saints and the Virgin Mary and the Latin invocations attached to the figures of the donor and his brother, the reverse side shows in the picture of the Crucifixion above the figure marked „reinhart" inscriptions in German, reading as follows: — „Do mān czalt von cristi geburt mccclrrrv (1385) iar am sant wenzeszlaus tag wart disse tafel volbracht von dem Eirbn̄ Reinhart von Mülhusen burger zu Prag stifter diss. kappel und aller ander ir zu gehörd. Bittent got daz er im gnedig sey amen." Above the head marked „Eberhart" the inscription reads: „Do mān czalt von cristi geburt tusend dry hundert und achzyg iar an dem fritag vor sant gyldn tag starb Eberhart von Mülhusen burger czu Prag Reynhartz Bruder stifters disser kapell. Bittend got vor in."

The altar, the first definitely dated and at the same time completely preserved work of Czech panel painting, still shows close dependence on Theodoric's style, with which it shows numerous, conspicuous points of agreement, especially in the typicality of the heads. For a late period of origin, on the other hand, speak the elongation and mobility of the figures and the advanced disintegration of the solid forms by light, by which features the work strongly reminds one of the altar of St. Lawrence's Chapel at Marienburg. A certain coarseness of form, slackness of technique and superficiality of workmanship bear witness that in the Mulhouse altar there is preserved a belated and peripherally coarsened offspring of Theodoric's style, characteristic of the artistic standard of second-class painters who worked for wide circles of burghers and borrowed compilatively from the Court art of the previous painting generation.

169.—174.   # THE MASTER OF THE TŘEBOŇ ALTAR. — THREE PANELS   Plates 88.—112.
FROM THE PASSION CYCLE. — About 1380.

Prague, National Gallery, Inv. No. O 476, 477 and 1266.

a) 169. Plates 98.—92. Christ on Mount Olivet. — 170. Plates 93.—95. Ss. Catherine, Magdalene and Margaret (reverse side of the preceding panel). — b) 171. Plates 96.—101. The Resurrection. — 172. Plates 102.—104. Ss. James the Less, Bartholomew and Philip (reverse side of the preceding panel). — c) 173. Plates 105.—108. Laying in the Sepulchre.

— 174. Plates 109.—112. Ss. Giles, Gregory and Jerome (reverse side of the preceding panel).

Lime-wood, canvas-covered, gesso ground with incised drawing, tempera. The dimensions of the first two pictures are alike, being h. 132, w. 92 cm. The state of the paintings may be said to be very good. They have turned somewhat dark with dirt, but beyond that they have suffered no other damage. Nothing is known of these panels having ever been restored.

All these three panels were apparently at one time the component parts of a wing altar, very likely the main altar, placed originally most probably in the Church of St. Giles at the Augustine Monastery at Třeboň. Records preserved since 1378 speak of the consecration of altars dedicated to St. Mary Magdalene, St. Augustine and other saints. In view of the fact that the work on the vault of the church proceeded in 1380, it is to be assumed that the wing altar only came into being and was set up in its place after this date. The panels from the dismantled altar were made over as a gift to various churches in the Třeboň area in the first half of the XVIIIth century. The pictures with Christ on Mount Olivet and the Resurrection went to the small church of St. Magdalene, whence they were sent to Prague in 1868 and purchased for the National Gallery in 1872. The dimensions of the third panel are: Height 135, width 93 cm. Its frame is the original one, and the state of the painting is good. The picture underwent restoration between the years 1909 and 1911 which limited itself to the mere preservation of the panel. In the course of a second repair, in 1913, the damaged places were repaired and numerous repaintings removed. The last restoration took place in 1922. Although the dimensions of the picture do not altogether correspond to those of the other two panels, it is regarded on grounds of style as a component part of one and the same altar. The panel came at some time unknown to Domanin near Třeboň, where it was placed in a chapel built in 1895. It was purchased for the National Gallery in Prague in 1921. Whilst the first two of these panels must be regarded as an expression of the Master's own style, this expression would appear to have been influenced by the creative conception of a younger hand that was working with the Master on the picture.

The work of the Třeboň Master appears as the supreme synthesis of spiritual conception and naturalistic vision, which was as much a symptom of those times as a personal contribution of the painter. Although his appearance was not wholly unprepared by the work of the group which preceded him (the Emmaus Crucifixion, the cycle of mural paintings on themes from the Apocalypse in the Virgin Mary Church at Karlštejn Castle), the Třeboň Master's work as a painter produces the effect of something novel, even revolutionary. By way of reaction to a loosening in style, the Master of the Třeboň Altar introduces a new stylistic idea and stylistic unity, a new order of plasticity and formal discipline. By reviving the rhythmic (though not as yet linear) principle in composition and in his system of folds he already marks the passing over to formalism about the year 1400. Perhaps that is why his work has a more conservative effect than the styleless naturalism of the Theodoric school. In actual fact the Master of the Třeboň Altar, too, is a great innovator in his sympathy toward natural form, in his view of space logically built into depth, in his apparently new chiaroscuro construction of form and combination of colour and light. For him, chiaroscuro is a space-creating instrument as much as an important medium of expression. Light no longer serves the purpose of breaking the solidity of bulk as it had in the school before him, but rather to dissolve the local colour and transpose it into tone. Also new is the Třeboň Master's view of the human figure, ennobled and refined by him in the proportioning, movement, gestures and attitudes of his figures. By this, too, the Třeboň Master already prepares the style in vogue about the year 1400. On the expressive side, the Master of the Třeboň Altar appears more as a sensitive, almost mystically inspired story-teller than a dramatiser of epics. — The analogies which link the Master of the Třeboň Altar with Western art are not so far-reaching as to force the assumption of his dependence on the school to which Broederlam belongs. As it is, the principal work of the latter painter, the Dijon altar, is by all calculations younger by a number of years (1394). It is rather a case of parallel development in the problem of naturalism and its means of plastic expression. The influence of the Třeboň Master's style on Czech and Central European creation was most profound, but substantially it remained uncomprehended by his contemporaries, so much so, that at the end of the XIVth century there was neither in Bohemia, nor in the rest of the cultural region of Central Europe an artist who could have developed from the Master of the Třeboň Altar on the way which in the West led from Broederlam to van Eyck. In spite of divergent, isolated attempts to place the Master of the Třeboň Altar chronologically into a later period and thus to deprive him of his importance for the evolution of art, his dating must remain what it hitherto was, that is to say about 1380—1390, mainly because only this dating allows a logical explanation of the style of Czech panel painting about the year 1400. In this relation the epitaph of Jan of Jeřeň, dated 1395, is a convincing terminus ante quem.

THE CRUCIFIXION. — WORKSHOP OF THE MASTER OF
THE TŘEBOŇ ALTAR. — Before 1400.

Prague, National Gallery, Inv. No. o 577.

Pine-wood, canvas-covered, gesso ground with incised drawing, tempera. H. 125, w. 95 cm. The state of the painting is good. Retouched with wax paints in 1932.

This is a part of an unknown altar. Neither is it known when it came to be placed in the chapel at Sv. Barbora near Třeboň, where it remained until the abolition of the chapel during the reign of Joseph II. It passed subsequently into private hands in Třeboň, whence it was acquired by purchase for the Prague National Gallery.

The picture must be regarded as having been produced in the workshop of the Master of the Třeboň Altar. Although the chromatic modelling, the form of folds and the rendering of head types show that its painter was a well-taught pupil of the Master, his composition, his building-up of space and his arrangement of figures show that he still clung to the older patterns of which the Emmaus Crucifixion comes close to his conception on these points. The view that the Vyšší Brod Crucifixion was a first step toward the Crucifixion from the chapel at Sv. Barbora cannot be accepted. It may be assumed, however, that judging by the small difference in measurements and the stylistic affinity, the picture is a part of a presumed altar probably also of Třeboň provenance, to which the Adoration of the Child panel, referred to under Catalogue No. 176, likewise belonged.

176. THE ADORATION OF THE CHILD. — SCHOOL OF THE
MASTER OF THE TŘEBOŇ ALTAR. — Before 1400.

Hluboká Castle.

A wood panel, canvas-covered, gesso ground with incised drawing, tempera. — H. 125,5, w. 93 cm. Considerable repaintings, enamel for the most part worn off. During the restoration in 1930, in the course of which some of the crudest repainting was removed, the restorers found the rather indistinct monogram of a renaissance restorer with the year 1516 added.

The provenance of the picture is not known.

On its iconography, the panel represents a combination of three scenes, i. e. the Birth of the Lord, the Adoration of the Child and the Annunciation to the Shepherds. The first and third scene already appear in combination in the oldest Czech book and panel painting. An exact evaluation of this panel is rendered difficult by the repaintings which changed the original colour character of the picture. As far as can be judged from the present state of the picture, its painter derived his total conception, composition, the folding of the garments and the figure types from the work of the Master of the Třeboň Altar. He failed, however, to reach the level of his model both in his construction of space — muddled and even backward — and in the quality of the work and method of painting, which already signifies a departure from the chiaroscuro principle of the Master of the Třeboň Altar. With these features, too, the Hluboká panel would be seen to fit into the evolutionary line of the end of the XIVth century. This panel is apparently a component part, together with the Crucifixion picture mentioned under Catalogue No. 175, of an altar. The bad state of its preservation does not allow of its being ascribed to the same painter's hand.

177. THE MADONNA ARACOELI; — SCHOOL OF THE MASTER
OF THE TŘEBOŇ ALTAR. — About 1400.

Prague, National Gallery, Inv. No. o 1457.

Lime-wood with gesso ground, incised drawing, tempera. H. 72, w. 48 cm.

Original frame, 11 cm wide, bearing paintings of prophets and female saints. Top left hand corner shows David, top right hand Isaiah; bottom left hand corner shows Jeremiah, bottom right hand Ezekiel. The left hand vertical moulding shows from top to bottom Ss. Catherine, Margaret and Ursula, the right hand vertical moulding from top to bottom Ss. Barbara, Dorothea and Apollonia. The state of the painting is good. The gold of the background is considerably worn off.

The provenance of the picture is not known. It was purchased from the Lindpaitner Gallery in Berlin in 1928. The scrolls held by half-figures of prophets bear Latin inscriptions, referring to the persons depicted.

In this picture is met for the first time the painted frame which, in the first half of the XVth century, was to become a characteristic feature of Czech panel painting. The origin of this type of ornamentation is to be sought in Byzantine painting, from where it most probably found its way via Italy to Bohemia, gaining great popularity there. Save for a few small divergencies, this Madonna picture is a faithful copy of the smaller picture (h. 29, w. 22 cm) painted on parchment and deposited amongst the treasures of St. Vitus Cathedral in Prague; according to tradition, this picture was brought from Italy as a gift from Pope Urban V to Emperor Charles IV in 1368.

This Madonna type, which in Byzantine iconography is called „Agiosoritissa" or „Chalkopratissa" was taken over from Byzantium by Italian painting, by which it was handed down to posterity in a number of replicas. Of these, the one nearest to the picture in St. Vitus Cathedral is the much venerated Madonna in the Roman church of Santa Maria in Aracoeli, from which the Czech copy took over everything as regards type, forms and style without attempting to interpret the type thus taken over in any contemporary painters' language. The stylistic character of the centre part of the picture differs plainly from the stylistic character of the figures on the frame, but the uniform manner of embossing proves that both parts of the picture emanated from one and the same workshop. The frame pictures manifest an undeniable influence of the Master of the Třeboň Altar, not only in the chiaroscuro merging of the colours and in the development of form by painting, but also in the folds. The more elongated shape of the heads, the mobility of the figures as well as the more schematic conception of the garments are, on the other hand, divergent features. Naturalism in details and a somewhat dramatic accent already go beyond the limits reached by the art of the Třeboň Master; they point to an evolutionarily more advanced group around 1400.

178.   THE VYŠŠÍ BROD CRUCIFIXION. — Before 1400.   Plates 126.—129.

Prague, National Gallery.

Oakwood, canvas-covered, gesso ground with incised drawing, tempera. H. 129,5, w. 98 cm. The state of the painting is good. The panel, the background of which as well as the heads of the Virgin and St. John were repainted, was restored in Prague in 1938.

From time immemorial the picture was kept at the Monastery of Vyšší Brod. It was loaned to the National Gallery in Prague in 1938, whence the occupants carried if off to Germany in 1940. In 1947 it was returned to the National Gallery in Prague, as restituted property. No support can be lent to the view that the picture is an early work of the Master of the Třeboň Altar. Many stylistic features show that the time of the picture's origin must be sought in a younger set of painters, nearer the year 1400. Of these features, particular mention must be made of the strictly symmetrical filling of space, the striving for balanced composition and a linear, rhythmical construction. It is also scarcely to be assumed that a painter of such eminence as the Třeboň Master would have gone over in his evolution from agitated forms to forms as tranquil in expression as can be seen on the wings from Sv. Majdalena. Many features related to the Třeboň altar, such as the facial types and the folds (cascading draperies and long lappets) and the tonality of the picture show that the painter of the Vyšší Brod Crucifixion grew up in touch with the art of the Master of the Třeboň Altar, from whom, however, he differs fundamentally by his stressing of the spiritual side of the event, and rises, in the expression of the heads and gestures of the figures, into a dramatically agitated, even pathetically exaggerated language. On the other hand it would not do to overlook some archaic features of style such as, for example, the naturalistically intended, ugly type of Christ's head, forcefully reminding one of the Crucified One of the Mulhouse Altar, or the loop motives of the garment hems, which likewise point to the style current in the Sixties of that century. Finally, the question easily arises as to whether the accentuation of the expressive component of the picture, too, may not perhaps represent a return to the school of the Vyšší Brod master, especially to the last picture of the Vyšší Brod Cycle (Descent of the Holy Ghost) and the Košátky panel. — It would, therefore, seem that here is proof of a complex crossing of stylistic currents, of which one flowed into the Vyšší Brod Crucifixion indubitably from the work of the Master of the Třeboň Altar, whilst the other sprang from the older Czech tradition and whilom school of the Theodoric style, which here re-echoed in the same way as it did in the contemporary manuscripts of Wenceslas IV. (The coloured reproduction of the picture No. 127 and the black and white reproduction of the pictures Nos. 128—129 are in keeping with the state of both prior to the restoration in 1938).

---

179. MADONNA BETWEEN ST. BARTHOLOMEW AND Plates 130.—132.
ST. MARGARET. — About 1400.

Hluboká Castle.

Wood panel, canvas-covered, gesso ground with incised drawing, tempera. H. 110, w. 125 cm. Thickly repainted in all parts, especially in a portion of St. Bartholomew's cloak.

The picture may have been originally in the chapel of Český Krumlov Castle. In the last century it stood on the altar of the Holy Virgin Chapel at Protivín Castle, whence it was transferred to Hluboká Castle.

The picture appears as a work of transition and a connecting link between the art of the circle around the Master of the Třeboň Altar and the younger, already formalistical style. As in the case of the Vyšší Brod Crucifixion here, too, some features of form, style and composition show that they have been compilatively derived from older Czech creations. However, they are fewer in number and manifest themselves less prominently than in the Vyšší Brod Crucifixion. On the other hand, there is a noticeable addition of motifs, which, particularly in the system of folds, form already a clear first step towards the style of 1400 (zig-zag hems of garments). Here also a formal polish is employed, and a plastic modelling of bulk, a dominance of line and elegance in figures, and types of faces conspicuous by their soullessness. The Hluboká panel is neither the work of the Master of the Třeboň Altar, nor is it directly dependent on his school. Finally, mention should be made that, perhaps for the first time in the history of European painting, a Persian rug of the Serabend type has been used to drape the throne of the Madonna in this picture, and is seen in an absolutely faithful reproduction

---

180.—181. EPITAPH OF JAN OF JEŘEŇ (two fragments). — 1395. Plates 133.—135.

a) 180. Plate 134. Seated Virgin Mary with Child Jesus (left part of the panel). *b)* 181. Plates 133., 135. St. Bartholomew and St. Thomas (right part of the panel).

Lime-wood, canvas-covered, gesso ground, tempera. — The epitaph comes from the St. Vitus Cathedral on Hradčany, where it was placed seemingly not far from the tomb of Jan of Jeřeň in the Chapel of Ss. Simon and Jude. Jan of Jeřeň was a canon of the Chapter of Prague, a Licentiate of Canon Law and Archdeacon at Hradec Králové. The epitaph was, at some time unknown, cut apart and pieces of it were discovered only during this century in the shops of Vienna.

a) 180. Plate 134. SEATED VIRGIN MARY WITH CHILD JESUS.

Vienna, in private possession.

H. 61, w. 36 cm. — The background, the ground, throne, crown and haloes are new. The figure of Mary is well preserved with all the enamels, only slightly retouched in places. The lower part of the panel, on which there was the beginning and the continuation of the text which is preserved in part on the second fragment, was cut off.

The fragment passed by purchase into private hands in Vienna in 1920.

b) 181. Plates 133., 135. ST. BARTHOLOMEW AND ST. THOMAS.

Prague, National Gallery, Inv. No. O 1268.

H. 64,5, w. 49,5 cm. Both figures are relatively well preserved in their paint structure, and so are the inscription on the lower part of the panel and the gold of the haloes. The ground has been totally repainted, the gold of the background has worn off down to the base and renovation has taken place. There are isolated retouchings in the outlines of both the figures and the book. The repainting was done between the years 1910 and 1915.

This fragment was discovered at an auction sale in the Vienna Dorotheum in 1910, and in 1911 it was made over as a gift to the Kaiser Friedrich Museum in Berlin. From there it was acquired through the Haberstock Gallery in Berlin for the National Gallery in Prague in 1921.

Underneath the picture appear pieces of a Latin inscription reading: „ . . . nonagesimo q'nto in illa silba zoph Obiit . . . Jerzen liceń in decret̄ Cano^c9 p̄geń et opolień et . . m Symonis et Jude in ecclia prageń sepultus" (. . . nonagesimo quinto in illa sillaba zoph (May 15th) obiit . . . Jerzen licenciatus in decretis canonicus pragensis et opoliensis et . . . Sanctorum Simonis et Judae in ecclesia pragensi sepultus).

These two fragments used to form a whole, which, to be complete, should have added to it, in the space between the Virgin Mary and the Apostles, the figure of the donor. (Results of X-ray examination of the fragments). The composition scheme of the picture has its forerunners in the older Czech paintings. — This particular panel is important primarily because it represents the first definitely dated example of a new Czech style and, at the same time, the first step in its evolution. Although connecting links are here evident with the art of the Master of the Třeboň Altar which in everything, but especially in its view of the human figure, in its rendering of faces and its fold system worked out the patterns for a new style, there can no longer be any talk of a connection either with a workshop or a school. True enough,

the epitaph springs from the art of the Master of the Třeboň Altar, but it reacts to it with a new inclination to idealism and reshapes it with a typically formalistic view of style, through which Czech art in all its elements passed about the year 1400, aiming away from the individualistic manifestation of the Třeboň Master at a stylistic generalization and unity.

The epitaph, containing all the marks of the style current about the year 1400 „in nuce", forsakes first of all the spaciousness and chiaroscuro painting principle of the last school, replacing it all by a decorative handling of relief, plastic expression and clear colourfulness of local tones. At the same time the picture revives the idea of a linearly rhythmic articulation of the picture space which the first school of Czech panel painting used to employ. Symptomatic is also the cult of formal beauty, which is here cultivated to the detriment of the expressive side. Connected with this is a striving for the sculptural elaboration of solid forms, the self-sufficiency of a drapery which almost swallows up the body, and the calligraphic play of a line which outranks the paint and, in some places, already leads to ornamentalisation.

182.   THE DUBEČEK PANEL. — Before 1400.   Plates 136.—140.

Prague, National Gallery, Inv. No. O 693.

Pine-wood, canvas-covered, gesso ground with incised drawing, tempera. — H, 118, w. 96,5 cm, with original frame. This picture is well-preserved in its colouring, but it is mechanically damaged to a considerable extent and the frame in its greater part has been repainted. The entire upper part of the picture surface is warped and the paint partly peeled off. The gold of the haloes and in the background is partly repainted. On the border of the right hand third of the picture there is a lengthy fissure, in which the painting is disturbed and touched up. Partly restored in Prague, 1920.

The panel comes from the Gothic church of St. Peter in Dubeček, near Prague. It was donated by

an unknown canon. Discovered in 1891. Passed into the possession of the Prague National Gallery in 1892.

This picture belongs to the same style group as the epitaph of Jan of Jeřeň, and stands on about the same level of evolution. The close affinity between these two panels does not, however, justify the assumption of a workshop common to both. Certain divergencies in formal conception (fold motives) and method of painting show that here we are concerned with a work somewhat more conservative both as a whole and in details (with a poorer grasp of the rhythmic principle) and a work of lower artistic quality.

183.   MATER DOLOROSA. — Before 1400.   Plate 141.

Církvice, Parish Church of St. Vincent.

Wood, canvas-covered, gesso ground, tempera. H. 88, w. 75.5 cm. This picture shows considerable repainting. In particular, Christ and the low wall on which He is lying are later repaintings across Mary's cloak, which is visible underneath. The background is totally repainted, there are fairly large retouchings

on the hands, and a number of other interferences. The paint has come loose in several places. The contours of Mary were partly covered up by the repainting of the present background, fresh outlines having been drawn.

The exact provenance of the panel is not known,

but it has been in the parish church of Církvice near Kutná Hora since the XVIIth century. It was inserted into the altar dating from the year 1685, at which time most probably the background of the picture was provided with a silver plate of hammered design.

This panel, hitherto almost unnoticed, was thought to be a Pietà of much more recent origin. To-day it is evident that the figure of Christ is a subsequent addition made some time after 1450, and the panel a mutilated part of the original picture which apparently represented a bust of the Mater Dolorosa. This figure clearly proves that the original picture was a work of high quality, the stylistic and formal features of which agree with other panels from the end of the XIVth century (the type of the face is derived from the schools around the Master of the Třeboň Altar). The drapery, however, does not possess the high, accentuated plasticity of the folds and the wealth of cascaded hangings with open tubules of other pictures dating from about 1400. From this it may be deduced that the picture falls as regards its origin into the beginnings of a style in the course of development, probably into the last decade of the XIVth century.

---

184. THE ST. VITUS MADONNA. — About 1400. Plate 142.—143.

Prague, National Gallery, Inv. No. DO 991 (formerly one of the treasures of the Metropolitan Cathedral of St. Vitus, Inv. No. 259).

Wood, canvas-covered, gesso ground, tempera. H. 51, w. 39,5 cm. The picture is preserved in a practically undamaged state and in its original, contemporary, carved frame. Only some minor retouchings in Mary's cloak, background regilt, with a new capreolary ornament.

It is probable that the picture was directly destined for the St. Vitus Cathedral in Prague. It was loaned to the Prague National Gallery in 1940.

The St. Vitus Madonna most likely derives iconographically from an older prototype, in which there must have already been determined the basic distribution of material as well as the bodily position of the Child Jesus. Close similarities of the picture with miraculous Madonnas (such as the Krumlov Madonna) transcend the limits of a merely evolutionary parallel and point to the plausible possibility of the painting having been directly influenced by works of sculpture. The style of the picture fully corresponds to the developments in Czech painting about the year 1400 as documented in contemporary miniatures (the Vulgata in Karlsruhe, 1400). The St. Vitus Madonna fits in there with its ingenious technique (modelling by means of enamels) and its lyrical tenderness of expression. The direct relation of the picture to other very similar Madonna pictures (the Madonnas of Lnáře and Zlatá Koruna and the Stará Boleslav relief) cannot be safely proved, but replicas bear witness to the rapid and copious spread of the type, in the evolutionary series of which the St. Vitus Madonna forms so far the first known link. With its formal perfection, the picture signifies one of the high points of Czech style about the year 1400.

---

185. THE LNÁŘE MADONNA. — After 1400. Plate 144.

Lnáře, Monastery Church of the Holy Trinity.

Lime-wood, gesso ground on parchment, tempera. H. 44,5, w. 40 cm. Only the middle part is original. On the left and right the picture has been complemented by two sections of an oval and finished by the application of oil paint in the XVIIth or the beginning of the XVIIIth century. The middle part is very well preserved; the only repainting done was in the case of the haloes (gilding) and of the entire background, whilst repairs were effected in several places (particularly on the covering of Mary's head. Work of preservation and partial cleaning was done in 1927.

The panel is of unknown origin and was brought to Lnáře according to credible legend in 1682.

The Lnáře Madonna looks like a replica of the St. Vitus Madonna, to which it also approximates in the general style of its plastically stressed forms and many individual particulars. Its quality is beneath that of the St. Vitus specimen, from which it differs most noticeably in its greater rigidity of form, more schematic drawing and indifference of expression. Despite this, it may be regarded as a work done in the first decade of the XVth century; this is borne out also by the technical features of the picture, which make it differ from all late replicas.

Prague, National Gallery, Inv. No. DO 246.

Wood, tempera on gesso ground, with canvas. H. 68,5, w. 50 cm. The background is regilt with bronze, considerable repainting with red paint appears on the cloak. In the scarlet and blue parts of the cloak there are only local retouchings of damaged places. In 1908 the picture underwent partial restoration.

The picture was most probably intended directly for the Cistercian Monastery in Zlatá Koruna. In 1938 it was loaned to the National Gallery in Prague.

It was formerly regarded as the prototype of the miraculous Marian picture, which in these days is being designated as a St. Vitus type of Madonna. It does not, however, have any direct connection with the latter, as can be seen when the two are compared with each other, or when it is compared with some kindred pictures. The picture is probably the work of an imitator who made a free adaptation of his model. The lack of independence in the work is also confirmed by formal shortcomings which would be impossible in a work of a creatively working artist (the flesh of the body of the Child Jesus between the fingers of Mary's right hand, the motif of the cloak thrown over the left shoulder, the motifs of the cascading draperies, the badly drawn hand of Child Jesus and the wrong placing of the ears). The flattening of the forms, the deviation from the rhythmic principle, the dryness of the drawing and stylisation, the loud local colouring and a general coarsening of form are proof of the later origin of the picture, which stands on about the same stylistic level as the Crucifixion (No. 188) and the Roudnice Altar, that is to say about the year 1410.

187.   THE SEATED MADONNA OF JINDŘICHŮV HRADEC. — About 1400.   Plate 146.

Prague, National Gallery, Inv. No. O 1482.

Lime-wood, canvas-covered, gesso ground, tempera. H. 25, w. 19 cm. The layers of paint in the upper third (gold background, wings of the angels and partly also their figures) are ruined. During repairs in 1931 the repaintings were removed and the damaged parts stopped. The rest of the picture is in a fair state of preservation, including the enamels. Originated probably in Jindřichův Hradec. Purchased in 1931 from private owners in Prague for the Prague National Gallery.

As regards its origin, the picture would seem to fit into the period of full development of the Czech 'beautiful' style which finds its classical expression in it. With its fine modulation of colours and its mellow valeur-modelling of form it approaches the St. Vitus Madonna, together with which it represents the supreme manifestation of the Czech style about 1400, with all the signs of the formalistic aesthetics and idealism of the period in the sensuous permeation of the subject. Something analogous in book painting can be found in the Missal of Zbyněk Zajíc of Hazenburk, dating from the year 1409.

188.   THE CRUCIFIXION. — About 1410.   Plate 147.

Berlin, Deutsches Museum, Cat. No. 1662.

Pine-wood, canvas-covered, gesso ground, tempera. H. 85, w. 81 cm. The picture, including the enamels, is very well preserved. In some places slight retouchings of the cloak of John and the covering of Christ, also in the hair of John next to the damaged halo and the hair of Christ. The original gold is partly rubbed off, but only in Christ's halo has it been regilt over relatively larger spaces.

The provenance of the picture is not known. It was acquired in 1908 in Petrograd for the Deutsches Museum, Berlin. With its great formality, the picture still belongs to the classical creations of the Czech 'beautiful' style, but certain tendencies to mannerism and a certain decorative flattening (affecting also the draperies) tend to put forward the origin of the picture into a somewhat later period. The picture cannot be linked with any other preserved relic, but it can be said that it stands on about the same level of evolution as the Zlatá Koruna Madonna and the Roudnice Altar. However, both these works are beneath the high value of the Berlin panel.

Lime-wood, canvas-covered, gesso ground, with incised drawing, tempera. — H. 90, w. 68 cm, including original frame. — State before restoration: The greater part of the picture had been repainted with a thick layer of paint. Only a small part — the mantle and head covering of the Madonna — belong to the old layer. The remainder, that is the brown background with aureole, the face, hair and crown of the Madonna, the entire figure of the Child and, finally, the painting of the frame were subsequent additions dating from the time of repainting some time in the XVIIIth century; into that period also falls the excision, in the surface of the original golden clasp of the Madonna's mantle, of a circular recess for a reliquary. During the restoration, finished in 1946, the removal of all repainting uncovered the original, almost intact Gothic painting including the enamels. Even the lightness and colourfulness of the picture appeared almost untouched. The gold in the background and on the frame was in many places rubbed through and the silver foil itself, which formed the base for the gilding, had darkened through oxidisation. The scaled-off parts of the original ground for the gold and colours were replaced by a white, chalky putty; the upper part of the frame was also added, whilst the painting proper needed practically no stopping.

The picture was discovered in a cloister of the Capuchin Monastery in Roudnice in 1929. No older provenance of the picture is known, but it would seem indubitable that it was painted for Roudnice,

the place where so many outstanding works of Czech panel painting were found, most probably for the archbishop's residence or for the Augustinian Monastery church. Loaned to the Prague National Gallery in 1939.

The repairing of the picture brought to light what is for the time being the oldest example of the iconographic type which, some time later, was adopted from the miraculous Vyšší Brod Madonna and applied to the Budějovice Madonna. The fact that here one has to do with a long divined prototype, to which all other Marian pictures of this type stand in the relation of replicas to a model is proved not only by the as yet unpainted frame (the frame of the replicas is invariably painted on), but also by what the picture has to say in its style. The attractive facial type, both of the Madonna and the Child Jesus, the soft chiaroscuro modelling of the form and the sentiment of the expression appear to us still like an echo of the style of the Master of the Třeboň Altar.

On the other hand the formal polish, the formalistic folding of the drapery and the bright, shining colourfulness of the picture allow the surmise that it came into being at the time of the appearance of a new aesthetic of style and under the potent influence of the contemporary plastics at the end of the XIVth century. Thus the Madonna of Roudnice is one of the most valuable manifestations of the Czech 'beautiful' style at the initial stage of its development.

190.   THE BUDĚJOVICE MADONNA. — After 1400.   Plates 149.—151.

České Budějovice, Municipal Museum, Inv. No. N I 45.

Wood, canvas-covered, gesso ground, tempera. H. 95,5, w. 75 cm in the original, painted frame. The state of preservation is good on the whole. In some places, the contours of the centre panel appear somewhat blurred. On the Madonna's mantle the paint is partly washed off and local retouchings show, particularly in the large red fold underneath the body of Jesus. The enamel and top layers of paint on Mary's mantle are for the greater part torn down. Otherwise the centre picture is well preserved as regards the flesh tint and the golden background. The figures on the frame, particularly on the bottom moulding, are damaged in places, the paint having

parted from the gilt base. These places are slightly retouched. In the course of repairs, undertaken in 1934 in Prague, the new gilding and repainting dating from the end of the XIXth century were removed and the most deteriorated parts retouched.

Nothing is known of the provenance of the picture, but it most probably originated in České Budějovice. It was donated to the infirmary chapel of the Holy Trinity at the latter place, and was finally handed over to the local museum at the end of the XIXth century.

The figures on the upper frame represent, from left to right, the following: St. Paul, a group of

Czech saints headed by Ss. Wenceslas and Adalbert, also St. Peter. On the right hand vertical moulding are painted St. Philip, St. Vitus and St. Catherine, on the left hand vertical moulding are Ss. James, Wenceslas and Barbara. On the bottom moulding are Ss. Ursula, Dorothea and Apollonia.

Formerly the Budějovice Madonna used to be regarded as the oldest preserved picture of this type. To-day it is clear that it is nothing but a replica of the Roudnice Madonna, which has assumed that position. A comparison of the two pictures proves the Budějovice Madonna to be an undoubted copy which, although it imitates the type and form of the pattern with precision, betrays at the same time a divergent idea, observable in the linearly more plastic conception of form, particularly in the formulation of face types. This points to an already more ad-vanced stage of stylistic development after 1400. Although the picture still adheres firmly to the basis of this style, some of the motifs are a symptom of the incipient disintegration of the stylistic canon, which would seem to put forward the date of the picture's origin to about 1410. Particularly the manneristi-cally felt figures on the frame bear out such a dating. The Budějovice Madonna therefore is probably on the same level as the Zlatá Koruna Madonna, but surpasses it by a standard of painting which is outstanding. There is, however, a feature common to both in that they both represent Southern Bohemian replicas of prototypes the origin of which must be sought in Prague. The connection of the České Budějovice Madonna with the St. Vitus Veraicon is fairly close, yet a workshop common to both cannot be presumed.

191.   THE ST. VITUS VERAICON. — After 1400.   Plates 152.—156

Prague, Holy Cross Chapel of the Metropolitan Cathedral of St. Vitus.

Pine-wood panel, frame of lime-wood, canvas-covered, gesso ground, tempera. H. 62, w. 50,5 cm with the original, painted frame. Apart from in-significant places showing small retouchings the pic-ture is very well preserved. The original gilding is partly rubbed off, down to the red under-painting. During the repair in 1936 the panel was reinforced, the missing portions of the moulding were stopped and these places touched up. The later gilding of the frame and of the middle panel were also removed.

The picture was most probably directly destined for the St. Vitus Cathedral in Prague, and is still at that place of destination.

On the frame can be seen the figures of Czech saints, being, on the left hand vertical moulding on top, Ss. Vitus, Adalbert and Ludmila, whilst on top of the right hand vertical moulding there are Ss. Wenceslas, Prokop and Sigismund. On the horizontal part of the moulding are half-length figures of angels holding scrolls with appropriate inscriptions.

The incised drawing on the gilt background of the centre panel and the dotted embossing of the haloes and garment hems prove indisputably that the whole picture and the frame came into being at one and the same time. But technical points of agree-ment, too, speak for the contemporaneity of the middle picture and its frame. The Veraicon on the middle panel is a copy which in many respects departs from the Byzantine pattern. In the small pictures on the frame there appears the same loo-sening of strict rigidity as in the case of the Budějo-vice Madonna, to which the St. Vitus Madonna is very closely akin. This fact notwithstanding, it can-not be presumed they came from one and the same workshop.

192.—205.   CYCLE OF THE CAPUCHIN MONASTERY, PRAGUE.   Plates 157.—170.

FOURTEEN PANELS WITH THE HEADS OF CHRIST, THE VIRGIN MARY, ST. JOHN THE BAPTIST AND THE APOSTLES. — Before 1410.

Prague, National Gallery, Inv. No. DO 932—945 (former Capuchin Monastery Church of the Virgin Mary in Prague IV.)

Lime-wood, tempera on gesso ground without canvas. — The pictures are of unequal dimensions, varying in height between 47,5 and 49 cm and in width between 34 and 35,7 cm. — State before repair: The wood beneath four of the pictures to-tally ruined by ravages of the death-watch beetle; other pictures in fairly good condition, the rest intact. The state of the painting was not found satisfacto-ry. In the first place, all the panels were covered with a thick layer of varnish, which, in turning brown, darkened the painting to a considerable degree and gave it an unduly warm tone. The background of all the pictures was repainted with a thick layer of oil paint. In the course of repair work done in 1942 the first task was to render firm and secure the wood of the damaged panels, then to remove the varnish coating from the paintings, and, finally, to take off the compact deposit of the repaintings. Underneath the latter were discovered dark, blueish-green backgrounds with a dark-brown surface coating, which proved to be older than the repainting, albeit not the original. After the removal of the brown coatings from the background and the contours of the heads and after swabbing off the retouchings and the repaintings on the cloaks, that is to say all the later additions, the holes were stopped and finished with retouches, for the greater part only in the background. The painting proper was either not touched up at all, or only to a very small degree in the course of the 1942 restoration.

The provenance of the Cycle is not known. Nothing could be ascertained as to the time the Cycle came to the Prague monastery of the Capuchin Fathers, which institution was only founded in 1600. Its Prague origin, however, is more than probable. The Cycle was loaned to the Prague National Gallery in 1939, where during its exhibition an attempt at reconstruction was made by the joint framing of the panels in two frames of seven pictures each.

The whole Cycle comprises fourteen heads: Christ, the Virgin Mary, St. John the Baptist and the Apostles, who are identifiable only in parts. They are Ss. Peter, Paul, John the Evangelist and Bartholomew, whilst seven further apostles cannot be determined.

The Cycle is perhaps an incompletely preserved typological series called Deésis (praying), the centre of which was formed by Christ with the Virgin Mary on the left and St. John the Baptist on the right side; they were joined on both sides by apostles and possibly also by further saints. This typological series came into being at the beginning of the Middle Ages in the composition of the Last Judgment; from the three central figures it very soon spread in Byzantine art — particularly in Italo-Byzantine art — into a voluminous corpus until, at the end of the XIIIth and in the XIVth century, it represented the first germs of an Iconostasis. Judging by the position of the heads, the Cycle formed originally one complete row of heads more than six metres long, which most probably was placed on the screen between the nave and the choir.

The Capuchin Cycle owes its rise most probably to an effort to imitate a Byzantine pattern imported from abroad, which not only conditioned the whole basic scheme, but even affected the style of some of the pictures (Christ, the Virgin Mary, some of the heads of the Apostles). In other respects, however, the foreign pattern was adapted quite in the spirit of the style of the time in its full development. Pointers to this are facial typicality, accuracy, purity and plasticity of form. The stylistic analogy with the so-called Ambrass sketch-book in Vienna is such as to justify the assumption that both works emanate from one and the same workshop. However, some of the heads, with their realistic sharpness of facial expression, would seem to tend toward goals farther ahead.

(The illustrations No. 158 and 159 show the state prior to restoration, the rest the state subsequent to it.)

206.   THE DEATH OF VIRGIN MARY. — About 1410.   Plate 171.
Nuremberg, Germanisches Nationalmuseum. Inv. No. Gm 1119.

Lime-wood, canvas-covered, gesso ground, tempera. H. 38, w. 32 cm, with the original, painted frame. The state of preservation is very fair, unrestored. — Probably the right-hand half of a diptych.

The picture is of unknown provenance. It was acquired in 1926 from an art dealer's shop in Frankfort-on-Main for the Germanisches Nationalmuseum in Nuremberg. With its formal features the picture belongs to the group of works between the St. Vitus Veraicon and the Capuchin Monastery Cycle, which it approaches with its figure-types and supple folding of the drapery. Some signs, however, speak for the period of an incipient stylistic mannerism.

207.   ANNUNCIATION OF THE VIRGIN MARY. — About 1410.   Plate 172.
Budapest, Szépmüvészeti Múzeum, Inv. No. 3142.

Wood, gesso ground with incised drawing, tempera. — H. 31.5, w. 25.3 cm.

The picture was acquired from the estate of M. Jankowich, who died in 1846. It is probably a part of a diptych.

Similarities, down to close details (figures, drapery, the method of modelling, the haloes, etc.) to the Nuremberg panel of the Death of the Virgin Mary justify the assumption of a workshop common to both these works. Only the difference in their dimensions forbids one to consider the Budapest picture as the second, untraceable half of the Nuremberg diptych.

WITH THE PICTURE OF THE DEATH OF THE VIRGIN IN THE CENTRE. — About 1410.

Prague, National Gallery, Inv. No. O 1464—1466.

A triptych with wings painted on both sides. Lime-wood, canvas-covered, gesso ground tempera. — H. 147, width of centre 118.5, width of wings 45 cm. The coloured surfaces are in a fair state of preservation in their structure; only in the paintings of the inside have the finest enamels been lost in parts, and the brilliance of the colours has become dimmed. Restoration work was done on the pictures at the beginning of this century and, again, in 1929 (Prague).

The altar was probably painted for the Church of the Virgin Mary in Roudnice. It was subsequently dismantled and reassembled during the last but one restoration. It remained in its place of destination until 1928, when it was purchased for the Prague National Gallery.

The centre panel shows the Death of the Virgin Mary; the left wing inside shows Virgin Mary the Protector, the right wing inside The Man of Sorrows; the left wing reverse shows the Mater Dolorosa, the right wing reverse the Man of Sorrows.

The Roudnice altar is fundamentally the work of one master, for the differences between the centre panel and the inside of the wings spring from a stylistic subjection to a traditional scheme. The reverse side of the wings, characterised by a coarsening of types, a more marked attention to line and more dramatic treatment, must be ascribed to a younger, and, to some extent, more progressive assistant. — The inner sides of the wings and the centre of the triptych show so numerous agreements with the Capuchin Monastery Cycle and the Ambrass Sketch-Book that a direct influence of this workshop on the Roudnice altar must be assumed. Quite conspicuous in the Roudnice altar is a weakening of the sense of space and of rhythmic surface composition, a lack of talent for composition and of interest in the expressive side of the action. The principal tendency of the work is decorative, aiming primarily at colour effects. This work, too, signifies the beginnings of stylised mannerism and, at the same time, of a decay in style. Into the same circle also belongs the drawing of St. John the Evangelist in the Municipal Archives at Brno.

THE MASTER OF THE RAJHRAD ALTAR. — SIX

213—218. Plates 181.—192.

PICTURES OF THE PASSION CYCLE AND THE LEGEND OF THE HOLY CROSS. — Before 1420

a) 213. Plates 181.—183. Carrying the Cross. — *b)* 214. Plates 184.—186. The Crucifixion.—*c)* 215. Plate 187. The Last Supper. — *d)* 216. Plates 188.—189. Christ on Mount Olivet.—*e)* 217. Plates 190.—191. The Resurrection.—*f)* 218. Plate 192. The Finding of the Holy Cross.

Pine-wood, canvas-covered, gesso ground, tempera. Of an extensive altar originally composed of about four wings, there remained preserved six pictures: two large ones (Carrying the Cross and Crucifixion) which evidently formed the centre of the altar, and four smaller pictures (Last Supper, Resurrection and Finding of the Holy Cross) which are the remnants of the wings. From these panels it can already be seen that on this altar two cycles were combined: the traditional passion cycle and the cycle carrying the legend of the Holy Cross.

The provenance of the altar cannot be ascertained to any degree of safety, but it is most probably of Moravian, perhaps of Olomouc origin.

a) 213. Plates 181.—183. THE RAJHRAD ALTAR: CARRYING THE CROSS.

Brno, Provincial Museum. Inv. No. A 626.

H. 99, w. 147 cm. — In spite of a great deal of damage, the character of the original colour has survived. The gold of the background and halo as well as the helmets of the soldiers were crudely repainted with thick bronze. Moreover, there are many retouchings of damaged parts. The picture has not been cleaned and has not undergone any restoration lately.

Since the last century the picture was deposited at the Benedictine Monastery in Rajhrad, and was purchased in 1938 for the Provincial Museum in Brno.

The Carrying of the Cross, together with five other pictures that are grouped under the joint designation of the Rajhrad Altar can be regarded on the basis of style, dimensions and technical details as works of one entity, notwithstanding that, in their style, painting technique, colouring and folding of drapery, differences between them do appear.

These differences may be explained by the joint labour of various painters, an arrangement which used to be the rule with arks of large dimensions. It was probably the principal master's hand that painted the broad centre picture which are most uniform in style and most painstaking in execution, the same hand also doing its share toward the other pictures (mainly in the case of the Mount Olivet panel). To the hand of one or the other assistant must be ascribed the Last Supper and Mount Olivet panels which, although of lesser quality, nevertheless follow closely the work of the Master. Perhaps from the same hand comes also the Finding of the Holy Cross, which, however, is less akin to the centre panels than the preceding pictures. Lastly, the hand of some further assistant of the workshop betrays itself in the Resurrection picture, which differs in colouring, drawing and manner of painting. The maximum number of assistants that may be surmised, therefore, is two. The principal master springs directly from the Czech formalistic style of the period after 1400 and continues in it, yet at the same time he also strives to overcome the mannerisms of the time and to create a new style. Being a split personality, however, the Master of the Rajhrad Altar did not know how to attain a new synthesis, the more so as the style on which he built up his work was already inwardly exhausted and condemned to extinction. Characteristic of the Master of the Rajhrad Altar is a wavering between tradition and new stylistic currents, which causes a dualism of expression, first of all of a type portrayal which partly retains the formulation of the 'beautiful' style, partly reaches out for a naturalistic expression in the faces of figures of secondary importance to the action; further his treatment of folds in which he alternately uses formalist and more sober, simplified, traditional forms. In the end this duality transfers itself even to the basic conception, which vacillates between the hieratic and the narrative. The conspicuous presence of naturalistic elements is connected on the one hand with the rise of empiricism, on the other hand with a new wave of influences emanating from the Franco-Flemish circle (Jacquemart de Hesdin) communicated by the Czech book-painting of the Antwerp Bible character (1402) the Martyrology from the Barcelona Museum, the Sedlec Antiphonal (1414) and the Boskovice Bible. The main feature of the new artistic faith of the Master is his narrative tendency, which in places attains a tone that is of the moral-depicting genre, with an eminent sense of actuality. But in these components in which the painter shows his allegiance to the older tradition, he very frequently makes breaches in stylistic strictness and rigidity. This shows up in the folding style of the draperies which stiffen to the semblance of tinplate and in a composition of rhythmically undulating relief which, however, no longer fully respects the requirements of the harmony of the 'beautiful' style. The idea of space did not progress beyond the time prior to 1400, even though efforts to deepen space by diagonals were not lacking. Lifelike naturalistic heads and movements of the figures are peculiarities of the Master, who here departs from the sacred pathos of the Master of the Třeboň Altar whom otherwise he takes for a starting point for some of his types, and, partly, also for the chiaroscuro method of painting. The style logic which would seem to place the Rajhrad Altar between the altar of Roudnice and the group of the Vyšší Brod Madonna, as well as the similarities with the dated Litoměřice Bible of 1411—1414, entitle us to give the Rajhrad work a place in the more advanced second decade of the XVth century. Very close to the Carrying of the Cross picture is a woodcut of the same theme, which is kept at the National Library in Vienna and is possibly of Moravian origin. What the mutual relations in this case have been cannot be exactly determined.

b) 214. Plates 184.—186. THE RAJHRAD ALTAR: THE CRUCIFIXION.

Prague, National Gallery, Inv. No. O 1584.

H. 102, w. 142 cm. The picture is cut down on both the vertical sides, i. e. by several centimetres on the right, and by about two centimetres on the left. The painting is very well preserved, including most of the enamel, with the original gold. During the repair done in 1936 in Prague the panel wood was reinforced, whilst the later gilding as well as most of the repaintings and retouchings were removed.

The picture was discovered in 1935 in the Church of Ss. Philip and James in Olomouc-Nové Sady, whither it was brought from another Olomouc church, that of St. Maurice in the year 1784, together with ten additional panels which were subsequently destroyed. The picture was purchased for the Prague National Gallery in 1937.

The composition scheme of the picture, which belongs to the iconographic type of 'great' calvaries is akin to the miniature painting of the Missal of Zbyněk Zajíc of Hazenburk, and particularly to the Crucifixion panel from Sv. Barbora (No. 175). Judging by the stylistic and technical analogies, there is no doubt that the picture at one time formed a part of the Rajhrad Altar. Although it is the work of one and the same hand that painted the Rajhrad picture mentioned under a) 213, it is more conservative in its conception of space, more consistent in the rhythmical composition of the surface and the harmonious distribution of the composition material, as also in the reserved manner in which it unfolds the story. These considerations, which to some extent weaken the realistic component of its painter's art were evidently forced upon him by the theme of the picture.

c) 215. Plate 187. THE RAJHRAD ALTAR: THE LAST SUPPER.

Brno, Provincial Museum, Inv. No. A 624.

H. 97, w. 59.8 cm. Besides the bronzing over of the gilt background and the haloes, the picture shows retouching of damaged places, particularly in the outlines of the figures, most of all of the heads. The history of this picture is the same as that of a) 213.

Whilst in style the picture is closely related to the centre pictures of the altar, it lacks their careful execution (compare, for example, the head of St. John in its different handling), and is, therefore, apparently an artisan's work. Of all the other panels of the altar, it comes nearest to the Mount Olivet picture, but is harder than this and less mobile in its rendering.

d) 216. Plates 188.—189. THE RAJHRAD ALTAR: CHRIST ON MOUNT OLIVET.

Brno, Provincial Museum, Inv. No. A 625.

H. 97.5, w. 59.5 cm. The picture, which fundamentally is well preserved, shows but few retouchings and repaintings. The outlines of all the heads were filled in. The repaintings were only partly removed during the last restoration which was carried out in Prague in 1936. At that time the later gilding was also removed. The history of the picture is the same as that of a) 213.

The picture is probably the work of an assistant directly dependent on the principal master of the altar, to whose hand must be ascribed the heads of all three of the sleeping apostles. With its careful painting and effort to create individuals which culminates in an almost naturalistic head of St. Peter, it differs considerably from the other parts of the picture, which are executed hastily and fairly superficially. Both in its style and technical detail this picture comes nearest to the large panels of the altar.

e) Plates 190.—191. THE RAJHRAD ALTAR: THE RESURRECTION.

Brno, Provincial Museum, Inv. No. A 627.

H. 100, w. 62 cm. The picture shows considerable repainting, different from that on the other Rajhrad panels. It has been regilt with gold foil, retouched and repainted over large spaces.

Its history is the same as that of a) 213.

Stylistically, formally and technically the picture differs largely from the other panels of the Rajhrad Altar. The differences show particularly in the light and bright colouring and treatment of the drapery in the spirit of the formalistic style, albeit in a conception amply different from that of the principal master of the altar. However, the identical principles of composition, conception of the figures and embossing of the haloes point to one and the same workshop and to this picture's being a part of the joint whole. It would therefore appear that this picture is the independent work of an assistant of the master, who, in a common school, knew how to preserve his individuality. Although dependent on the master, he indubitably had his own, older schooling.

f) 218. Plate 192. THE RAJHRAD ALTAR: FINDING OF THE HOLY CROSS.

Brno, Provincial Museum, Inv. No. A 628.

H. 97, w. 60 cm. This picture was spared repainting and retouching comparatively more than any of the other Rajhrad panels. The gold was brushed over with bronze, the contours of the crowns and the haloes of St. Helen were traced out in a dark line. Otherwise there are a few retouchings in the upper half of the picture. Completely repainted are the cloaks of St. Helena and the Emperor. There are some small retouchings in damaged places of the painting. The picture shows considerable mechanical injury. Unrestored.

The history of the picture is the same as that of a) 213.

The scheme of this scene, fairly rare in the XIVth and the beginning of the XVth century, is ostensibly of French origin. As compared with French miniatures (for example the Milanese fragment of the Hours of the Duke of Berry), the Czech panel combines two successive scenes, i. e. the Finding of the Holy Cross proper and its Testing by the miraculous resurrection of a dead man.

This panel, like the preceding one, differs from the style of the centre panels, but in its composition principle and the heads, as well as in the system of folds, painting technique and narrative qualities of the subsidiary figures, it shows complete relation to them. Certain divergencies and a not very careful execution of the work betray the hand of an assistant dependent on the master, perhaps the one who created the Last Supper and Mount Olivet pictures.

ADORATION OF THE THREE KINGS. — About 1420. Plate 193.

České Budějovice, Municipal Museum, Inv. No. NI. 11.

Lime-wood, canvas-covered, gesso ground, tempera. H. 112.5, w. 61 cm. The cutting down of the panel on the left-hand side ruined the figure of the third King. The reverse side of the panel shows traces of having been originally painted on. The picture is in a rather dilapidated state, with the paint scaled off in places. The restoration to which the picture was subjected in Prague in 1932 removed the repaintings, and covered the bare spots with a neutral tone.

This panel is possibly a fragment of an altar wing the original provenance of which is unknown. It was purchased in the Seventies of the XIXth century in the vicinity of Želnava.

The picture belongs to the trend in Czech painting of the first quarter of the XVth century which, although it sets out from the style of the period about 1400, draws also on other sources in keeping with the sources of the Master of the Rajhrad Altar. The panel is fairly strongly affected by the influence of the Master of the Třeboň Altar, which conditioned the spacial construction of the hut. In its colouring, it is built up of soft and subdued tones. Certain signs of a further loosening in style as compared with the Rajhrad Altar advance the date of the picture to a somewhat later period. The picture belongs to a rather conservative current of Czech painting of the period.

220.—221. MADONNA OF ST. THOMAS'S CHURCH. — About 1420. Plates 194.—198.

Brno, Provincial Museum.

Lime-wood, canvas-covered, gesso ground, tempera. H. 43.5, w. 30.5 cm, with the original, painted frame. A panel with painting on both sides, the painting on the reverse being on parchment. Both sides of the picture show considerable damage. In particular, whole portions of the gilding together with their ground have scaled off the frame, as also off the reverse side and the lower part of the centre panel. The enamels are rubbed off in places, particularly on the body parts, but elsewhere they are excellently preserved. During the last restoration, effected in Prague in 1936, the panel was made firm, the paint fixed, repainting removed, the parchment on the reverse was made fast and indispensable retouchings were carried out. The picture emanates from the chapel of Mary the Virgin in the Brno Church of St. Thomas. It passed into the ownership of the Arts and Crafts Museum in Brno, whence it was later loaned to the Brno Provincial Museum.

a) 220. Plate 194.—197. MADONNA WITH CHILD JESUS. (Front of panel).

In the top left-hand corner of the picture God the Father with His hand on the scroll bearing the appropriate Latin text. On the frame are half-length figures of saints, being: on the left moulding Ss. Andrew, Dorothea and Apollonia, on the right moulding Ss. John the Evangelist, Ursula and Anna. In the centre of the top moulding is St. John the Baptist, in the centre of the bottom moulding St. Mary Magdalen.

b) 221. Plate 198. VERAICON. (Back of panel).

The Madonna combines the composition scheme of the St. Vitus Madonna with the type of the Roudnice Madonna in Mary's head. With the position of the right hand and the type of the infant shown in it, the picture is closer akin to the Zlatá Koruna than the St. Vitus panel. The Veraicon on the back is in its formulation similar to the St. Vitus Veraicon, but is in the flesh tint brighter and nearer to the front side of the picture. Judging by the style of the drawing, the drapery (reduced, less articulated and stiffer), the figure and colouring, the picture may be put amongst works which arose about 1420. There are no sufficient grounds on which it could be ascribed to the Master of the Rajhrad Altar.

Ceské Budějovice, Municipal Museum.

Wood, canvas-covered, tempera. H. 57, w. 57 cm, with the original, painted frame. Both sides of the panel bear paintings, the back painting being on parchment strips. The condition of the picture is bad. The centre picture on the front side is relatively better preserved. During the restoration, undertaken in Prague in 1922—1923, the paints and parchment strips were made fast, the picture was stopped and the worn-off places were toned up.

The panel was presented to the České Budějovice Museum as a gift in 1893. It probably came from Zlatá Koruna. Indubitably of South Bohemian origin.

a) 222. Plate 190. ADORATION OF THE CHILD. (Front of panel.)

Besides appearing soiled and coarsely gilded altogether, the picture had been toned up in the places where the paint flaked off after the buckling of the base. The frame with figures of female saints shows considerable damage so that only about half the original painting was preserved. In some places, local retouchings appear besides later gilding.

As on the Hluboká panel, so in this picture the older scene of the Birth of our Lord had been replaced by the scene of the Adoration of the Child and connected with the scene of the Annunciation to the Shepherds. For the first time in Czech panel painting, the Child Jesus is placed in a manger. For the first time, too, the, the figure of St. Joseph is left out in this scene. Above the manger and in the hands of the herald angel is an inscribed scroll with the customary Latin text. The moulding shows half-length figures of female saints. On the bottom moulding are from left to right: Ss. Elizabeth, Ludmila, Anna, Mary Magdalen and Hedwig. On the top moulding from left to right: Ss. Barbara, Dorothea, remnants of the figure of St. Jerome, a piece of

the cloak of another female saint, and St. Lucia. On the left vertical moulding are, beginning from the top, an unknown holy nun and some unidentified female saint, also Ss. Margaret, Genevieve and Catherine.

b) 223. Plate 200. CHRIST ON MOUNT OLIVET (back of panel).

Of this picture, only the torso has been preserved. Besides the ruined bottom half of the middle picture and the right-hand side with two extensions into the top half, the rest of the painting also has a series of holes which at one time were partly retouched, and during the last restoration were partly toned up. The haloes and the silver of the helmets of the first three soldiers were regilt.

The picture appears to be a work of artistic and evolutionary prominence and representative of the progressive current which strove for a new synthesis in the joining of the expiring Czech formalism and the style of the Master of the Třeboň Altar, with the Franco-Flemish influences transmitted here again by the contemporary Czech miniature of the martyrologia type in the Barcelona Museum. Evidence of the anti-formalistic tendency of the picture, which tries to stand up to the manneristic softness of the late 'beautiful' style and its calligraphy, can be seen primarily in the attempts at reform of the older folding method by a harder conception of drapery and in the strengthened line. At the same time an increasing narrative content, an uncommonly clear building up of space in the construction of the hut, with evident first steps towards a perspective distribution of the material in planes and particularly the deepening of the scene on the back of the panel by a blue sky in the place of a golden background (for the first time in Czech panel painting) are signs which can only be explained by the action of alien, Western influences.

224.　　ST. BARBARA. — About 1420.　　Plate 201.

Prague, monastery gallery of the Royal Canonry of the Premonstratensian Fathers at Strahov.

H. 75,5, w. 53,5 cm, with the original frame. The picture shows considerable repainting.

The origin of the panel is not known.

The picture shows a loosening in the composition of the cloak with, at the same time, a greater rigidity of line and a breaking away from the decorativeness

of the older school. The lyrical sentiment still shows the connections between the panel and the style prevalent about 1400. The panel is most probably of Southern Bohemian origin, but for the time being it cannost be linked up with any known relic.

THE LAST SUPPER. — About 1420.

Plate 203.

Kremsmünster, Monastery Gallery.

Pine-wood, canvas-covered, gesso ground, tempera. H. 30, w. 20,5 cm, with the original, painted frame. The picture is in a fair state.

With the Last Supper of the Rajhrad Altar this panel is akin only in its composition scheme, which, however, appears in this case more loosely treated and broken up, so that any direct connection between the two is out of question. The folding of the cloak rather bears witness to a later date of origin.

226.

THE MASTER OF THE VYŠŠÍ BROD MADONNA: THE MADONNA OF VYŠŠÍ BROD. — After 1420.

Vyšší Brod, the monastery church of the Virgin Mary.

Wood, canvas-covered, gesso ground, tempera, with incised outlines. H. 97,5, w. 75,5 cm with the original, painted frame. The state of preservation is good. Except for certain parts of Mary's cloak, the picture has not been repainted, nor restored.

It was most probably destined for the Vyšší Brod church of Mary the Virgin, and has remained at its place of destination ever since.

On the top moulding are shown angels holding scrolls bearing the text of the invocation; on the left-hand moulding are Ss. Apollonia, Margaret and Simon; on the bottom moulding are, from left to right half-length figures of Ss. Wenceslas, George, Ursula, Dorothea, Prokop, John the Baptist and Giles.

The picture is a later copy of the prototype, the oldest example of which is the Roudnice Madonna. It does vary, though, in that it uncovers the right hand of the Madonna (this motif being subsequently repeated by only a few of the later replicas).

Stylistically, the frame figures of the Vyšší Brod Madonna appear as a typical manifestation of a step in the new evolution. Their style sets out from the reforming efforts of the painting school of the se-

cond decade of the XVth century, but it does not continue with the logical development of the problems suggested by it. Its roots are still firmly set in the Czech style from the beginnings of the XVth century, but it strives to surpass its formal principles by new ones, the most conspicuous of which are the painting hardness and firm setting of the lines, a stiffening of forms and unrhythmical rendering of the garments. The dark and ample colouring, too, is an expression of a changed stylistic feeling, which simultaneously aims at an overvaluation of the contents by departing from the lyricism of the 'beautiful' style. Singularly, but less daringly and strikingly than in the work of the Master of the Rajhrad Altar does naturalism here seek expression (see the donor). — The Vyšší Brod Madonna is closely, sisterly connected with the Wroclaw Madonna and the other works grouped around her. Ostensibly from the same painter is the altar with the Crucifixion picture in the centre, Nos. 227—231. Analogies with the book-paintings point to some time after 1420 as the date of origin of the picture. The workshop of the Vyšší Brod Madonna may be safely assumed as having been located in Southern Bohemia.

227.—231.

THE MASTER OF THE VYŠŠÍ BROD MADONNA: TRIPARTITE WING ALTAR WITH THE CRUCIFIXION IN THE CENTRE. — After 1420.

Prague, National Gallery, Inv. No. O 1570—1572.

Pine-wood, canvas-covered, gesso ground, tempera. The wings painted on both sides, the reverse sides without canvas covering. Centre: H. 155,5, w. 87,5 cm. Wings: h. 154,3, w. (left) 43,5, (right) 44 cm. A triptych with the original framing of the inner pictures, the outside of the wings being frameless. The painting is well preserved, including the enamels; there are only some damaged places, especially on the centre picture. The picture has been

neither cleaned, nor restored. In 1941 the loosened film of colour was fixed.

The provenance of the picture is not known. The altar originally came from the private collection of Karl von Reininghaus, a Styrian collector. From there it passed into the O. Nierenstein (Neue Gallerie) art shop in Vienna in 1932 and was purchased in 1936 for the Prague National Gallery.

The centre picture shows the Crucifixion. On the

front side top of the right wing is St. Elizabeth and St. Helen, below St. Barbara and St. Ursula; on the front side top of the left wing is St. Anne, below St. Magdalen and St. Lucia. On the back of the left wing is Mary Salome with her two sons John the Baptist and James the Elder, on the back of the right wing is Mary Cleophas holding by the hand her sons, two on each side, being James the Less and Joseph the Just and Simon and Jude respectively.

The centre picture of the altar repeats the composition scheme of the Crucifixion on the Rajhrad Altar. This work, too, sets out from the traditional Czech style of the period after 1400 (types, drapery and colouring, indifference to space), but a more advanced grade of evolution is evidenced by a considerable loosening of the stylistic canons, noticeable in the suppression of the rhythmic principle, the unorganized fold system and by a certain vacuity in expression. Here already appears a failure to grasp the inner canons and substance of the 'beautiful' style, from which the painter took over only the outward features and painting usages. There also appear the first signs of rusticalisation, linked up with which is also a drop in the standard of painting craftsmanship and artistic style. This altar on the one hand and the picture of the Vyšší Brod Madonna on the other show such striking similarities in colouring, treatment of folds, types of figures and technique that it is possible to speak of one and the same master. It needs pointing out, however, that unlike the Vyšší Brod Madonna, which was a miracle-working picture designed for adoration, our altar is a more hastily executed work in which the share of the workshop must have been considerable. Other closely related works (such as the altar at Hýrov and the altar at Zátoň) are without doubt of South Bohemian provenance, and that is why this altar probably likewise originates from there. Its inception can be placed in the first quarter of the XVth century, which would be in accord with the contemporary evolution of Czech book-painting.

232.　　　　THE WROCLAW MADONNA. — After 1420.　　　　Plate 214.

Wroclaw, Archiepiscopal Diocesan Museum. Cat. No. (of 1932) 136.

Soft wood (pine), frame of lime-wood, canvas-covered, gesso-ground, tempera. H. 93, w. 73 cm, with original, painted frame. In very good state, only in some places touched up and repainted.

The picture comes from the Wroclaw Cathedral, having been transferred from there to the Archiepiscopal Diocesan Museum in 1903.

The left-hand vertical moulding shows St. John the Baptist, underneath him the donor. The right-hand vertical moulding shows St. Nicholas, underneath him St. Barbara. The top horizontal moulding shows two angels, the lower likewise two angels. Above the donor and in the hands of the angels and St. John the Baptist are scrolls with the usual Latin texts.

In the centre the picture repeats an already traditional type, showing lack of comprehension of some of the detailed motifs. The figure ornaments of the frame are on the same evolutionary plane as the Vyšší Brod Madonna, from which, however, they differ by a more plastic feeling, more organic arrangement of the draperies, a better composition of harmonies, a greater vitality and a richer inner expression. The Wroclaw Madonna also excels over the Vyšší Brod Madonna by the quality and more careful execution of its painting. The master of the Wroclaw Madonna must, therefore, be regarded as an artist of higher creative aims, but as one who probably went through the same workshop as the master of the Vyšší Brod Madonna. Thus the two pictures do not directly depend on each other. Nearest to the Wroclaw Madonna is the panel from Náměšť. With the other works in this group the picture is connected merely in a general way. It is most likely of South Bohemian origin and has come to Wroclaw evidently as an importation. Chronologically it cannot be far removed from the Vyšší Brod Madonna, which picture may perhaps be slightly older.

233.—234.　　　　THE NÁMĚŠŤ PANEL. — About 1430.　　　　Plates 215.—218.

Brno, Provincial Museum. Inv. No. A 38.

Wood, canvas-covered, gesso ground, tempera. H. 87,5, w. 95 cm. Both sides of the panel are painted on. Seemingly the only remnant of a lost altar. Provenance unknown. The panel was made over as a gift of Náměšť-upon-Oslava to the Brno Museum in the middle of the XIXth century.

a) 233. Plate 215. THE MARTYRDOM OF ST. APOLLONIA (inside of panel).

The colours are soiled, but preserved for their greater part. In places they are rubbed off. The picture appears touched up in places where the paint has flaked. Major interference with the brocade garments of the Emperor and Empress. The original gilding of the background and the haloes is faultlessly preserved. The picture has undergone no restoration so far. In the bottom right-hand part of the picture a scroll with inscription, the Latin text reading as follows: „Dñe ihū xp̄e tibi ofeo'dentes meos promunere p̄co." (Domine Jesu Christe tibi offero dentes meos, pro munere praeco).

b) 234. Plate 216.— 218. THE MARTYRDOM OF ST. CATHERINE (outside panel).

The outer side is in a worse state of preservation, the enamels being either damaged by dirt or rubbed off, including even in places the basic layer of paint. The silver background was found blackened and the paint in many places scaled off. Slight retouching on some of the more badly damaged places. Otherwise the picture was not cleaned, nor restored. There are Latin texts on the inscription scrolls, as follows: „Suscipe dne de⁹ spm̄ nr̄m". (Suscipe domine deus spiritum nostrum). — „Ecce videte potēciā (potentiam) dei mei". — „Heu · nobis · heu · nob[is].—" „Ignis accēsus (accensus) est ī [n] furore meo". —

The Náměšť panel is a work of considerable evolutionary importance. The stylistic base for the painter of this panel is still the Czech tradition of the beginnings of the XVth century, and he does not (with the exception of the inscription scrolls, used here for the first time to such an extent and so decoratively) digress on the whole from the stylistic direction taken by the school of painters between 1420 and 1430. With all its style and colouring, the panel to-day comes nearest the altar of the master of the Vyšší Brod Madonna (Nos. 227.—231). In its treatment of draperies, the form of the haloes, figures and a series of subsidiary features the Náměšť panel is so closely akin to the Vyšší Brod altar that there is more in it than a mere contemporary affinity. In the chiaroscuro method and technique of the painting, but chiefly in the careful underpainting of the pictures of the Náměšť panel there is shown a considerable kinship with those of the pictures of the Rajhrad altar in which we surmise a direct participation of the Master. — Quite new traits here are the highly dramatic rendering of the scenes and the uncommon intensity of the expression, which is in direct contrast to all of the hitherto lyrical and epic Czech tradition, and, particularly, to the paucity of expression shown in the altar of the Master of the Vyšší Brod Madonna. In this one may detect a faint echo of Austrian influences, without, however, attaching unduly great value to them. As to any connection with the art of the first generation of Late Gothic, one cannot as yet begin to consider it. The motif of the inscriptions scrolls and the more pointed shaping of the draperies advance the time of the panel's origin to about the year 1430.

235.—237. THE HÝROV ALTAR.— THREE PANELS OF A DISMANTLED   Plates 219.—221.
TRIPARTITE WING ALTAR, SHOWING THE PICTURE OF THE MADONNA WITH THREE DONORS IN THE CENTRE. — About 1430.

Prague, National Gallery, Inv. Nos. O 1396—1398.

Wood, canvas-covered, gesso ground, tempera. Centre panel 83 cm high, 102,5 cm wide, the wings 84 cm high, 45 cm wide. The wings are in the original frames. The centre panel and the right wing in particular show considerable damage, the paint appearing rubbed off in places right down to the base. The top enamels are rubbed off. The centre panel underwent total repainting in the XVIIth century. In its course, the donors were turned into the Three Kings and, simultaneously, the architectures together with the garment of St. Margaret on the left wing were renovated, whilst the bottom half of the right wing was painted over altogether. The repaintings on the wings were partly removed prior to 1912, at Vyšší Brod. The altar was restored afresh in Prague during 1923 and 1924.

The triptych comes from the Church of Ss. Philip and James in Hýrov, near Vyšší Brod, from where the centre picture was transferred to the gallery of the Vyšší Brod Monastery in 1910, the wings having been brought there somewhat earlier. The triptych was loaned to the National Gallery in Prague in 1923 and acquired for it by purchase in 1936.

On the centre panel is shown the Madonna with

the Child and the donors, to whom is attached a scroll with the wording of a Latin invocation. The right wing shows St. John the Baptist, the left wing representing St. Margaret.

The centre panel shows the conserved, basic theme of the Madonna being adored by the three donors, as formulated in the Czech painting of about the year 1400. In spite of their conformity, down to their most minute details, the wings must be regarded as the work of a hand other than that which painted the centre picture. This is evidenced by the finer and more painstaking workmanship employed in their making, as also by the different chromatic scale. The affinity in types, drawing and drapery formation is

proof of the close connection between the altar and the group of the Vyšší Brod Madonna, yet the connection is not close enough to conclude from it that the two groups are the work of one and the same master. It is more likely that the Hýrov altar is the product of a somewhat later workshop circle. Quite noteworthy is the degree of naturalism reached in the figures of the donors, whom the painter dressed in clothes exactly as worn in their time, and in whose portraits he even attempted to capture the principal individual traits. Placed in juxtaposition to the Náměšť panel, the Hýrov altar would appear more conservative and with deeper roots in the tradition of the country.

238.—240.   THE ZÁTOŇ ALTAR. A TRIPARTITE WING ALTAR WITH   Plates 222.—227.
THE CRUCIFIXION PICTURE IN THE CENTRE. — After 1430.

Prague, National Gallery. Inv. Nos. DO 215.—217.

Pine-wood, canvas-covered, gesso ground, tempera. Centre 168 cm high and 92 cm wide, wings 42 cm wide. Original framing. The wings were originally painted on both sides, but now the outer side is completely ruined. The pictures are in a bad state of preservation. All the top enamels were rubbed off and the coloured appearance was totally changed. There was no repainting of any importance. The altar was superficially restored in 1900 and partially repaired in 1923 in Prague, when the painting was fixed and slight retouchings were applied. In 1941 there was a fixing of the coloured layer which had worked loose.

The altar emanated from the Church of St. John the Baptist in Zátoň, where it evidently represented the main altar and was most probably commissioned for that church direct. In 1900 it was taken to Český Krumlov, whence it was loaned to the Prague National Gallery.

On the centre panel is the Crucifixion. On the top part of the left wing is St. John the Baptist preaching (with inscribed scroll showing a Latin text); the bottom part shows the Baptism of Christ (with inscribed scroll bearing a Latin text); on the top part of the right wing is the Beheading of St. John the Baptist, the bottom part showing Salome before Herod.

The Crucifixion repeats in all the principal figures the altar scene of the Master of the Vyšší Brod Madonna (Nos. 227—231), but its scheme is recast and filled with a new feeling. For the Zátoň altar is the work of a painter who reacted to the soulless cult of form of the preceding school, by an ever-ascending

effort to restore dramatic vigour to the scene and to put feeling into his subject. It signifies therefore a decisive departure from the static conception and formalism, and a new stressing of the story element, now deepened by a new wave of narrative feeling and human sympathy. In this, as also with the painter's interest in the present and his efforts at characterisation he is at one with the Náměšť panel which, however, he does not reach in his painting quality that, in some places, reaches a level almost of vulgarity (advanced ornamentalisation of draperies). On the formal side, the Zátoň altar is bound by ties of considerable affinity to the altar of the Master of the Vyšší Brod Madonna (Nos. 227—231) and to the other works of this style group, particularly to the Hýrov altar. The Zátoň Altar is probably the work of a painter who passed through the workshop of the Master of the Vyšší Brod Madonna. The characteristics of the landscape space rest on the coulisse principle of high horizons, known already from the Czech book-painting of the period after 1400. The conception of the interior architectural space (after the Košátky panel very likely the first attempt at the creation of an interior) still remains based also on the trecento conception of rectangular space which, however, does not coincide with the space of the picture and with which the figures are not really connected. The ornamental motif has its origin in the mural painting of the period of Charles IV; it appears again in the later Visitation picture of Krumlov, and the Visitation painting which bears the escutcheon of the noble family of the Švamberks.

Vienna, Kunsthistorisches Museum. Gallery No. 1734.

Pine-wood, tempera, on gesso ground, without canvas. (The inner side is canvas-covered). H. 134, w. 75 cm. Corners of the top part lopped off at a later date. Panel painted on both sides; probably the left wing of a lost altar.

The exact provenance of the picture is not known. Up to the year 1917 the picture was placed in an open passage of the pilgrimage church of Kreuzberk near Český Krumlov. From there it was acquired by the State Gallery in Vienna, only to be finally taken over by the Kunsthistorisches Museum of Vienna in 1922.

a) 241. Plate 228. Ss. PETER AND PAUL. (Inner side of panel).

The painting is almost totally ruined, so that only fragments of the figure of St. Peter in outline remained, as also minute remnants of the figure of St. Paul, which is almost totally rubbed off. An angel holds scrolls, the right one bearing the text „·s·petrus·".

b) 242. Plate 229. MATER DOLOROSA (outer side of panel).

The outer side, depicting the Mater Dolorosa, is comparatively better preserved. The golden background is of more recent origin.

The Mater Dolorosa here probably formed the counterpart to the Man of Sorrows, as in the Roudnice Altar. The picture has no close connection with the Zátoň Altar, from which it differs considerably by its high quality, colouring, the design of the folds and technical execution. Neither is this panel in any close connection with the other pictures of this school. With its outstanding level of execution and profound pathos of expression the Mater Dolorosa on the whole stands unique.

243.—244.   FRAGMENT FROM ČESKÉ BUDĚJOVICE: VISITATION   Plates 230.—231.
OF THE VIRGIN MARY AND CHRIST THE GARDENER. — After 1430.

České Budějovice, Municipal Museum, Inv. No. N I.43

Wood, tempera on gesso ground, inner side canvas-covered. H. 79, w. 49.5 cm. The panel, painted on both sides, has original frame on the inner side. The panel is the top half of the right wing of a folding altar, cut down obliquely at the bottom.

The restoration, undertaken in Prague in 1938, removed the repainting from the heads, the raiment of the Virgin and other, smaller repaintings; it also removed retouchings, stopped the holes with putty, and cleansed and toned up the picture.

The panel comes from Kugelvejt and was acquired for the Municipal Museum of České Budějovice after 1876.

a) 243. Plate 230. THE VISITATION OF THE VIRGIN MARY. (Inner side of the panel.)

The top enamels totally rubbed off down to the ground.

b) 244. Plate 231. CHRIST THE GARDENER. (Outer Side of the panel.)

The outer side is in a still worse state of preservation: the lower half of the figure is missing, the painting is covered all over with old varnish, and a series of retouchings are seen. On its inner side, the panel repeats the type of a box-like inner space as known from the Zátoň altar. The types of the figures, the soft modelling of the form (originally sure to have been softer still) and the fluent, pliable arrangement of the draperies all prevent the picture to be placed in any very late period of time. On the contrary, it seems it is here a question of work connected with the school of about 1430. Although it has a composition scheme common to the other pictures on this subject, the panel nevertheless has no direct stylistic connection with any of them, being in fact unique amongst the works produced in South Bohemia. The pregnancy of both the women is indicated by the figures of the babes in the ovals placed on the abdomen.

245. FRAME OF THE ROUDNICE RELIQUARY. — After 1430. Plate 232.

Roudnice Castle Museum, Inv. No. VIII. Fa. 8.

A glass-panelled box reliquary with a wooden, painted frame. Tempera on a thick gesso layer without canvas-covering. H. 30, w. 28, thickness 3.5 cm.

Excellently preserved, including enamels, the gold worn off in places. Not restored.

The reliquary was found under the altar in the chapel of Roudnice Castle in 1816, and was given a place in the Castle Museum.

On the left-hand vertical moulding is St. Dorothea, on the right-hand moulding St. Catherine; the bottom horizontal moulding shows St. Peter (with a scroll bearing a Latin text), the top showing the Man of Sorrows.

On comparing the writing on the scrolls of the relics with a similar reliquary also kept in Roudnice from the year 1464, it can be seen that the writing on our reliquary is older and can claim to belong to the first half of the XVth century. In the drapery of the figures is found the supreme expression of the style of pointed hems seen conspicuously in another work, the altar of the Master of the Vyšší Brod Madonna at the National Gallery in Prague. The stylistic purity of the folds, the freshness of the rendering and charm of the figures all speak in favour of an origin of the work at a time of still unabated stylistic tension, that is to say for the period toward the end of the first third of the XVth century. It has nothing in common with the Visitation picture bearing the family crest of the noble house of the Švamberks. Any later dating is also disproved by the complete lack of Late Gothic fold motifs.

246.—248. THE MASTER OF THE CARRYING OF THE CROSS, Plates 233.—236. FROM VYŠŠÍ BROD. — THREE PANELS FROM DISMANTLED ALTAR. —After 1430.

a) 246. Plate 233. Visitation of the Virgin Mary.
b) 247. Plate 234. Adoration of the Child. —
c) 248. Plates 235.—236. Carrying of the Cross.

a) 246. Plate 233. VISITATION OF THE VIRGIN MARY.

Prague, National Gallery, Inv. No. Z 300.

Wood, canvas-covered, gesso ground, tempera. H. 100, w. 70 cm. In a good state of preservation, retouched in places. Restored in Prague in 1927.

The picture represents a fragment of a larger altar group, probably combining the Marian with the Passion Cycle. It is of unknown provenance, and passed in 1945 from private ownership in Kamenice near Prague into the possession of the Prague National Gallery.

At the heads of both figures are scrolls with appropriate Latin texts.

The picture is a part of an altar to which also belongs the fragment of the Carrying of the Cross from Vyšší Brod and the Adoration of Christ picture in Budapest. That there is a connection between them is proved by the dimensions of the panels, the uniformity of figure types, treatment of the folds, embossing, the painting style and technique. Judging by the fragment of the Carrying of the Cross, the whole altar and, therefore, also this picture is of South Bohemian provenance. The painter of the panel and of the other two pictures combines in his iconographic scheme the types and colouring of the older Czech tradition with the new Lower Austrian achievements which came to the fore with their school of the early Twenties of the century, particularly in their fold motifs (the style of long pleats bluntly turning up from the ground, the motif of cut-down „cornucopias", long, extending tips, etc.) and, perhaps, also in the use of inscription scrolls, unless, which is possible, the knowledge of them was imparted by the graphic art. The Visitation picture of the Viennese Master of the Friedrich Altar is repeated in some motifs almost literally by our picture, so that one is led to assume a contact between the South Bohemian workshop and Vienna, as also a direct influence of the master of the Friedrich Altar, though only through his earliest works. This is one of the first attempts to overcome the stylistic crisis in Czech painting by the direct reception of foreign influences.

b) 247. Plate 234. ADORATION OF THE CHILD.

Budapest, Szépművészeti Múzeum, Inv. No. 1636.

Pine-wood, canvas-covered, gesso ground, tempera. H. 100, w. 72 cm. Very good state of preservation, minor retouchings in places. Unrestored.

The picture was acquired by Jankowich Miklós de Vádas in Budapest at the beginning of the XIXth century, most probably through some Austrian agents. It was taken over after his death (1846) by the Szépmüvészeti Múzeum, Budapest.

The scrolls bear the usual Latin inscriptions.

The picture agrees in style, dimensions, figures, technique and embossing with the foregoing panel. It is the work of one and the same master, and a part of one and the same altar.

c) 248. Plates 235.—236. CARRYING OF THE CROSS, FROM VYŠŠÍ BROD.

Prague, National Gallery, Inv. No. O 1399.

Wood, canvas-covered, gesso ground, tempera.— H. 100, w. 41 cm. The picture appears much damaged, being cut down on both sides, no less than one third of the lower left-hand side having been lost that way, including the canvas. However, the remaining parts are in good condition and the enamel is well preserved. Restored in Prague in 1924.

The panel comes from the monastery gallery in Vyšší Brod. It was loaned to the Prague National Gallery in 1923, passing to that institution in 1936 by way of purchase.

A scroll with Latin text is between the two groups of figures.

The coincidence of dimensions, style, figure type, technique and embossing of the background with the preceding picture leads to the conviction that this panel, too, is the work of one and the same master and a part of the same altar as the two foregoing ones.

249. ANNUNCIATION OF THE VIRGIN MARY, FROM VYŠŠÍ BROD. After 1430. Plates 237.—238.

Prague, National Gallery, Inv. No. O 1395.

Pine-wood, canvas-covered, gesso ground, tempera. H. 101.5, d. 66 cm. The painting, originally on both sides of the picture, is badly damaged. In the left-hand bottom corner a big rectangular piece of the canvas covering, with its paint, had been torn out, as also, a long strip upwards from it, to a point above the head of the angel. Besides this, the paint layer had also flaked off in several other places, together with its ground. The restorations, effected in 1924 and 1932 made fast the loosened painting, toned up the missing parts and applied some retouchings.

The panel represents evidently a fragment of an altar, but its exact provenance is not known. It comes from the monastery gallery in Vyšší Brod, whence it was loaned to the Prague National Gallery in 1923. It was bought for the National Gallery in 1936.

The scrolls bear the usual Latin texts.

In many formal features, the figures, tke curves and cut of the folds, the manner of embossing and colouring the panel shows such a kinship with the Master of the Carrying of the Cross of Vyšší Brod that if it were not for its different dimensions the picture could be regarded as a part of the same dismantled altar. The common provenance would likewise tend to prove it. Nevertheless, the panel is the work of some other painter who, although more conservatively informed, was also influenced by Lower Austrian painting and probably was directly connected with the work of the Master of the Carrying of the Cross.

250. THE SKALICE CRUCIFIXION (from Soběslav). — After 1430. Plates 239.—241.

Prague, National Gallery, Inv. No. DO 222.

Wood, canvas-covered, gesso ground, tempera. H. 181.5, w. 134 cm. The picture shows considerable damage, particularly on the fissures between the boards. There are numerous holes in the group of soldiers to the left of Christ. The enamel is preserved in but very few places. The first restoration of the picture took place in Vienna in 1886, the second in Prague in 1928. During the second restoration the paint was made fast, the missing places were stopped and retouched.

This picture is probably the centre of a wing altar.

The panel comes from the Church of Ss. Simon and Jude in Skalice, whence it was later taken to the Municipal Museum in Soběslav, to be finally loaned (in 1928) to the Prague National Gallery.

The figure of the donor has attached to it a scroll bearing a text with the usual invocation.

The principal figures and motifs show a repetition of the composition principle of all Czech Crucifixions with three Crosses from the early part of the XVth century. The Skalice picture presents, however, a number of new motifs (Christ with His eyes closed, the Hussite clothing of some of the soldiers, etc.). On the formal side the panel shows many foreign features supplied here, too, by the Lower Austrian school of painting in the Twenties of the XVth century (Hans von Tübingen) not only as regards arrangement of the composition, but also in the figures, drawing, drapery and advanced degree of naturalism. The picture, which is of a low artistic standard, is of importance primarily from the point of view of cultural history.

251.—252. THE MADONNA OF DOUDLEBY AND THE ADORATION   Plates 242.—243.
OF THE CHILD. — About 1440.

Doudleby, near České Budějovice, Church of St. Vincent.

A panel which was originally painted on both sides, only to be at some later date cut apart and divided into two pictures. Tempera, painted only on the front side of the panel on a gesso ground canvas, whilst the Adoration picture on the reverse side is only painted on a thin gesso ground without canvas. — H. 112, w. 84 cm. The panel was restored and cut in two in Vienna, in the year 1904.

The panel was directly destined for the Early Gothic Church of St. Vincent in Doudleby, where it hung from times immemorial. To-day it is in the temporary custody of the National Gallery in Prague.

a) 251. Plate 243. THE MADONNA OF DOUDLEBY.

Apart from the repainting of the gold background there are only minor local retouchings. To the donor is linked a scroll bearing a Latin text of invocation.

Iconographically this picture shows its derivation from the Byzantine type of Odigitria, in the later derivative of Psychostrosia. Our picture has, on the whole, preserved the typological scheme near to Byzantine patterns, but some of the deviations it shows are ascribable to the Italianate development of the basic type.

b) 252. Plate 242. ADORATION OF THE CHILD.

Considerable damage was caused to the picture by the painting being transferred to canvas. Whole parts, particularly in Mary's figure, were repainted. A series of retouchings spread over the whole surface. The moral-depicting motif of St. Joseph cooking victuals, first used by Czech painters in mural paintings decorating the cloisters of Emmaus Monastery in Prague at the end of the third quarter of the XIVth century.

The basically Byzantine type of the Madonna is here adapted in the Gothic sense (type of face, modelling of drapery and colourfulness) and in its technical execution it corresponds to other Czech Madonnas from the beginning of the XVth century. In the Adoration of the Child the space development of the landscape resembles the landscape painting of French miniatures round about 1400, the knowledge of which was passed on here by some of the older works of the kind of the Adoration of the Child from České Budějovice, but our picture remains far below the latter's level owing to the vagueness of its idea of space. The preponderantly epic tone — in which lies the principal charm of the picture — together with the advanced ornamentation of the drapery is evidence of the steady rusticalisation of the Czech style. The artisan level, together with these symptoms, as well as considerable analogies in the style of the folds with the library bible of the Strahov Monastery in Prague, dated 1446, point to a comparatively late date of origin in the Forties of the XVth century.

253.—256. ALTAR WINGS FROM SV. MAJDALENA. — PANELS OF   Plates 244.—245.
A DISMANTLED, QUINQUEPARTITE WING ALTAR. — After 1440.

Prague, National Gallery, Inv. Nos. O 1378—1381.

Wood, tempera, on thin gesso ground, without canvas. H. 123, w. of extreme wings 21,5, of inside wings 28 cm. Considerable repainting was applied to the picture during the last restoration, carried out in Vienna in 1910, when the damaged parts were touched up. The reverse sides of the panels were rendered completely valueless through repainting.

The panels represent fragments of a larger altar ensemble. They emanate ostensibly from the Church of St. Giles in Třeboň, whence they were transferred in the XVIIIth century to the Church at Sv. Majdalena near Třeboň, and, finally, to the Třeboň Castle Museum. They were bought in 1923 for the National Gallery in Prague.

Prior to its dismantling, the altar can be imagined as having had in its centre an ornately decorated panel

78

in front of which stood the statuette of the Virgin Mary, now on show at the Municipal Museum of České Budějovice and likewise originating from the church at Sv. Majdalena. When opened, the ark showed from the left: St. Matthew, St. Assumpta with Child, the Man of Sorrows and St. Giles. When closed, it showed the following pictures, starting from the left: the Herald Angel, St. Othmar(?), St. John the Baptist and Mary the Virgin receiving the Annunciation.

Like the Madonna of Doudleby, the altar from Sv. Majdalena's represents a provincially coarsened and artisan-conceived work of very conservative style. This general stylistic position, and its somewhat popular narrative element, together with the similarity of the figure-types, drawing and colouring are points of contact which link the altar with the Madonna of Doudleby to an extent which justifies the assumption of a workshop common to both. Some of the features already point to the picture of the Krumlov Madonna in the Prague National Gallery, a work which came into being after 1450. The stylistic formation of the statuette of the Virgin Mary would also point to a comparatively late period.

257.—269.   THE MASTER OF THE ALTAR AT ST. JAMES'S. —   Plates 246.—260.
THIRTEEN PANELS FROM A DISMANTLED, QUINQUEPARTITE WING ALTAR. — About 1440.

a) 257. Plates 246.—247. The Annunciation. b) 258. Plate 248. The Visitation of Virgin Mary. c) 259. Plate 249. Adoration of the Child. d) 260. Plates 250.—251. Three Kings Adoring the Child. e) 261. Plate 252. Christ's Sacrifice in the Temple. f) 262. Plate 253. Capture of St. James.—g) 263. Plate 254. St. James tends the Sick. h) 264. Plate 255. Death of St. James. i) 265. Plate 256. Moving the Body of St. James. j) 266. Plate 257. Philetus Sent to St. James. k) 267. Plate 258. St. James Treats Philetus. l) 268. Plate 259. Philetus Frees Hermogenes. m) 269. Plate 260. Hermogenes Receives Staff from St. James.

These thirteen pictures, of almost identical dimensions, preserved from the past and at present fairly scattered over various places, are linked by us as one altar complex representing both a Marian Cycle and the Legend of St. James. These panels evidently formed the wings of an altar the centre part of which may have consisted of pictures of wide format or of wooden sculpture. The legend of Hermogenes was preserved in its fulness on four panels and the St. James Cycle must likewise be deemed complete, whilst of the Marian Cycle only five panels came to be preserved; their number is incomplete and needs the addition of three pictures which for the time being cannot be traced. In a reconstruction of its most probable appearance, the altar in its closed state would show scenes from the Hermogenes legend; on being first opened, the Marian Cycle would appear, and, finally, the completely opened-out altar would show in its centre either the said wooden sculpture or other space-filling objects, whilst the wings would bear pictures from the legend of the martyrdom of St. James. — The St. James Legend appears for the first time in Early Gothic art. In our altar the Cycle has been simplified, a number of scenes being assembled into one picture on the panels in each case.

The provenance of the altar is not known, but we surmise that it was destined for some church in Moravia, perhaps for the Church of St. James in Brno. In their majority the pictures passed at times unknown into the hands of Austrian owners, from whom they gradually found their way into the art market during recent times.

a) 257. Plates 246.—247. THE ALTAR AT ST. JAMES'S: THE ANNUNCIATION.

Prague, National Gallery, Inv. No. DO 248.

Pine-wood, canvas-covered, gesso ground, tempera. H. 82,5, w. 75 cm. Well-preserved on the whole, showing only some disturbed places. The gold is new in parts. Restored and cleaned. The picture was found, in company with five other panels, amongst the property of the late Baroness M. Redl in Lower Austria in 1930; it was bought in a Prague art shop by R. Morawetz, together with the Visitation picture. In 1939 it was loaned to the National Gallery in Prague.

The scheme of the picture comes nearest to the Annunciation picture from Vyšší Brod. Stylistically the picture maintains the composition in vogue at the beginning of the XVth century, but it already adds a few elements that are new. It must be considered as the work of a studio assistant to which the master himself has lent his hand by touching up the figure and, it seems, also the head of the angel and the head of Mary.

b) 258. Plate 248. THE ALTAR AT ST. JAMES'S: THE VISITATION OF THE VIRGIN MARY.

Prague, National Gallery, Inv. No. DO 249.

Pine-wood, canvas-covered, gesso ground, tempera. H. 82, w. 75,5 cm. The gold was partly renewed, but otherwise the picture is well preserved including the top enamels. It was also cleaned. The history of the picture is the same as that of No. 257. The scheme sets out from the Visitation picture of the Master of the Carrying of the Cross from Vyšší Brod. The motif of the door half ajar was, however, no longer comprehended by the painter. There is no direct connection between the two pictures. Our picture is a work of lesser stature, pointing to the labours of an assistant's hand, probably the same that painted the Adoration and, in part, also the Annunciation picture.

c) 259. Plate 249. THE ALTAR AT ST. JAMES'S: ADORATION OF THE CHILD.

Vienna, Kunsthistorisches Museum. Gallery No. 1738.

Pine-wood, canvas-covered, gesso ground, tempera. H. 81, w. 75 cm. Very good state of preservation. Only the gilt background appears damaged and regilt in parts.

The panel was acquired at the Viennese Dorotheum auction sale of the Hoffmann Collection for the Kunsthistorisches Museum in 1910. — The scrolls show the usual Latin texts.

The picture is closely related to the Adoration in České Budějovice. It is most probably the work of an assistant of the Master of the Marian Cycle, the same who painted the Visitation and, partly, also the Annunciation. The figures of the shepherds, the landscapes, the pronouncedly decorative character of the scrolls and to some extent also the colouring, point to an interrelation with the more advanced St. James Legend. Compared with the Adoration of the Three Kings, however, our panel appears to have been painted far more superficially.

d) 260. Plates 250.—251. THE ALTAR AT ST. JAMES'S: THE CAPTURE OF ST. JAMES.

Prague, National Gallery, Inv. No. O 1485.

Pine-wood, canvas-covered, gesso ground, tempera. H. 82,5, w. 75 cm. The picture is well preserved without any repaintings or retouchings, the gold in the background being rubbed off in places. Newly cleaned and varnished.

It was acquired for the National Gallery in Prague from the André art shop in Prague in 1932.

In its composition scheme, the picture repeats the Adoration in the Municipal Museum of České Budějovice, but there is no direct relationship between the two. The picture is most probably the work of the Master of the Marian Legend, the master of the workshop which gave rise to the St. James Altar. His work betrays itself in the greater elasticity of the

drawing, the fresher and more careful painting and in a number of details. Here, too, is most apparent a dependency on the Czech painting of the first two decades of the XVth century.

e) 261. Plate 252. THE ALTAR AT ST. JAMES'S: CHRIST'S SACRIFICE IN THE TEMPLE.

Nuremberg, Germanisches Nationalmuseum, Inv. No. Gm 306.

Fir-wood, canvas-covered, gesso ground, tempera. H. 82,5, w. 75 cm. The state of preservation is good on the whole, without retouchings of any importance, only the gold being renewed. Unrestored.

Judging by the compactness of the colouring, the drawing, careful execution and some of the detail, the picture appears to be the work of the principal master of the workshop like the Adoration of the Three Kings. The masculine figures show an apparent connection with the St. James Cycle.

f) 262. Plate 253. THE ALTAR AT ST. JAMES'S: CAPTURE OF ST. JAMES.

Prague, National Gallery, Inv. No. O 1578.

Lime-wood, canvas-covered, gesso ground, tempera. — H. 82,5, w. 75 cm. Well preserved on the whole, though some enamels worn and the gold partly rubbed off.

Bought in 1937 for the Prague National Gallery from Mrs. Scharmitzer in Vienna.

The scrolls bear Latin texts reading as follows: „herodes · fec^t apprehēd^{s}e · s · iacobū (Herodes fecit apprehendere sanctum Jacobum)". — „Abiathar misit funem ī collū s iacobi".

This picture, like all the following pictures from the legend of St. James are apparently the work of one and the same hand, differing stylistically to a marked degree from the principal master. The distinguishing marks are here primarily a greater expressiveness in, and a sharper definition of the faces of some of the figures, the colouring and use of the scroll device. These novel elements, the origin of which we think to lie in the Lower Austrian region, are here combined with the older Czech style after 1400 into a new synthesis, albeit of no high artistic level. The general modelling and rather poor enamelling is common to the St. James Cycle in its entirety, the basic conception of which in the matter of landscape and interior space, figures and raiment remains within the tradional framework. Alien elements are here still in an absolute minority.

g) 263. Plate 254. THE ALTAR AT. JAMES'S:
ST. JAMES TENDS THE SICK.

Austria, private property.

Up to 1907, the picture was in the Baron Uhl
Collection, in 1937 it was discovered in Austrian
ownership. No further data could be ascertained.
The scrolls show Latin texts, reading as follows:
„·S·iacobe·aplé i^{v}x libera·me" (Sancte Jacobe, apo-
stole Jesu Christi, libera me). — „Cui·s·ia In noīe
i^{v}x' exurge san^9." (Cui sanctus Jacobus: In nomine
Jesu Christi exurge sanus).

In its construction, composition, figures, types
and arrangement of garments it resembles the preceding picture.

h) 264. Plate 255. THE ALTAR AT. ST. JAMES'S:
THE DEATH OF ST. JAMES.

Brno, Provincial Museum, Inv. No. A 571.

Pine-wood, canvas-covered, gesso ground, tempera. — H. 82.5, w. 75 cm. The background has
been gilt over, the top enamels were for the greater
part preserved. The picture has not been cleaned.
Its restoration was effected from 1930 to 1932.

The panel was acquired in 1932 from a Vienna
art shop by way of exchange.

The scrolls bear the following Latin inscriptions:
— „Iussu herodis decolat^2·s· ia C̄ciosia" (Iussu
Herodis decolatur sanctus Jacobus cum Iosia). —
„Discipuli tulūnt corp^9 2 navi īpo". (Discipuli tule-
runt corpus et navi imposuerunt.)

Naturalistic elements can be traced in the picture,
particularly in the figure of the executioner and the
vista of the city in the background. The picture was
painted by the same painter, and just as cursorily, as
the foregoing ones.

i) 265. Plate 256. THE ALTAR AT ST. JAMES'S:
MOVING THE BODY OF ST. JAMES.

Vienna, Kunsthistorisches Museum, Inv. No. 1816.

Pine-wood, canvas-covered, gesso ground, tempera. — H. 82, w. 75.5 cm. The gilt background was
partly regilt and the picture shows local retouchings.

The panel was acquired in 1932 from Lower
Austrian owners for the Kunsthistorisches Museum
in Vienna.

The scrolls bear the following Latin texts: —
„Discipuli petūt sepltura" (Discipuli petunt sepul-
turam). — „Lupa ondit (ostendit) boues indo-
mitos".

The scenic arrangement of the ground-plan supports the impression of spatial depth. Stylistically,
the panel is closely allied with the other pictures

of the cycle, and is the work of the same hand. In
its numerous corrections and general manner of
painting one can see the cursoriness of workshop
work.

j) 266. Plate 257. THE ALTAR AT ST. JAMES'S
PHILETUS SENT TO ST. JAMES.

Prague, National Gallery, Inv. No. O 597.

Pine-wood, canvas-covered, gesso ground, tempera. H. 82.5, w. 76 cm. Local retouchings. During
the restoration, carried out in Prague in 1935, the
later gilding and repainting was removed.

As indicated by the coloured background, the
panel, together with three further panels, was a part
of the outer side of the altar wings depicting the
beginnings of the legend of St. James. It was
acquired, with two others, in 1889 from Mrs. Dot-
zauer's estate for the Prague National Gallery.

The scrolls show Latin wording, reading as follows: — „herōgenes· misit philetū ad iacobū". —
„S ia· philetū corā oib^9 rac̄onabilit c̄ovicit". (Sanctus
Jacobus Philetum coram omnibus racionabiliter con-
vicit.)

The colouring seen to-day, differing to some
extent from the other panels of the legend, is conditioned by the state of its preservation. Judging
from the identical principles of composition,
figure types, painting technique and striving after
a deepening of space, this panel may be held to
be, like the other pictures, a part of the St. James
altar and the work of the same painter.

k) 267. Plate 258. THE ALTAR AT ST. JAMES'S:
ST. JAMES TREATS PHILETUS.

Prague, National Gallery, Inv. No. O 599.

Pine-wood, canvas-covered, gesso ground, tempera. H. 82.5, w. 75 cm. The state of preservation
is the same as that of the preceding picture.

The history of the picture is the same as under
No. 266.

The scroll shows the Latin inscription: — „·S·iaco·
misit· phileto sudariū suū."

l) 268. Plate 259. THE ALTAR AT ST. JAMES'S:
PHILETUS FREES HERMOGENES.

Austria, privately owned.

The description of the picture is the same as under
No. 263.

The scroll shows the Latin inscription: — „S·ia·
dixit· philete solue h'mogenem". — „philetus soluit
hermogenem".

Stylistically the picture belongs to our group and,

seemingly, is the best preserved part thereof. The scrolls here have a preponderantly decorative purpose.

m) 269. Plate 260. THE ALTAR AT ST. JAMES'S: HERMOGENES RECEIVES STAFF FROM ST. JAMES.

Prague, National Gallery, Inv. No. O 598.

Pine-wood, canvas-covered, gesso ground, tempera. — H. 82.5, w. 75 cm. The state of preservation is the same as under No. 266. During the restoration, done in Prague in 1935, the later gilding and the repainting of the background were removed.

The provenance is the same as under No. 266.

The scrolls are inscribed in Latin as follows: — „hermogenes· petit· aligd'signū". — „·S·iaco· dedit. ei· baculum". — „Jacobe apl'e (apostole) miser'e· nobis".

As regards an evaluation of the picture, the conclusions expressed in respect of the preceding pictures of the St. James legend also apply in this case.

The literary pattern for the St. James Cycle of the St. James Altar must be sought in the St. James Legend, the first concluding phase of which is represented by the so-called Historia Compostellana from the first half of the XIIth century, broadened subsequently by further additions into a definite shape. This late redaction also became the pattern for the old Bohemian (Czech) Passional which was preserved in the manuscript of the Prague National Museum, wherein all the material epic parts of the Latin original were preserved.

Judging by the stylistic and technical side of the pictures, there were two artistic individualities who worked on the altar. One of them, the more conservative of the two, painted and supervised the painting of the Marian legend, whilst the other, more progressively informed, carried out the pictorialisation of the St. James Legend. To the master of the workshop it is therefore possible to ascribe the Adoration of the Three Kings and, possibly, also of the Sacrifice in the Temple, besides the final touches to the other pictures of the Marian Cycle, which otherwise are merely the work of a poorly gifted assistant who had to depend on the Master and partly also on a fellow assistant.

The workshop cannot be linked up with the Master of the Rajhrad Altar. Its leading painter was an independent personality deeply rooted in the tradition of the Czech style after 1400, who was only partially influenced by the formal elements of the art of the Rajhrad Altar's Master. Into his conservative style there enter some elements that are novel (painting method, colouring, motifs of expression, principles of composition and scrolls with texts), which, in the work of a younger and more penetrating assistant and painter of the St. James Cycle, assume a greater importance under the influence of the Lower Austrian painting in the decade from 1420 to 1430. However, even he remains in substance on the traditional basis. His art is not Late Gothic — neither in intention, nor in effect — in fact it has remained totally untouched by Late Gothic. — The Master of the St. James Altar is the last outstanding personality of the Czech painting school; his work at the same time marks the end of an evolution almost a hundred years old.

270.   MADONNA OF H. M. THE KING OF ENGLAND. — About 1440.   Plates 261.—263.

London, Buckingham Palace.

Wood, tempera, on gesso ground. H. 59.5, w. 48 cm. — The state of preservation is very good. As far as is known, the picture has not been restored. It is in the original, painted and embossed frame.

The exact provenance is not known. The panel passed, at some date unknown (prior to 1906) from the Wallerstein Collection into the possession of H. M. the King of England, and is now in the Buckingham Palace Collection in London.

The paintings on the frame show scenes from Mary's life, as follows: — On the top moulding the Annunciation, the Visitation and the Adoration of the Child, on the left moulding the Adoration of the Three Kings, on the right moulding Christ's Sacrifice, on the bottom moulding the Resurrection, the Descent of the Holy Ghost and the Death of the Virgin Mary.

Iconographically, the centre picture has no close connection with any known type of miracle-working Madonna; only distantly does it remind one of the Roudnice type. In composition scheme the frame pictures are very near to the pictures of the Marian Legend of St. James's Altar, although in some of them considerable loosening in composition may be observed. As the drawing, and particularly the drapery in this whole picture are close to those of the St. James altar, the possibility cannot be excluded of a close connection between the two works. In any event, the panel may be placed in approximately the same period.

Prague II, Parish Church of St. Stephen Major.

Lime-wood, canvas-covering not ascertained, gesso ground, tempera. — H. 70, w. 61 cm with the original, painted frame. The picture is well preserved, showing minor local retouchings. The gold mostly bronzed over. During the repair done in 1878, the repainted background both on the picture and the frame as well as most of the later additions were removed and the whole picture was touched up and regilt.

Most probably the picture was intended directly for the Parish Church of St. Stephen's in the New Town of Prague, where it has been in place since the year 1573.

On the frame are pictures of scenes from the life of the Virgin Mary. On the upper moulding, from the left are the Annunciation, the Visitation and the Adoration, the right-hand vertical moulding showing the Circumcision; the bottom moulding from right to left shows the Adoration of the Three Kings, the Sacrifice in the Temple and the Descent of the Holy Ghost, the left-hand vertical moulding showing the Death of the Virgin Mary.

The centre picture repeats with small variations the type of the Roudnice Madonna. The frame pictures repeat the older, current Gothic schemes of scenes from the Marian Legend, manifesting the later stylistic characteristics more decisively than the frame pictures of the Madonna of the King of England.

Stylistically these pictures are approximately on a level with the Marian Cycle of the Altar at St. James's, lacking the expressly late features. The fluid rendering of the draperies and the softly painted faces point to the second third of the XVth century. The date inscribed on the back of the picture, 1472, is most probably false.

Prague, National Gallery, Inv. No. O 495.

Pine-wood, canvas-covered, chalk base, tempera. H. 41.5, w. 31.5 cm, with the original, painted frame. The state of preservation is a very good one. Neither restored, nor cleaned.

The centre picture depicts the Madonna's Ascension, with the Assumpta in a sunlit flower-garden standing on a crescent. On the upper moulding of the frame from left to right are Ss. Margaret, Catherine, Barbara and Dorothea, on the left-hand vertical moulding from top to bottom are Ss. Apollonia, Genevieve (?) and two donors; the right-hand vertical moulding shows Ss. Agnes, Ursula and Clara, the bottom moulding Ss. Magdalena, Anna and Jerome.

Iconographically the picture ranks with the group of Czech Assumptas standing on a crescent in a flower-garden, all of which, in panel and book-painting, can be placed chronologically in the second half of the XVth century (the Assumptas of the White Mountain, Deštná, Dubany, etc.). A stylistically interesting example of the retrospective orientation in the Czech school of panel painting round about 1450, when after previous attempts to overcome formalism and to reform style by admitting foreign, Western and Austrian influences, a way out is sought from a long-protracted stylistic crisis in a return to the indigenous tradition. This phenomenon can be particularly well observed in the South Bohemian region, where the evolution went on uninterruptedly, continuously from the beginning of the century, in a numerically large group of relics tied to each other by a considerable stylistic and thematic affinity. Characteristics of the 'beautiful' style here renewed are the figure types, the fastidious fold system and the soft tonal modelling of forms. Lanna's Assumpta is free from all the alien stylistic accents which penetrate into the other relics of the period with motifs of the broken style. In many respects it is closely related to Lanna's Madonna picture, but the disputed question as to whether both these pictures have originated in one and the same workshop cannot be definitely decided because of the bad state of preservation of Lanna's Madonna. The existing difference in the treatment of draperies need not upset the assumption of their close connection with each other, even an absolute promiscuity of folding styles that can be frequently observed in one and the same relic (as in the case of the Visitation bearing the family crest of the Švamberks).

THE ASSUMPTA OF THE WHITE MOUNTAIN. — About 1450.

Plate 267.

Prague, National Gallery, Inv. No. O 1269.

Tempera on canvas. — H. 146.5, w. 99 cm. Considerably damaged by the peeling and rubbing off of paint in large spots.

Acquired in 1921 for the National Gallery in Prague. Said to originate from the older monastery on the White Mountain.

In the corners of the picture can be seen the Evangelists with scrolls bearing appropriate Latin texts. Angels are holding scrolls with a Latin text of the beginnings of the Marian Antiphonal.

Iconographically, this picture agrees with the other pictures of this subject about the middle of the XVth century. It has in common with Lanna's

Assumpta the fold-style of Mary's cloak, with its repeated undulating motif. Otherwise it is very close to the Deštná Assumpta, particularly in its figure types, and in the Late Gothic features of the crumpled folds of the secondary characters and the treatment of the inscription scrolls.

The picture used to be regarded as a Late Baroque copy, but this presumption is contradicted by the whole, inimitable stylistic and colouring structure. The unusual feature is the tempera painting on canvas without a wooden panel, but this may be due to the canvas having been taken off the panel later.

THE LANNA MADONNA. — About 1450.

Plate 268.

Prague, National Gallery, Inv. No. O 494.

Pine-wood, canvas-covered, gesso ground, tempera. — H. 50.5, w. 38.5 cm with the original, painted frame. The state of preservation is very bad, all the enamels having been rubbed off. Unrestored.

Pictures on the frame: On the top moulding from left to right Ss. Barbara, Apollonia and St. Catherine, on the left-hand moulding Ss. Dorothea and Lud-

mila, on the right-hand moulding Ss. Margaret and Magdalena, and on the bottom moulding St. Peter, with a winged arrow in the middle and St. Christopher on the right.

Lanna's Madonna is a replica of the Roudnice type. By the style of the frame-pictures it approaches Lanna's Assumpta, but differs from it in the broken-style motifs of the drapery.

THE DEŠTNÁ ASSUMPTA. — About 1450.

Prague, National Gallery, Inv. No. O 724.

Pine-wood, canvas-covered, gesso ground, tempera.— H. 144, w. 111 cm. The pigments including the enamels are well preserved throughout the picture, almost without a single fault. During the restoration, carried out in Prague in 1942, the varnish was taken off.

This picture of unknown provenance passed as a gift from private ownership in Jindřichův Hradec to the Chapel of St. John in Deštná near Soběslav in 1811. In 1895 it was acquired for the Prague National Gallery.

The scrolls show the usual Latin texts.

The panel repeats the basic Assumpta type changed into a miracle-working picture, with donors. The formalistic style of the early XVth century is here crossed with Late Gothic elements, in the broken folds of the drapery and in a noteworthy naturalism in the rendering of the heads of the donors and the vegetation. It came into being in the same workshop as the Roudnice type of Madonna in České Budějovice (No. 276) and belongs to the same cycle as the Visitation picture from Český Krumlov. It is the most valuable and largest-dimensioned work of this late period.

MADONNA. — About 1450.

Plate 271.

České Budějovice, Municipal Museum.

Lime-wood, canvas-covered, gesso ground, tempera. — H. 72, w. 53 cm, with the original, painted frame. The picture is damaged only on the bot-

tom part and on the bottom moulding of the frame. Otherwise it is well preserved. Partly repaired in 1845, otherwise not restored.

The picture was bought in 1922 by the Municipal Museum in České Budějovice from private owners in Čtyři Dvory near České Budějovice. The vertical mouldings show angels with scrolls, bearing the usual Latin inscriptions. The bottom moulding shows a fraction of a Latin text, with invocation.

This Madonna repeats the Roudnice type. Stylistically the picture is so closely related to the Assumpta of Deštná that the assumption of a workshop common to both is justified.

277. VISITATION OF THE VIRGIN MARY FROM ČESKÝ KRUMLOV. Plate 272.
About 1450.

Prague, National Gallery, Inv. No. DO 218 (Owned by A. Schwarzenberg).

Wood, canvas-covered, gesso ground, tempera. H. 88.5, w. 71 cm. The colours are in many places rubbed off down to the base.

This picture of unknown provenance was kept until 1923 at the Český Krumlov Castle, and was loaned in that year to the National Gallery in Prague.

It repeats the traditional iconographic scheme and is on the same stylistic level as the Assumpta of Deštná, but does not reach the latter's level and is the work of some other hand.

278. VISITATION OF THE VIRGIN MARY. — After 1450. Plate 273.

Prague, National Gallery, Inv. No. O 673.

Lime-wood, canvas-covered, gesso ground, tempera. H. 57, w. 57.5 cm, with the original, painted frame. Well preserved on the whole. During the restoration, carried out in Prague in 1935, the more recent gilding was taken off the centre of the panel, which was cleaned but not touched up.

Judging by the coat of arms shown, the order for the painting of the picture must have been placed by some member of the South Bohemian noble family of the Švamberks. No closer details of its provenance are known. It was bought for the Prague National Gallery from A. Wiehl, of Prague, in 1891.

In the corners of the frame moulding are shown the figures of the four evangelists, with their names in Latin. Besides them there is on the top moulding St. John the Baptist (left) and St. Jerome, on the left-hand vertical moulding St. Andrew and below him St. Margaret; on the right-hand moulding is St. Bartholomew and St. Apollonia, bottom left is St. Cecilia, bottom right is St. Clara.

The composition scheme was taken over from the established type of the visitation, but its painter failed to a considerable extent to grasp details. This non-comprehension, together with the linear schematic arrangement of the drapery with the first motifs of the broken, Late Gothic style and the indication of landscape in the background window, all bear witness to a late origin of the picture. The panel relates closely to the Brussels Madonna and the Madonna from Krumlov at the National Gallery in Prague.

279. THE BRUSSELS MADONNA. — After 1450. Plate 274.

Brussels, in the M. van Gelder Collection.

Wood, tempera, H. 44, w. 33 cm.
Of unknown provenance.
The Madonna repeats in a free manner the basic Roudnice type. Stylistically, with its way of seeing the figures, the flattening of shapes and the fold motives, it is closely akin to the Visitation picture which bears the crest of the Švamberk family.

280. THE MADONNA OF JINDŘICHŮV HRADEC. — About 1460. Plate 275.

Jindřichův Hradec, Castle.

Wood, canvas-covered, gesso ground, tempera. H. 80.5, w. 68.5 cm with the original, painted frame. The picture is well preserved on the whole, and is unrestored.

The exact provenance is unknown.
In the corners of the frame are the four evangelists with appropriate Latin texts on the scrolls. — On the frame are scenes from the life of the Virgin Mary

and busts of Old Testament prophets. The cycle begins in the left-hand bottom corner and each scene has related to it two Latin inscriptions on the prophets' scrolls: the Annunciation, the Adoration of the Child and the Adoration of the Three Kings. The left-hand vertical moulding shows the Circumcision of Christ, the right-hand vertical moulding the Resurrection; the top horizontal moulding shows the Ascension of the Lord, the Descent of the Holy Ghost and the Death of the Virgin Mary.

This simplified replica of the Roudnice type is evidently painted directly in accordance with the pattern of the Vyšší Brod Madonna (with both hands uncovered). In style, the frame pictures show a number of Late Gothic characteristics, chief amongst them being the broken folds, the architecture of the huts and the landscape background. Influence of illustration models may be safely assumed in this case. The picture has no close connection with the Viennese Madonna.

281.—282.   THE VIENNESE MADONNA. — About 1470.   Plates 276.—277.

Vienna, Kunsthistorisches Museum, Gallery No. 1783.

Lime-wood, canvas-covered, gesso ground, tempera. H. 33.5, w. 26.5 cm. The panel is painted on both sides and is in its original, painted frame. During the restoration, carried out at the beginning of this century, the panel was cleaned and most of the holes were touched up.

The picture was acquired in Český Krumlov in 1878, and was taken over by the Kunsthistorisches Museum in Vienna in 1927.

a) **281. Plate 276. MADONNA WITH THE CHILD** (front of panel).

The picture is well preserved in its colour structure, and appears to be disturbed only in some places.

On the frame: On the top moulding from the left Ss. Margaret, Magdalena and Apollonia, on the left-hand vertical moulding St. Dorothea, on the right-hand vertical moulding St. Catherine, on the bottom moulding from the left Ss. Ursula, Elizabeth and Barbara.

b) **282. Plate 277. VERAICON** (back of panel).

This side of the panel, too, has its colouring in the original state.

In the depiction of the Madonna, the picture adheres only loosely to the Roudnice type, which it varies in many motifs. The advanced fold-style shows that this is a late replica. The level of the work is somewhat crudely artisan.

COPIES

283.   THE MADONNA OF BŘEZNICE. — End of the XVth century.   Plate 278.

Březnice, Castle Chapel, now at National Gallery, Prague.

Panel of soft wood, dark-grey gesso ground, tempera. H. 41.5, w. 29.5 cm. Well preserved on the whole, only partly damaged owing to hammered silver crowns having been placed on the heads of Mary and Christ.

The iconographic origin of this Madonna is to be sought in the Byzantine „Odigitri" type which, in its turn, has a series of variants. Of the types derived from these, the nearest to the Březnice Madonna is the „Peribleptos" Virgin Mary, preserved, for example, in the icon of St. Clement's Church at Ochrida.

The back shows a Latin, Late Gothic inscription, according to which the picture was painted during the reign of King Charles IV in 1396 after the pattern of the Madonna picture of Roudnice, reputed to have been painted by St. Luke.

As shown by the colouring and the capreolary ornamentation on the golden background of the panel front, it is a case here of a Late Gothic copy of a picture kept in Roudnice. Thist lost Roudnice picture was presumably a work of Byzantine or, more likely, of Byzantine-Italian origin.

VERA EFFIGIES OF ST. WENCESLAS. — Copy after a picture from Plate 279.
the middle period of the XIVth century.

Prague, Municipal Museum, Inv. No. 9255.

Oil on copper. — H. 27.5, w. 18 cm. Satisfactory state of preservation.

The picture comes probably from the Augustinian monastery of St. Wenceslas in the New Town of Prague, abolished in 1784. It was acquired for the Municipal Museum in Prague in 1893.

Whilst the armour of St. Wenceslas is in keeping with the first half of the XIVth century, his face already bears signs of the style round about 1360. The copy evidently seeks to imitate the lost prototype, of the likeness of which a fair idea may be gained from the miniature painting in the Breviary of Jan of Středa (known as Liber Viaticus) dating from the period after 1360.

LIST OF PLATES

LIST OF PLATES

ERRATA

Plates 136—140: „Dubečko" should read „Dubeček"

Plate 193: Text should read „Adoration of
the Three Kings — About 1420"

Plates 244—245: For „Magdalena" read
„Majdalena"

Plate 246: „At" should precede „St."

REPRODUCTIONS

1. THE PREDELLA OF ROUDNICE. - Before 1350

2. THE PREDELLA OF ROUDNICE: St. John (detail)

MADONNA OF MOST. ▪ Before 1350

MASTER OF THE VYŠŠÍ BROD CYCLE: ANNUNCIATION OF THE VIRGIN MARY. - About 1350

MASTER OF THE VYŠŠÍ BROD CYCLE: BIRTH OF OUR LORD

MASTER OF THE VYŠŠÍ BROD CYCLE: BIRTH OF OUR LORD (detail)

7. MASTER OF THE VYŠŠÍ BROD CYCLE: BIRTH OF OUR LORD (detail)

8. MASTER OF THE VYŠŠÍ BROD CYCLE: ADORATION OF THREE HOLY KINGS (detail)

STER OF THE VYŠŠÍ BROD CYCLE: ADORATION OF THREE HOLY KINGS

STER OF THE VYŠŠÍ BROD CYCLE: CHRIST ON MOUNT OLIVET

11. MASTER OF THE VYŠŠÍ BROD CYCLE: CHRIST ON MOUNT OLIVET (detail)

12. MASTER OF THE VYŠŠÍ BROD CYCLE: CHRIST ON MOUNT OLIVET (detail)

MASTER OF THE VYŠŠÍ BROD CYCLE: CHRIST ON MOUNT OLIVET (detail)

MASTER OF THE VYŠŠÍ BROD CYCLE: CRUCIFIXION

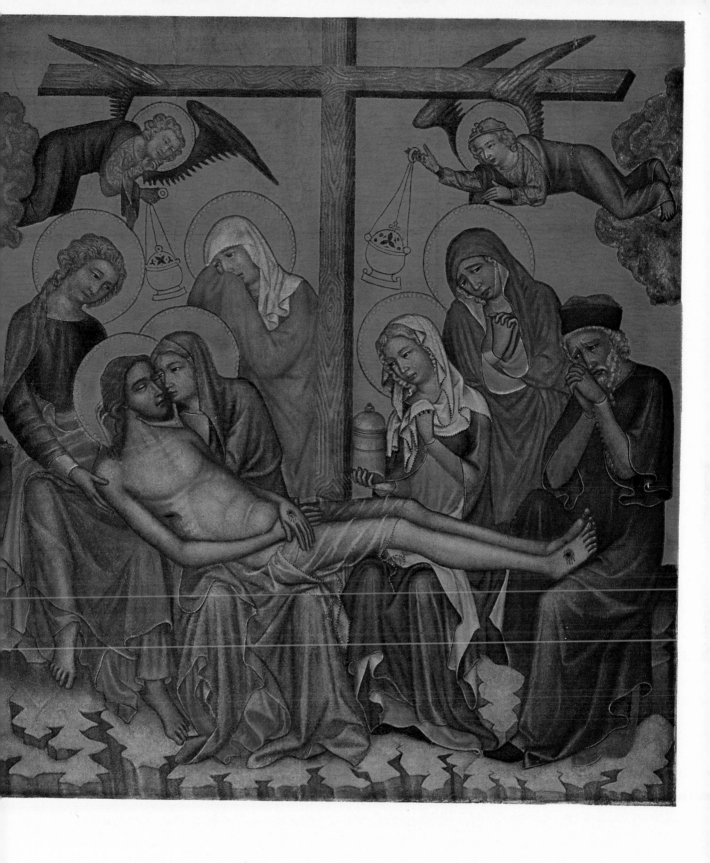

MASTER OF THE VYŠŠÍ BROD CYCLE: LAMENT FOR CHRIST

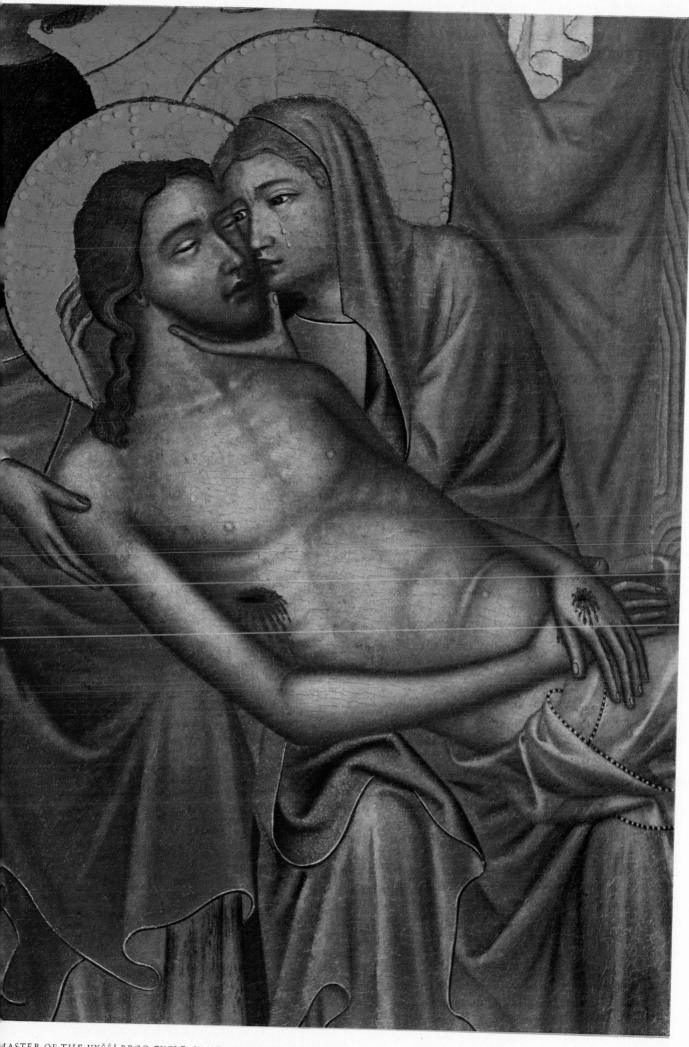

MASTER OF THE VYŠŠÍ BROD CYCLE: LAMENT FOR CHRIST (detail)

MASTER OF THE VYŠŠÍ BROD CYCLE: RESURRECTION

8. MASTER OF THE VYŠŠÍ BROD CYCLE: RESURRECTION (detail)

MASTER OF THE VYŠŠÍ BROD CYCLE: RESURRECTION (detail)

20. MASTER OF THE VYŠŠÍ BROD CYCLE: RESURRECTION (detail)

MASTER OF THE VYŠŠÍ BROD CYCLE: ASCENSION

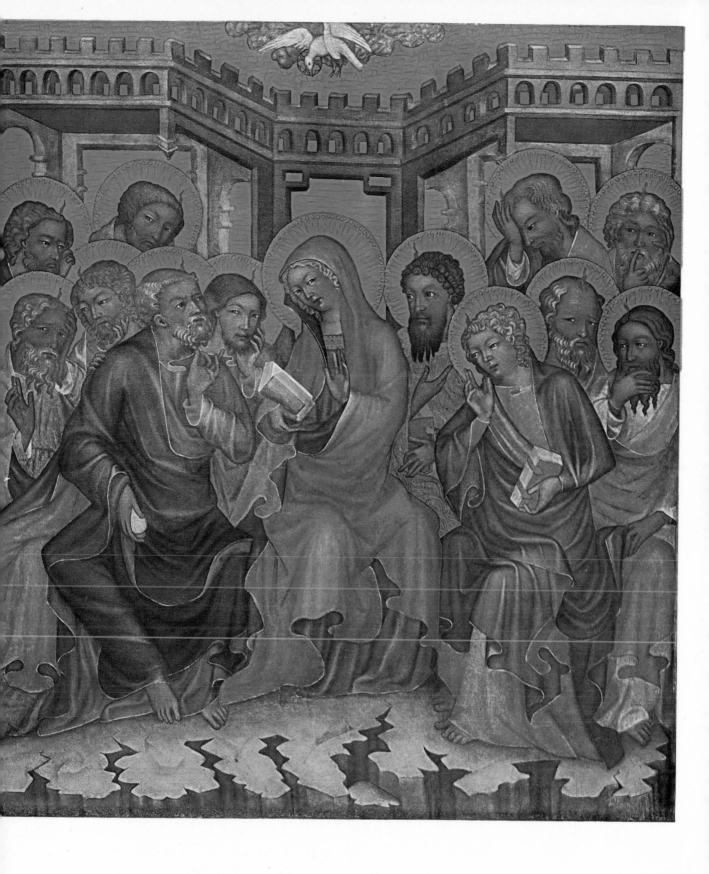

MASTER OF THE VYŠŠÍ BROD CYCLE: DESCENT OF THE HOLY GHOST

MASTER OF THE VYŠŠÍ BROD CYCLE: DESCENT OF THE HOLY GHOST (detail)

MASTER OF THE VYŠŠÍ BROD CYCLE: DESCENT OF THE HOLY GHOST (detail)

25. MASTER OF THE VYŠŠÍ BROD CYCLE: DESCENT OF THE HOLY GHOST (detail)

MADONNA OF VEVEŘÍ. - About 1350

MADONNA OF STRAHOV. - About 1350

28. MADONNA OF KLADSKO. - About 1350

29. MADONNA OF KLADSKO (detail)

MADONNA OF KLADSKO (detail)

MADONNA OF KLADSKO: Arnošt of Pardubice (detail)

32. MADONNA OF KLADSKO (detail). About 1350

THE KAUFMANN CRUCIFIXION
ter 1350

THE KAUFMANN CRUCIFIXION (detail)

35. THE KAUFMANN CRUCIFIXION (detail)

36. THE KAUFMANN CRUCIFIXION (detail)

37. HOLY TRINITY (VRATISLAV). - After 1350

EATH OF VIRGIN MARY (Košátky). · After 1350

39. DEATH OF VIRGIN MARY (detail)

DEATH OF VIRGIN MARY (detail)

DEATH OF VIRGIN MARY: St. John (detail)

. MADONNA BETWEEN ST. CATHARINE AND MARGARET. - About 1360

DONNA BETWEEN ST. CATHARINE AND MARGARET (detail)

44. MADONNA BETWEEN ST. CATHARINE AND MARGARET: St. Catharine (detail)

45. MADONNA OF ZBRASLAV. - About 1360

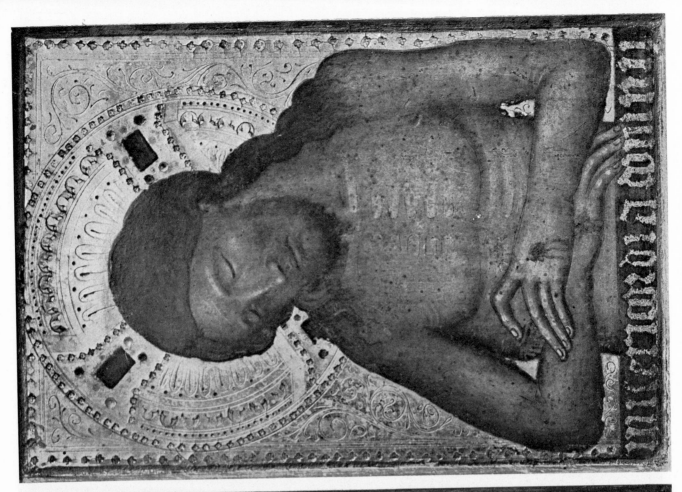

46, 47. VIENNESE DIPTYCH: Madonna. The Man of Sorrows. - About 1360

48. ROME MADONNA. - About 1360

49. VYŠEHRAD MADONNA (state after restoration). - About 1360

YŠEHRAD MADONNA (detail, state before restoration)

51. BOSTON MADONNA.- About 1360

52. MORGAN PANELS: ADORATION OF THREE KINGS. - About 1360

53. MORGAN PANELS: DEATH OF VIRGIN MARY

MASTER THEODORIC: ALTAR WALL OF THE HOLY CROSS CHAPEL, KARLŠTEJN CASTLE. · 1357-67, or 1365-67

MASTER THEODORIC: KARLŠTEJN CASTLE, WALL OF HOLY CROSS CHAPEL

56. MASTER THEODORIC: KARLŠTEJN CASTLE, HOLY CROSS CHAPEL, CORNER OF LEFT WINDOW RECESS

MASTER THEODORIC: KARLŠTEJN CASTLE, HOLY CROSS CHAPEL, CORNER OF RIGHT RECESS

MASTER THEODORIC: CRUCIFIXION

59, 60, 61. MASTER THEODORIC: TRIPTYCH (two angels, the Man of Sorrows, the three Marys)

62. MASTER THEODORIC: TRIPTYCH, THE MAN OF SORROWS (detail)

MASTER THEODORIC: ST. CLARA

MASTER THEODORIC: ST. HILARY

ASTER THEODORIC: ST. MARK

ASTER THEODORIC: ST. VITUS

MASTER THEODORIC: ST. CATHARINE

68. MASTER THEODORIC: ST. MAURICE

MASTER THEODORIC: HOLY KNIGHT

70. MASTER THEODORIC: ARCHANGEL URIEL

MASTER THEODORIC: PROPHET

72. MASTER THEODORIC: ST. PAUL, HERMIT

MASTER THEODORIC: FIVE HOLY BRETHREN

74. VOTIVE PICTURE OF JAN OČKO OF VLAŠIM
(state after restoration). · After 1370

VOTIVE PICTURE OF JAN OČKO OF VLAŠIM; UPPER PART OF THE PICTURE:
ST. SIGISMUND, CHARLES IV., MADONNA WITH CHILD JESUS, THE KING'S SON WENCESLAS, ST. WENCESLAS
(state before restoration)

VOTIVE PICTURE OF JAN OČKO OF VLAŠIM; LOWER PART OF THE PICTURE:
ST. PROKOP, ST. ADALBERT, JAN OČKO OF VLAŠIM, ST. VITUS, ST. LUDMILA (state after restoration)

77. VOTIVE PICTURE OF JAN OČKO OF VLAŠIM: ST. SIGISMUND AND CHARLES IV. (detail, state after restoration)

VOTIVE PICTURE OF JAN OČKO OF VLAŠIM: ST. ADALBERT (detail, state before restoration)

TIVE PICTURE OF JAN OČKO OF VLAŠIM: ST. WENCESLAS (detail, state after restoration)

80. VOTIVE PICTURE OF JAN OĆKO OF VLAŠIM: Jan Oĉko of Vlašim (detail, state after restoration)

CRUCIFIXION (from the Emmaus Monastery). - Before 1380

82. CRUCIFIXION (from the Emmaus Monastery, detail)

CRUCIFIXION (from the Emmaus Monastery, detail)

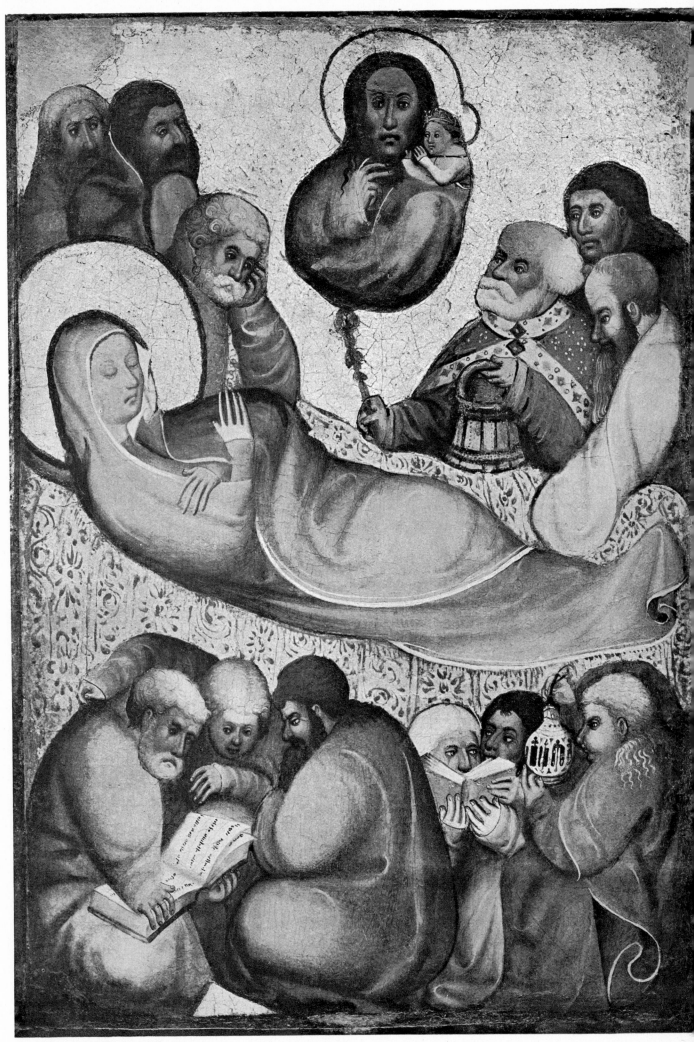

84. DEATH OF VIRGIN MARY. - About 1390

MULHOUSE ALTAR, Back part: Reinhart, Crucifixion and Eberhart. - 1385

86. MULHOUSE ALTAR, ALTAR CLOSED:
The Man of Sorrows and donor, Annunciation and Coronation of Virgin Mary, the Crucifixion

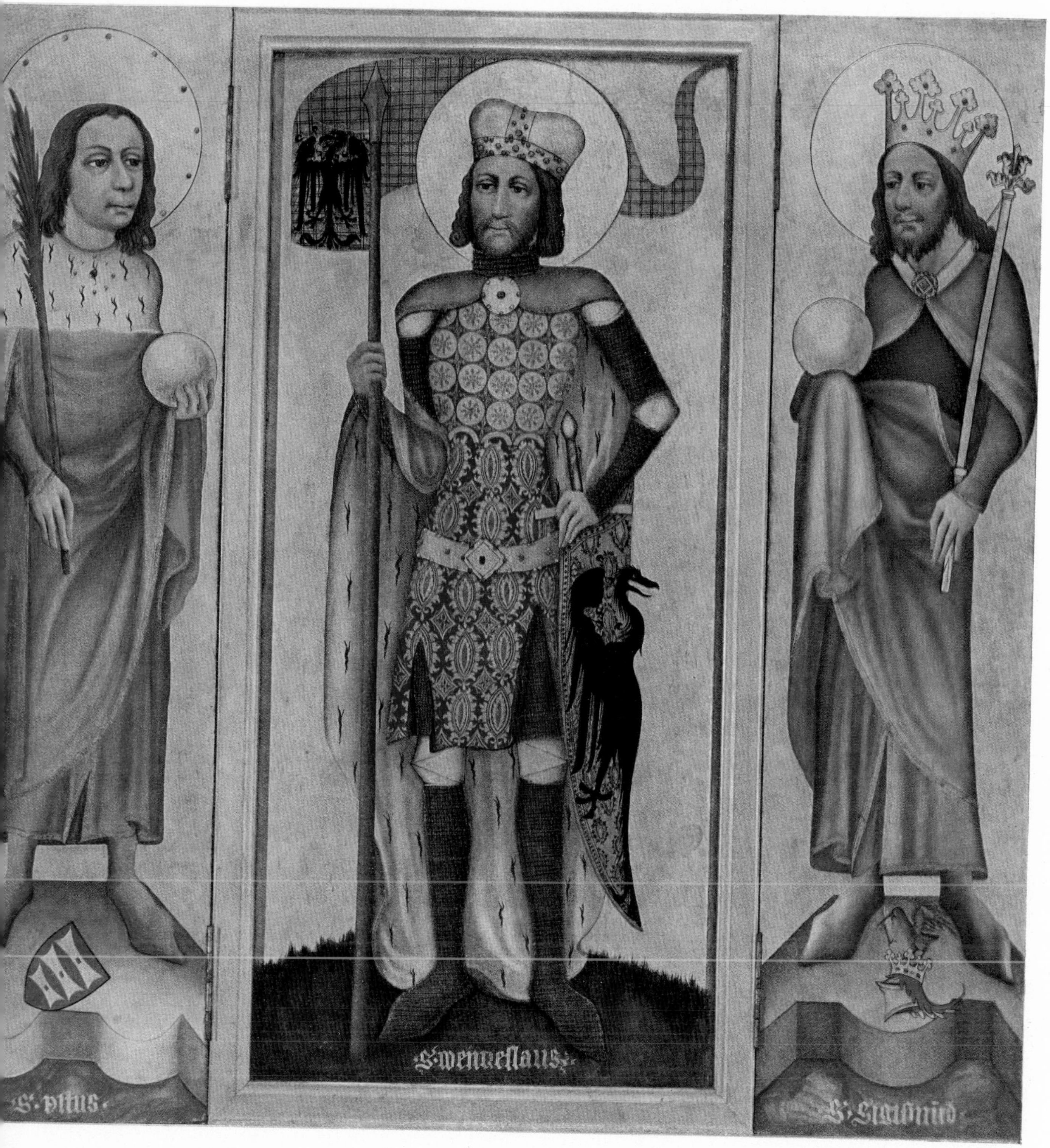

LHOUSE ALTAR, ALTAR OPEN: ST. VITUS, WENCESLAS AND SIGISMUND

ASTER OF THE TŘEBOŇ ALTAR: CHRIST ON MOUNT OLIVET. - About 1380

MASTER OF THE TŘEBOŇ ALTAR: CHRIST ON MOUNT OLIVET (detail)

90. MASTER OF THE TŘEBOŇ ALTAR: CHRIST ON MOUNT OLIVET (detail)

1. MASTER OF THE TŘEBOŇ ALTAR: CHRIST ON MOUNT OLIVET (detail)

92. MASTER OF THE TŘEBOŇ ALTAR: CHRIST ON MOUNT OLIVET (detail)

MASTER OF THE TŘEBOŇ ALTAR: ST. CATHERINE, ST. MARY MAGDALENE, ST. MARGARET (outer side of panel, picture No. 88)

MASTER OF THE TŘEBOŇ ALTAR: ST. MAGDALENE (detail)

95. MASTER OF THE TŘEBOŇ ALTAR: ST. MARGARET (detail)

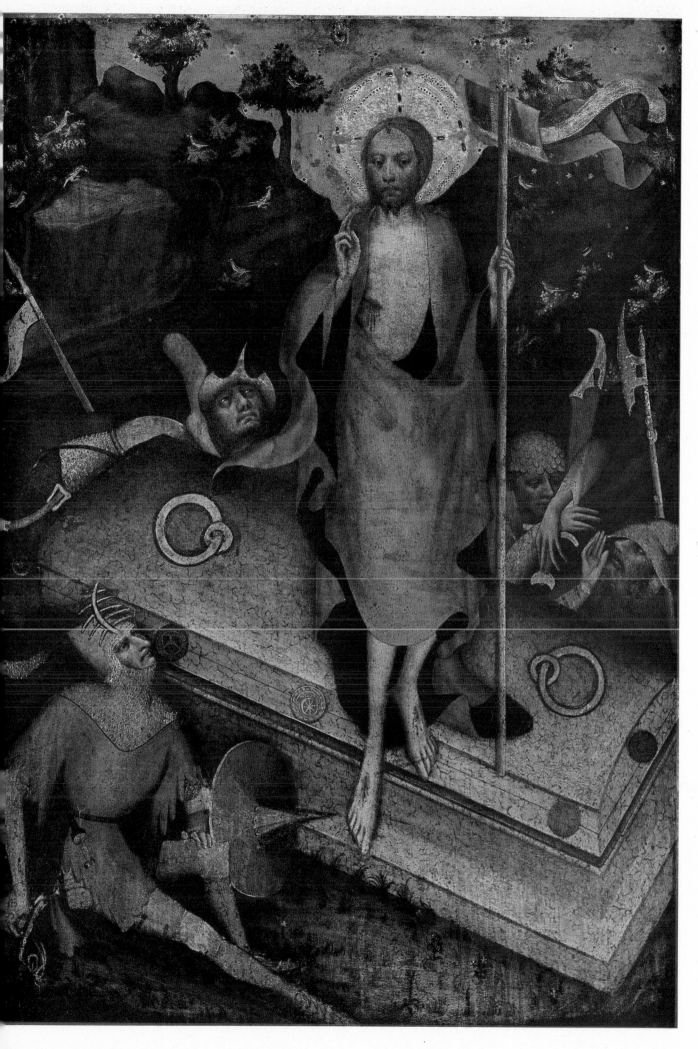

6. MASTER OF THE TŘEBOŇ ALTAR: RESURRECTION

7. MASTER OF THE TŘEBOŇ ALTAR: RESURRECTION (detail)

98. MASTER OF THE TŘEBOŇ ALTAR: RESURRECTION (detail)

99. MASTER OF THE TŘEBOŇ ALTAR: RESURRECTION (detail)

100. MASTER OF THE TŘEBOŇ ALTAR: RESURRECTION (detail)

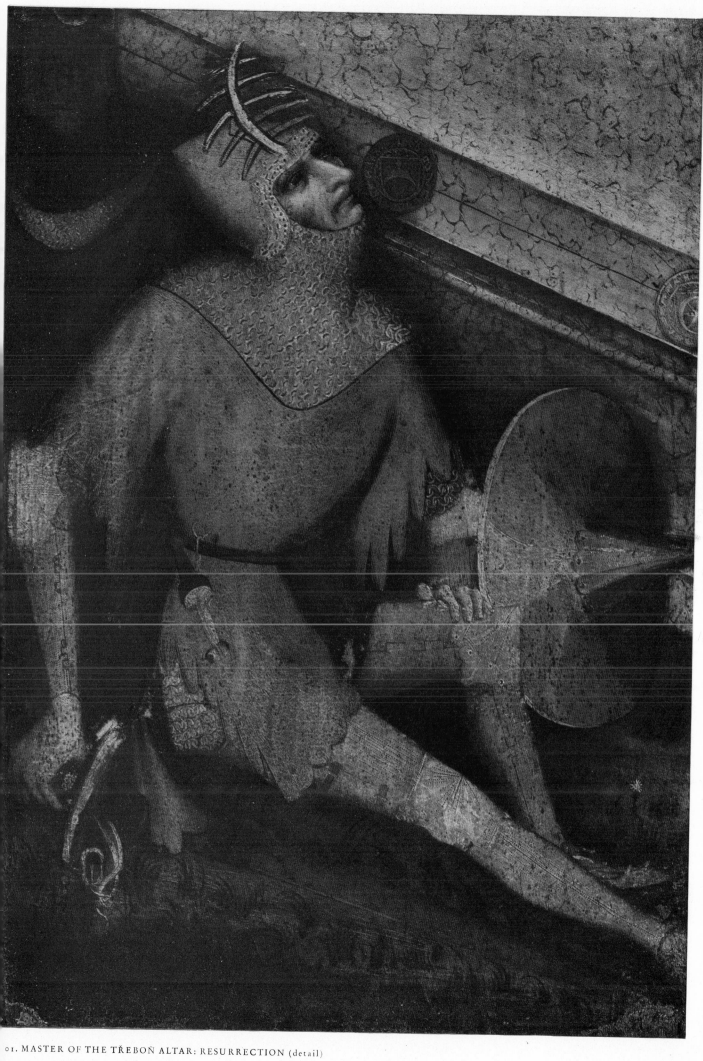

01. MASTER OF THE TŘEBOŇ ALTAR: RESURRECTION (detail)

02. MASTER OF THE TŘEBOŇ ALTAR: ST. JAMES THE LESS, ST. BARTHOLOMEW, ST. PHILIP (outer side of panel, picture No. 96)

3. MASTER OF THE TŘEBOŇ ALTAR: ST. BARTHOLOMEW (detail)

104. MASTER OF THE TŘEBOŇ ALTAR: ST. PHILIP

. MASTER OF THE TŘEBOŇ ALTAR: LAYING IN THE SEPULCHRE

. MASTER OF THE TŘEBOŇ ALTAR: LAYING IN THE SEPULCHRE (detail)

7. MASTER OF THE TŘEBOŇ ALTAR: LAYING IN THE SEPULCHRE (detail)

108. MASTER OF THE TŘEBOŇ ALTAR: LAYING IN THE SEPULCHRE (detail)

. MASTER OF THE TŘEBOŇ ALTAR: ST. GILES, ST. GREGORY, ST. JEROME (outer side of panel, picture No. 105)

MASTER OF THE TŘEBOŇ ALTAR: ST. GILES (detail)

III. MASTER OF THE TŘEBOŇ ALTAR: ST. GREGORY (detail)

MASTER OF THE TŘEBOŇ ALTAR: ST. JEROME (detail)

113. CRUCIFIXION: CHRIST (detail)

CRUCIFIXION

CRUCIFIXION (detail)

CRUCIFIXION (detail)

117. ADORATION OF THE CHILD. - Before 1400

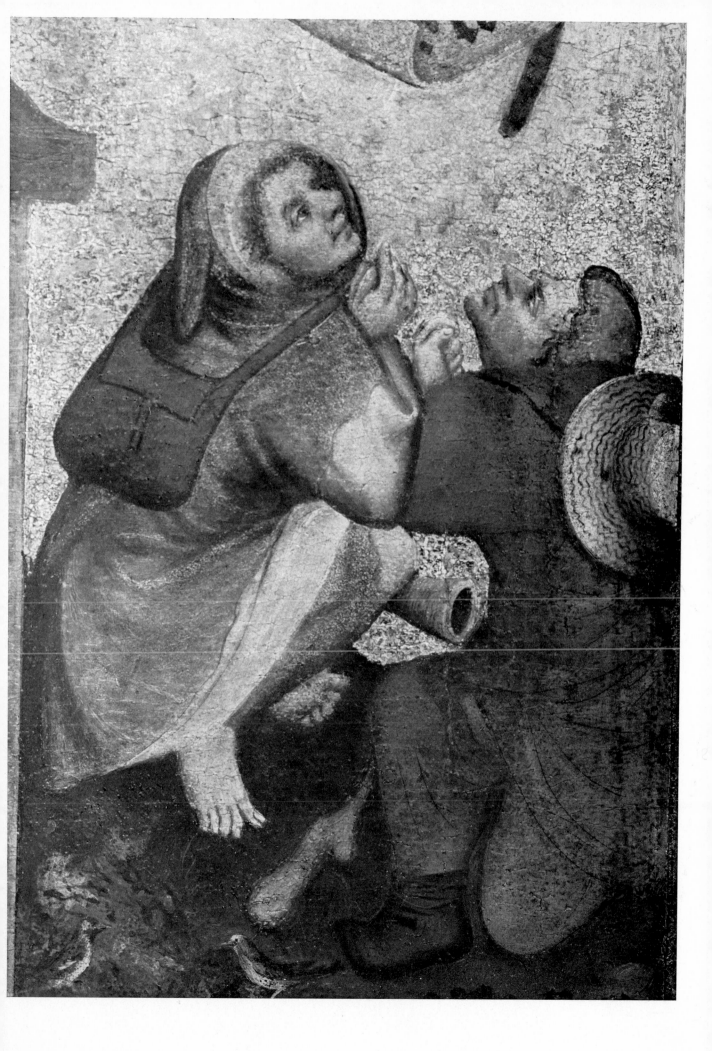

118. ADORATION OF THE CHILD (detail)

119. ADORATION OF THE CHILD (detail)

MADONNA ARACOELI. - About 1400

121.-122. MADONNA ARACOELI: ST. MARGARET AND ST. DOROTHEA (details of frame)

123. MADONNA ARACOELI, ST. URSULA (detail of frame)

124.-125. MADONNA ARACOELI, PROPHETS JEREMIAH AND EZEKIEL (details of frame)

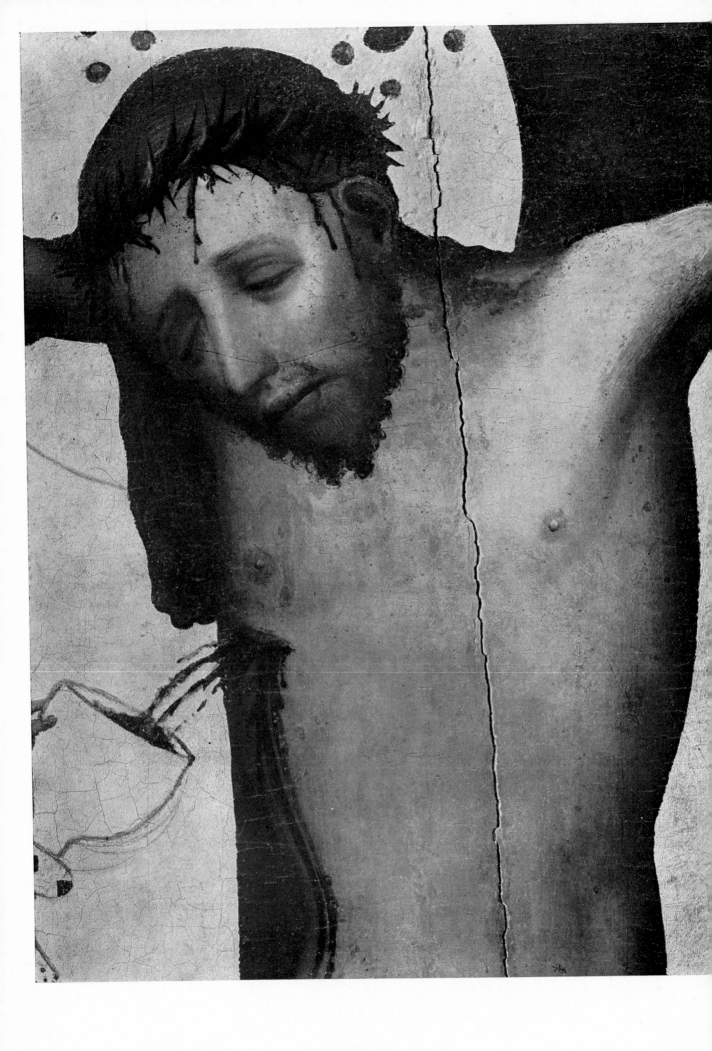

126. THE VYŠŠÍ BROD CRUCIFIXION: CHRIST (detail). - Before 1400

THE VYŠŠÍ BROD CRUCIFIXION. - Before 1400

128. THE VYŠŠÍ BROD CRUCIFIXION (detail)

129. THE VYŠŠÍ BROD CRUCIFIXION (detail)

130. MADONNA, BETWEEN ST. BARTHOLOMEW AND ST. MARGARET. - About 1400

131. MADONNA, BETWEEN ST. BARTHOLOMEW AND ST. MARGARET: St. Bartholomew (detail)

132. MADONNA, BETWEEN ST. BARTHOLOMEW AND ST. MARGARET (detail)

133. EPITAPH OF JAN Z JEŘENĚ: ST. BARTHOLOMEW AND ST. THOMAS. - 1395

134. EPITAPH OF JAN Z JEŘENĚ: VIRGIN MARY

EPITAPH OF JAN Z JEŘENĚ: ST. BARTHOLOMEW (detail)

5. DUBEČKO PANEL.- Before 1400

137. DUBEČKO PANEL: ST. ANDREW, bishop-saint and donor (detail)

38. DUBEČKO PANEL: ST. WENCESLAS (detail)

139. DUBEČKO PANEL: ST. ADALBERT AND ST. SIGISMUND (detail)

DUBEČKO PANEL: ST. PROKOP AND ST. LUDMILA (detail)

141. VIRGIN MARY · MATER DOLOROSA. · Before 1400

MADONNA OF ST. VITUS CATHEDRAL. - About 1400

MADONNA OF ST. VITUS CATHEDRAL (detail)

144. MADONNA OF LNÁŘE. - After 1400

5. MADONNA OF ZLATÁ KORUNA. - About 1400

146. SEATED MADONNA OF JINDŘICHŮV HRADEC. - About 1400

7. CRUCIFIXION. - About 1410

148. ROUDNICE MADONNA. - Before 1400

9. BUDĚJOVICE MADONNA. After 1400

150, 151. BUDĚJOVICE MADONNA: St. Wenceslas, St. Catherine (details of frame)

VERAICON (ST. VITUS). After 1400

153, 154. VERAICON (ST. VITUS): St. Adalbert and St. Wenceslas (details of frame)

155, 156. VERAICON (ST. VITUS): St. Ludmila and St. Prokop (details of frame)

157. CYCLE OF THE CAPUCHIN MONASTERY, PRAGUE: Christ (state after restoration). Before 1410

CYCLE OF THE CAPUCHIN MONASTERY, PRAGUE: Virgin Mary (state before restoration)

CYCLE OF THE CAPUCHIN MONASTERY, PRAGUE: St. Peter (state before restoration)

CYCLE OF THE CAPUCHIN MONASTERY, PRAGUE: St. John the Baptist (state after restoration)

161. CYCLE OF THE CAPUCHIN MONASTERY, PRAGUE: St. Paul (state after restoration)

162. CYCLE OF THE CAPUCHIN MONASTERY, PRAGUE: Apostle (state after restoration)

163. CYCLE OF THE CAPUCHIN MONASTERY, PRAGUE: Apostle (state after restoration)

164. CYCLE OF THE CAPUCHIN MONASTERY, PRAGUE: Apostle (state after restoration)

165. CYCLE OF THE CAPUCHIN MONASTERY, PRAGUE: Apostle (state after restoration)

CYCLE OF THE CAPUCHIN MONASTERY, PRAGUE: Apostle (state after restoration)

167. CYCLE OF THE CAPUCHIN MONASTERY, PRAGUE: St. John the Evangelist (state after restoration)

CYCLE OF THE CAPUCHIN MONASTERY, PRAGUE: St. Bartholomew (state after restoration)

169. CYCLE OF THE CAPUCHIN MONASTERY, PRAGUE: Apostle (state after restoration)

CYCLE OF THE CAPUCHIN MONASTERY, PRAGUE: Apostle (state after restoration)

171. THE DEATH OF VIRGIN MARY. About 1410

ANNUNCIATION OF VIRGIN MARY. About 1410

173. THE ROUDNICE ALTAR: Death of Virgin Mary, centre. About 1410

THE ROUDNICE ALTAR: Death of Virgin Mary (detail)

175, 176. THE ROUDNICE ALTAR: Virgin Mary the Protector, Christ the Sufferer (inner side of wings)

177, 178. THE ROUDNICE ALTAR: Mater Dolorosa, Christ the Sufferer and the donor with family (outer side of the wings)

THE ROUDNICE ALTAR (detail)

180. THE ROUDNICE ALTAR (detail)

181. THE MASTER OF THE RAJHRAD ALTAR: Carrying the Cross. Before 1420

182. THE MASTER OF THE RAJHRAD ALTAR: Carrying the Cross (detail)

THE MASTER OF THE RAJHRAD ALTAR: Carrying the Cross (detail)

184. THE MASTER OF THE RAJHRAD ALTAR: The Crucifixion

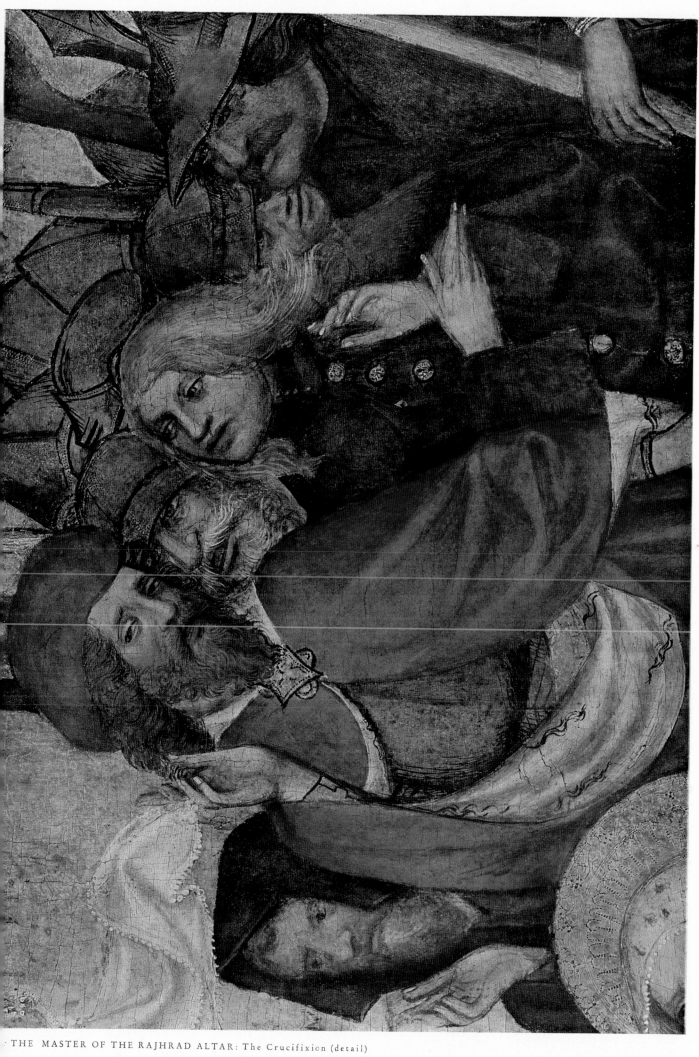

THE MASTER OF THE RAJHRAD ALTAR: The Crucifixion (detail)

6. THE MASTER OF THE RAJHRAD ALTAR: The Crucifixion (detail)

187. THE MASTER OF THE RAJHRAD ALTAR: The Last Supper

THE MASTER OF THE RAJHRAD ALTAR: Christ on Mount Olivet (detail)

189. THE MASTER OF THE RAJHRAD ALTAR: Christ on Mount Olivet

190. THE MASTER OF THE RAJHRAD ALTAR: The Resurrection

THE MASTER OF THE RAJHRAD ALTAR: The Resurrection (detail)

192. THE MASTER OF THE RAJHRAD ALTAR: The finding of the Holy Cross

193. THE MASTER OF THE RAJHRAD ALTAR: Adoration of the Three Kings

194. MADONNA OF ST. THOMAS'S CHURCH: Front side of panel. About 1420

195—197. MADONNA OF ST. THOMAS'S CHURCH: St. John the Baptist, St. Dorothea and St. Apollonia (details of frame)

MADONNA OF ST. THOMAS'S CHURCH: Veraicon (back of panel)

199. ADORATION OF THE CHILD: Front of the panel. About 1420

ADORATION OF THE CHILD: Christ on Mount Olivet (back of panel)

201. ST. BARBARA. About 1420

2. THE LAST SUPPER. After 1420

MASTER OF THE VYŠŠÍ BROD MADONNA: The Vyšší Brod Madonna. After 1420

204, 205. THE MASTER OF THE VYŠŠÍ BROD MADONNA: The Vyšší Brod Madonna, St. Wenceslas, St. George, St. Ursula, St. Prokop, St. John the Baptist, St. Giles (details of frame)

6, 207. THE MASTER OF THE VYŠŠÍ BROD MADONNA: The Vyšší Brod Madonna, St. Simon, donor (details of frame)

208. THE MASTER OF THE VYŠŠÍ BROD MADONNA: Crucifixion (altar centre). After 1420

209. THE MASTER OF THE VYŠŠÍ BROD MADONNA: Crucifixion, Mary Salome and Mary Cleophas (outer side of wings)

210. THE MASTER OF THE VYŠŠÍ BROD MADONNA: Crucifixion, St. Anna (inner side of wing, detail)

211. THE MASTER OF THE VYŠŠÍ BROD MADONNA: Crucifixion, St. Magdalene and St. Lucia (inner side of wing, detail)

212. THE MASTER OF THE VYŠŠÍ BROD MADONNA: Crucifixion, St. Elizabeth and St. Helena (inner side of wing, detail)

213. THE MASTER OF THE VYŠŠÍ BROD MADONNA: Crucifixion, St. Barbara and St. Ursula (inner side of wing, detail)

214. THE VRATISLAV MADONNA After 1420

THE NÁMĚŠT PANEL Martyrdom of St. Apollonia (inner side of panel). About 1420

216. THE NÁMĚŠŤ PANEL Martyrdom of St. Catherine (outer side of panel).

217. THE NÁMĚŠT PANEL Martyrdom of St. Catherine (detail)

218. THE NÁMĚŠŤ PANEL Martyrdom of St. Catherine (detail)

9. THE HÝROV ALTAR: Madonna with donors (centre). About 1430

220. THE HÝROV ALTAR: St. Margaret (left wing)

221. THE HỲROV ALTAR: St. John the Baptist (right wing)

222. THE ZÁTON ALTAR: Crucifixion, centre. After 1430

THE ZÁTOŇ ALTAR: Crucifixion (detail)

224. THE ZÁTOŇ ALTAR: Crucifixion (detail)

THE ZÁTOŇ ALTAR: (detail of right wing)

226, 227. **THE ZÁTOŇ ALTAR**: Sermon of St. John the Baptist and Baptism of Christ, Beheading of St. John the Baptist, Salome

228. MATER DOLOROSA: St. Peter and Paul (inner side) About 1430

229. MATER DOLOROSA (outer side of panel)

230. FRAGMENT FROM ČESKÉ BUDĚJOVICE: Visitation of Virgin Mary (inner side). After 1430

231. FRAGMENT FROM ČESKÉ BUDĚJOVICE: Christ the Gardener (outer side of panel)

232. FRAME OF THE ROUDNICE RELIQUARY. After 1430

233. THE MASTER OF THE CARRYING OF THE CROSS, VYŠŠÍ BROD: Visitation of Virgin Mary. After 1430

34. THE MASTER OF THE CARRYING OF THE CROSS, VYŠŠÍ BROD: Adoration of the Child

235. THE MASTER OF THE CARRYING OF THE CROSS, VYŠŠÍ BROD: Carrying of the Cross

236. **THE MASTER OF THE CARRYING OF THE CROSS, VYŠŠÍ BROD**: Carrying of the Cross (detail)

237. THE VYŠŠÍ BROD ANNUNCIATION OF VIRGIN MARY. After 1430

238. THE VYŠŠÍ BROD ANNUNCIATION OF VIRGIN MARY (detail)

39. THE SKALICE CRUCIFIXION. After 1430

240. THE SKALICE CRUCIFIXION (detail)

41. THE SKALICE CRUCIFIXION (detail)

242. MADONNA OF DOUDLEBY: Adoration of the Child (formerly back of the panel)

265. LANNA'S ASSUMPTA: Centre. About 1450

262, 263. MADONNA (H. M. THE KING OF ENGLAND): The Resurrection, Death of Virgin Mary (details of frame)

264. MADONNA AT ST. STEPHEN'S. About 1440

261. MADONNA (H. M. THE KING OF ENGLAND). About 1440

259. MASTER OF THE ALTAR AT ST. JAMES'S: Philetus frees Hermogenes

hermogenes · petit · aliqd · signu̅

Sacobe
apl̅e miserere · nobis

Siac̄o · dedit · ei̅ · baculum

160. MASTER OF THE ALTAR AT ST. JAMES'S: Hermogenes receives staff from St. James

251. MASTER OF THE ALTAR AT ST. JAMES'S: Three Kings adoring the Child (detail)

252. MASTER OF THE ALTAR AT ST. JAMES'S: Christ Sacrificed

253. MASTER OF THE ALTAR AT ST. JAMES'S: Capture of St. James

254. MASTER OF THE ALTAR AT ST. JAMES'S: St. James attends on the Sick

255. MASTER OF THE ALTAR AT ST. JAMES'S: Death of St. James

256. MASTER OF THE ALTAR AT ST. JAMES'S: Moving the body of St. James

257. MASTER OF THE ALTAR AT ST. JAMES'S: Philetus sent to St. James

258. MASTER OF THE ALTAR AT ST. JAMES'S: St. James treats Philetus

259. MASTER OF THE ALTAR AT ST. JAMES'S: Philetus frees Hermogenes

hermogenes·petit·aliqd·signū

Iacobe
 apłe miserere·nobis

Stacō·dedit·ei·baculum

260. MASTER OF THE ALTAR AT ST. JAMES'S: Hermogenes receives staff from St. James

261. MADONNA (H. M. THE KING OF ENGLAND). About 1440

262, 263. MADONNA (H.M. THE KING OF ENGLAND): The Resurrection, Death of Virgin Mary (details of frame)

264. MADONNA AT ST. STEPHEN'S. About 1440

265. LANNA'S ASSUMPTA: Centre. About 1450

266. LANNA'S ASSUMPTA

267. ASSUMPTA OF THE WHITE MOUNTAIN MONASTERY. About 1450

268. LANNA'S MADONNA. About 1450

269. ASSUMPTA OF DEŠTNÁ. About 1450

270. ASSUMPTA OF DEŠTNÁ (detail)

271. MADONNA. About 1450

272. VISITATION OF VIRGIN MARY (ČESKÝ KRUMLOV). About 1450

273. VISITATION OF VIRGIN MARY. After 1450

274. THE BRUSSELS MADONNA

275. MADONNA OF JINDŘICHŮV HRADEC. About 1450

276. VIENNESE MADONNA: Madonna (front of panel). About 1470

277. VIENNESE MADONNA: Veraicon (back of panel)

CONTENTS